Youth Work:
Emerging Perspectives
in Youth Development

Christopher R. Edginton
Christopher L. Kowalski
Steven W. Randall

Sagamore Publishing L.L.C.
Champaign, Illinois

Production Manager: Janet Wahlfeldt
Book design: Michelle R. Dressen
Cover design: Michael Morgan

ISBN: 1-57167-569-8
Library of Congress Catalog Card Number: 2004098668
Printed in the United States.

Sagamore Publishing, L.L.C.
804 N. Neil St.
Champaign, IL 61820
http://www.sagamorepub.com

10 9 8 7 6 5 4 3 2 1

IN MEMORY OF

Lynda Moore

CONTENTS

Foreword

Can you imagine a community without Girl Scouts or the YMCA or Junior Achievement? For decades, these youth-serving organizations have enhanced the quality of life in communities across the country. These youth-serving organizations have dedicated professional staffs and thousands of volunteers. And each year, college students prepare to work in these organizations to "make a difference" in the lives of young people.

American Humanics, a national alliance including 70 colleges and universities and 18 of the largest youth-serving national organizations, is dedicated to recruiting, educating, and certifying professionals to lead nonprofit organizations. These college graduates are the professionals who dedicate their lives to the development of youth. The disciplinary fields of social work, sociology, biology, psychology, education, and others provide research and theories upon which the principles and "best practices" are developed.

This text brings together the research, theories, and practices around youth development and utilizes the experiences and approaches tested by practitioners. A brilliant blending of theory and practice comes to life in this textbook. The richness of experience and the expertise of the three authors are evident throughout the text. The national organization of American Humanics recommends this textbook to the faculty at more than 70 campuses. We believe the material will enhance the educational experience of the 2500 American Humanics students to become tomorrow's leaders in youth-serving organizations.

Of special note are the chapters on mentoring and ethics. Learning about both of these areas is critical to providing quality experiences and positive leadership. Utilizing Greenleaf's work to shape the concept of youth professionals as leaders in the service of others broadens the awareness of leadership with a worthy purpose and mission. The central mission of American Humanics' alliance and member partnerships is leadership in the service of others. Authors Edginton, Kowalski, and Randall have provided an excellent textbook and reference source for organizations and individuals working with youth. We recommend this book to our university programs and to the youth-serving national organizations in our alliance.

Kala M. Stroup
President
American Humanics
Former University President
and faculty member
www.humanics.org

American Humanics is a national alliance of colleges, universities and national nonprofits with an innovative program and curriculum that educates, prepares and certifies college and university students for effective nonprofit leadership. It is the only national nonprofit organization meeting this need at the undergraduate level. To ensure student success, American Humanics provides leadership opportunities, internships, networking and scholarships as well as an innovative, experiential education.

The American Humanics alliance currently includes 70 colleges and universities, plus 17 national nonprofits and thousands of their local affiliates. More than 2,000 college students were enrolled in the American Humanics program during the 2003-2004 academic year. For more information please visit www.humanics.org, call 800-343-6466, or write to American Humanics, 4601 Madison Ave., Kansas City, MO 64112.

American Humanics Inc.

Preface

One's youth is a distinct stage of one's life. In many ways youth live in a separate world: a time and place with its own culture which provides significant opportunities for individuals to craft their identities, learn necessary life skills, expand their horizons, find their vocation, and develop the foundations for their adult life. Often the social gap between adults and young people makes it difficult for youth to learn from the experiences of their elders. Youth work represents an opportunity to bring young people and adults together—collaborative efforts that provide meaningful and insightful experiences for all involved.

This is an exciting time to explore youth work and youth development. Increasingly, the topic, as well as its concerns and issues, are a part of national consciousness and woven into our social fabric. American society is involved in an ongoing public discussion regarding youth, wherein attention is being directed toward understanding the needs and challenges faced by youth today. We are redefining, in a positive way, our perceptions of the contributions youth make to our ever-evolving culture. Further, significant efforts at focusing greater attention on the needs of youth, as well as enhancing the delivery of programs and services at the local, regional, state, and national levels, has occurred.

The literature of youth work and youth development is located in many disciplines and professional areas of study. Our effort is directed at creating a mosaic that portrays youth work and youth development as an emerging force in American society. Our focus is primarily directed toward assisting individuals in understanding the context of professional practice as related to youth work and youth development. We have borrowed heavily from existing frameworks in Europe, especially the United Kingdom, and from the emerging body of knowledge that is found in the efforts of philanthropic organizations and think tanks which have devoted a great deal of energy to studying the topic.

Our intention is to provide an introductory overview for the professional practice of youth work in the United States. There is little in the way of distilled information with a professional focus on the topic of youth work and youth development. As such, we have crafted a document that provides basic information regarding the status of youth and youth work in America today. Among the topics covered in this book are those dealing with adolescence as a life stage, historical perspectives, key terms and definitions of youth work and youth development, approaches and orientations to youth work, program and leadership strategies, ethics, multiculturalism, policy formulation, professional career development, and challenges and issues.

Acknowledgments

As is the case with any project of this nature, there are numerous individuals that have assisted us in formulating our ideas and helped us with the production of the manuscript. In particular, we would like to note that we have been greatly influenced by the contemporary works of Mark Smith and Tony Jeffs in the United Kingdom. We have learned a great deal from their writings as well as opportunities to interact with them personally. In addition, we are grateful for the leadership that Karen Pittman has provided to helping Americans better understand the concepts of youth work and youth development. We can think of no other person in the United States that has had a greater influence on shaping these topics as she has through her scholarly efforts.

From a historical perspective we also need to pay tribute to G. Stanley Hall, Jane Addams, John Dewey, and Jean Piaget. These individuals provided early inspiration for considering the unique challenges of youth. Our contemporaries over the years at the University of Northern Iowa have also helped us nurture and develop our ideas. In particular, we would like to thank Walter de Oliveria, Susan Hudson, Gordon Mack, Rheta DeVries, and Doug Magnuson.

Several individuals assisted us in the production of the manuscript. In particular we would like to acknowledge the support we have received from Karen Peterson, Terri Meehan, and Julee Jacobson. They were tremendously supportive of this effort, helping us to prepare the document. All of these individuals are extremely competent, capable, and professional in the execution of their duties.

Lastly, we would like to thank the following family members and friends. The senior author of this project would like to thank his family members who have been very instrumental in his professional work. Susan, Carole, David, and I are a team and have shared in our quest to improve the quality of programs and service for children and youth. They have been a steady source of inspiration, energy, and continuous effort above and beyond the call of duty. In addition, the senior author draws a great deal of joy from his grandchildren, Hanna and Jake. They are simply the greatest! Lana Kowalski, Pat Kowalski, Kari Kowalski, Kevin "Bob" Roberts, Chris Guidry, and David Hirner, have provided the motivation, encouragement and spots of humor to their son and friend as this work has progressed. Their dedication, passion and work ethic have inspired continual growth. Stefanie Donnell, Debra Williamson, Bill Williamson, Bill and Lorraine Randall, Angie and Scott Whiteman, and Eric Knoblock have provided unfailing and unconditional love and support to the most junior author of the document. To all of these individuals we would like to extend our deepest gratitude and appreciation.

We have dedicated this book to the memory of Lynda Moore, secretary to the Director of the School of Health, Physical Education and Leisure Services at the University of Northern Iowa. Tragically, Lynda died during the preparation of this document. Lynda was a patient person in working with this and many other projects. She helped us organize the effort, provided social and emotional support, and dedicated herself to ensuring that we were able to organize our efforts. Lynda was particularly adept at solving problems on the computer. She worked tirelessly at making sure that we had the precise layout for our materials as well as assisting us in identifying alternative terms that ensured that we were effectively expressing our ideas. We will miss Lynda Moore. Our lives have been enriched by her, and her presence will continue to be with us in the future.

CHAPTER ONE

Youth Today

INTRODUCTION

Youth are our most important asset (Edginton, 1997, p. 15). Often they represent and reflect our hopes, aspirations, and dreams for the future. Youth reflect and mirror many of our most cherished beliefs, values, and ideals. Yet, at the same time, today's youth create and advance fresh new perspectives that dramatically influence our culture. Youth have few preconceived notions; they approach the world with an innocence that enables them to see the world in a new and different light. "Today's youth will have a significant role in bringing about changes in technology, demography, economy, and politics" (Boyle, 2000, as cited in Delgado, 2002, p. 3). Major investments of time, capital, and commitment must be made in youth in order to nurture their development in the aforementioned areas (Haveman & Wolfe, 1994, as cited in Delgado, 2002). Without question, youth represent a complex social, cultural, political, and economic phenomenon; a prime force in American society whose aspirations require our best efforts.

Youth workers and youth service organizations have begun to play a more prominent role in American society. "The issue of promoting developmental opportunities for our nation's youth is not new" (Villarruel, Perkins, Borden, & Keith, 2003, p. ix). However, it is challenging to describe the efforts of youth workers and youth work organizations in a precise fashion. Multiple philosophies, orientations, and even assumptions concerning youth abound. Youth work and youth service organizations are found in nearly every sector of our society. It has become increasingly highly organized, complex, sophisticated, and evident in communities across America. Further, little is understood regarding the interaction, in the social context, of youth culture and the professional practice of youth workers and youth organizations.

The term youth development and the ideas and practices associated with it have emerged from the field of youth work, but they have extended beyond practice to influence local, state, and national decision makers in the public and private sectors (Hamilton, Hamilton, & Pittman, 2004, p. ix). Further, they suggest that youth development has risen from practice and that "practice seldom follows theory." Hahn and Raley (1998, p. 387) have raised the question of whether or not "there is a youth development field". These authors recognize that youth work is practiced in a variety of settings, but voice the question as to whether or not this work forms a profession. They ask "is youth development a profession, or simply a convenient organizing concept describing the field of specialized workers who have deeper and clearer ties to other professions?" (Hahn & Raley, 1998, p. 388). These authors conclude that there is greater need for definition and the strengthening of the field's theoretical knowledge base.

This book is an effort at more effectively identifying the theoretical knowledge base, as well as that knowledge base that is found in professional practice. We seek to more effectively define, clarify, organize, and extend the current body of knowledge that is available for the practice of youth work. Further, we seek to provide background information concerning the status of youth

in American society and the challenges and issues faced by youth today. This introductory chapter provides an overview of youth culture today.

DEFINING YOUTH CULTURE

Youth culture is defined as the unique symbols, beliefs, and behaviors that represent young people within society (Outhwaite & Bottomore, 1994). The idea of youth culture includes the different norms, rules, and regulations that encompass the grouping of youth. How, what, when, where, and whom may interact with youth is part of the youth culture. There are various actions and reactions that occur specific to the youth culture.

A primary component of youth culture is the incorporation of fads or trends. As discussed later in this chapter, trends have a profound impact on the economy. Within youth culture, trends play a pivotal role in the formation of identity. The wider youth culture, referred to as the mass or popular culture, revolves around the adoption of certain fashions, leisure pursuits, and lifestyle choices (Outhwaite & Bottomore, 1994). These fashions, leisure pursuits, and lifestyle choices affect how youth interact with others.

To understand the value youth culture plays in the overall composition of society, youth workers need to analyze the historical and psychological perspectives related to youth work. During the twentieth century, youths transitioned from "little adults" with no definitive norms, rules, or regulations to call their own, to a vibrant portion of the population, crying out for a humanistic representation in our society. As "little adults," youth were forced to conform to the norms and values of the adult population. Conformity of such magnitude drastically affected the psychological makeup of youth, often wearing them down mentally and physically and warping their interpretation and learning of such life skills as respect, integrity, and trust.

The pioneers in the field of youth work discussed in Chapter 3 paved the road for the establishment of a youth culture. Jane Addams, G. Stanley Hall, and Luther Gulick, to name a few, recognized the worth of youth and the need to help them develop into strong leaders. Their actions were the framework for acknowledging the importance of a youth culture. The formation and articulation of a youth culture is the recognition that the youth population is valuable, that their symbols, actions, and behaviors are a necessity for the prosperity of our society.

THE CONTEXT OF YOUTH WORK

Youth work has undergone a continual evolution, rearranging and shaping its services to form the body of knowledge and practitioners that currently exists. In the first two decades of the twentieth century, the concept of youth work was a radical idea formulated by individuals whose goal was to remove youth from life-threatening situations and help them develop into strong citizens of

society. Their goal was to eliminate exploitative youth labor and develop avenues for youth to exhibit creativity and begin to practice the skills needed for later stages in life, such as working together in groups, integrity, and reasoning.

As the original idea of youth work took hold in American society, community members began to formulate methods to reach youth and encourage such fundamental concepts as play and recreation. Organizations such as the Boy Scouts and the YMCA were stakeholders in this movement, emphasizing the importance of molding youth and guiding their actions.

PRACTICES AND PRINCIPLES FOR YOUTH DEVELOPMENT

Universal acceptance of the term youth development as a way of defining the efforts of youth workers and youth service organizations, is relatively new. In the past decade, there has been a great deal of interest and attention focused on development principles and strategies to be used in the practice of youth work. There is some agreement regarding the importance of a positive or prosocial approach to youth development. As a result, a number of principles for promoting youth development have emerged (Hamilton, Hamilton, & Pittman, 2004). Further, the application of approaches to learning, such as constructivism, has yielded additional ideas regarding the process of youth development. We offer the following as principles and practices upon which youth development strategies can be built.

Positive Orientation, Support, and Universality. A positive orientation builds on or accentuates the strengths of each and every individual youth. The emphasis in this area is that each youth has the right of access to those supports, which are necessary for their development. Such support should be provided in a way that does not stigmatize the individual based on race, ethnicity, class, gender, or individual condition. As Hamilton, Hamilton, and Pittman (2004, p. 11) write, " . . . opportunities should be available to all. Opportunities—to learn, explore, play, express oneself. . ."

Engagement, Empowerment, and Participation. Youth development best occurs through some form of engagement within which individuals have some say in their development. In other words, youth learn, explore, and grow in environments in which they have some active role in shaping. Simply stated, youth need a voice in those opportunities that are established to assist them in their development. Preparing youth as critical thinkers, problem solvers, and decision makers in a democratic society requires that they have a hand in the processes that influence their development. To empower youth means to enable them to have some influence regarding the life activities that influence their development.

Exploration, Experimentation, and Competence Building. Adolescence is often characterized as the process of becoming. It is a time in one's life of opportunities for exploration, experimentation, and competence building. Youth often seek opportunities to explore new ideas, relationships with others, and meaning within the context of society as a whole. Youth seek to develop their knowledge, skills, and competence in preparing for life. Youth need opportunities to fail, as well as a framework for development, which provides challenges of increasing complexity and support. Youth require opportunities that enable them to progressively develop their abilities to function successfully in society.

Safe Environments. All youth have the right to develop in environments that are conducive to positive growth. Such environments require that youth be physically, and psychologically safe. However, this does not mean that youth should not be challenged or exposed to risk, but rather they should be free from physical abuse and psychological trauma that impede their development. Increasingly, youth environments are punctuated, with violence, crime, physical and sexual harassment, bullying, and neglect. In order for youth to develop, they are best served when their environments, whether in the home, school, or broader community, are free of such barriers, which may be detrimental to development.

Autonomy. Youth seek autonomy and do not want to perceive that they are being controlled or compelled to act. Youth desire a level of independence and freedom of action. Conversely, youth also often seek adult support and guidance, and some structure to enable their development. As Friederich Fröbel (1897, p. 125) stated over one hundred years ago, the challenge is one of "systematizing play and directing it so as to make it more effective." Fröbel (1897, p. 125) ". . . knew that spontaneity must not be sacrificed to system, as the great value of play intellectually and morally depends on the freedom of the [individual] in expressing its own purposes and carrying out its own decision." The question then and the question today remains: How does the youth worker assist individuals in maintaining freedom, perfect spontaneity, and independence of action, yet provide support and guidance?

Becoming and Belonging. Youth work assists in the ongoing search for and development of their identity. We are all in the process of becoming, however, for youth, becoming is a quest of life. Youth ask the question consistently, "What will I become when I grow up?" In fact, as we become older, we continue to ask the question "What will I become when I become who I am to be?" Edginton (2000, p. 143) has written that youth are ". . . capable of learning, growing and perfecting themselves." In fact, to live and learn is to always be in the process of becoming. It is a continuous process that will be experienced throughout life. A part of the search for one's meaning in life is finding out where he or she belongs in life. Belonging refers to membership in an organization or association; simply put, a member in a group is a part of a broader community. Youth strive to belong to a group, to feel a sense of worth and inclusion that embraces them for who they are. Communities that develop support networks and strong relationships with youth, may be the group needed to facilitate a youth's quest to find out who he or she will become in life.

COMMUNITIES AND YOUTH DEVELOPMENT

Youth development does not take place in isolation. In fact, for effective youth development to be undertaken it requires the commitment of an entire community. All of the resources of a community can be brought to bear on the needs of youth. Clearly, the efforts of individuals, community groups, nonprofit organizations, government agencies, schools, religious organizations, civic institutions, and businesses have an important role to play in building a program of youth development in any community setting. Each of these different types of organizations, agencies, and institutions, as well as others, can work in partnership to strengthen a community's effort aimed at enhancing its youth development strategies.

As Perkins, Borden, Keith, Hoppe-Rooney, and Villarruel (2003, p. 6) have written ". . . youth development, either positive or negative, occurs as youth interact with all levels of their surroundings, including the other people in their environment such as family, peers, other adults, and members of their communities." These authors have suggested that community youth development may be defined as ". . . purposely creating environments that provide constructive, affirmative, and encouraging relationships that are sustained over time with adults and peers, while concurrently providing an array of opportunities that enable youth to build their competencies and become engaged as partners in their own development as well as the development of the community" (Perkins et al., 2003, p. 6). Further, Swisher, and Whitlock (2004, p. 216) have noted that communities ". . .are constituted by social interactions between residents. . .these relationships among youth, their friends and peers, parents, teachers and other adults in the community are important resources on which youth development efforts attempt to build." It is when ". . .youth are fully invested in their community and are empowered to provide direction, insight, and efforts around problem solving for the community. . ." that efforts are truly advanced (Perkins et al., 2003, p. 8).

The call to involve an entire community in the process of building strategies in support of youth development has resulted in the creation of a model of community organization referred to as the "capacity focus model." This model deviates from the traditional model of focusing on the problems of youth exclusively. The capacity focus model suggests that significant progress with youth must involve an investment of community members and their resources (Kretzmann & McKnight, 1993). The model requires that communities look within their own resource base in building for the future rather than seeking external support from outside sources.

The capacity focus model of community youth development has three main components: 1) targeting the assets of a community, 2) focusing the internal resources of a community to promote youth development, and 3) the development of relationships. As stated earlier, identifying or targeting the assets of a community is an important step in this model (Bogenschneider, 1996; Kretzmann & McKnight, 1993). A clear understanding of the resources that can be brought to bear is essential. Second, the capacity focus model for community youth development suggests that a community must develop itself from within. An internal focus creates a sense of ownership and provides a witness for youth and others that their actions in the community can in fact have a positive impact on youth. The last component involves the development of relationships within the community. This process of developing relationships is in effect the engine for building change within a community.

As noted, the capacity focus model involves calculating the assets that may exist within a community. The role of community members becomes one of aligning its assets together to build a strong future for youth (Kretzmann & McKnight, 1993). In any given community, the assets that may be available to support a program of youth development include community members, agencies, organizations, institutions, and other groupings that exist. Individuals and community organizations may bring together their unique talents, skills, and knowledge in a collaborative way to advance concerns related to youth.

Certainly youth workers must work in a collaborative fashion with such individuals and organizations to build partnerships that help identify concerns and solutions to challenges, locate resources, and/or provide guidance to a community's effort. Often community groups, such as volunteer organizations or clubs, are directly involved in issues that impact a given community. Such organizations with grassroots community origins and leadership capacities have the ability to address community concerns. Such individuals and organizations hold a great deal of influence within a community and have access to human, physical, and fiscal resources. They often have a depth of knowledge of a community that extends over a long period of time and can bring that perspective to bear upon the community.

Community institutions have varying levels of organization. The structure of organizations ranges from formal to informal. Organizations such as service or fraternal groups, civic groups, neighborhood associations, and others may have a significant amount of influence, power, or control within a community. More formally organized community groups, nonprofit organizations, government agencies, schools, religious organizations, civic institutions, and businesses may have a legal, moral or community-sanctioned mandate that provides

them with a great deal of influence. Such organizations often have as an important part of their vision or mission statements concerns for youth within a community. Many of these types of organizations have resources and can provide direct or in-kind support that may benefit a community's development of youth.

Community building for youth development is increasingly embraced throughout the United States. Efforts such as America's Promise, CityYear, and AmeriCorps are all reflections of strategies aimed at strengthening youth development within communities. Building collaborative relationships, partnerships, and other efforts aimed at connecting community resources are at the heart of this process. This process is built and renewed continuously between individuals, associations, and the institutions of the community. Such relationship building will strengthen the fabric of the community and solidify its efforts to develop youth within the community.

YOUTH IN AMERICA TODAY

There are 39 million youth between the ages of ten and nineteen living in America today (U.S. Census, 2000). This represents 14% of the population of the United States. By the year 2010, it is estimated that 42 million youth will be in this age range. In the year 2050, it is estimated that the youth population of America will be 53 million. As one can see, we live a society where the youth population is expanding. The influence of youth is ever present today and will increase in the future.

In this section of the book, a discussion of who and where our youth can be located, as well as future growth projections by region within the United States, will be outlined. In addition, we will explore how youth spend their time. The chapter will also include a discussion of the social health, physical health, educational attainment, and economic factors influencing youth today.

Who Are Our Youth?

The United States has become a "mosaic," with vibrant youth that possess various characteristics decorating the canvas of America. The diverse cultural groups of youth have inspired a whirlwind of change in the field of youth work. When analyzing the youth population, there are several groups that encompass significant portions of the population. Within America, there are 32 million youth who are Caucasian, 6.2 million youth who are African-American, and nearly 800,000 youth who are Asian, American Indian, Eskimo or from the Pacific Islands (U.S. Census, 2000). These statistics all increase as the projection is cast for 2050.

After looking at the statistics, the importance of incorporating a multicultural perspective is essential in youth work. As discussed in Chapter 8, multiculturalism is an integral part of youth development. The demographics of the youth population will continue to vary, thus creating a norm of daily interaction with vari-

ous cultures. Youth workers who can create programs and modify existing ones to meet the needs of the various cultural youth groups they encounter will enhance the existing field of youth development.

Social and Physical Health of Youth

Each day, millions of youth participate in activities that have life-altering effects on them. Some examples include sports programs, religious groups, support groups, after-school programs, and community services. Each one of these activities carries with it a specific value system and code of ethics that manage the interaction of youth. These interactions during the activities become the framework for how youth may engage others in a social setting. Youth learn verbal and non-verbal communication, how to work in groups, and active listening.

Many of these activities are the only outlets to which youth can escape and avoid the dangers associated with other parts of their social life. Drug and alcohol use and abuse, physical, psychological, emotional, and sexual abuse and neglect, unprotected sex, teenage pregnancy and parenting, delinquency, lack of physical fitness, violence, and crime are just a few of the obstacles that may negatively impact a youth's life. If there is not an opportunity to avoid these dangers and grow and interact with their peers, a youth may have lasting psychological, emotional, and physical scars.

- **Drug and alcohol use and abuse.** The age of first use of alcohol has decreased steadily over the decades, with sixteen years old as the most recent statistic indicating initial consumption. In 1998, one out of five teenagers were current alcohol drinkers and one out of thirteen were binge drinkers, consuming five or more drinks on one but no more than four occasions (Greenblatt, 2000). Since 1992, there has been a steady increase in drug usage among eighth, tenth, and twelfth graders with no differences in usage between males and females (Johnston, O'Malley & Bachman, 1996). The number of juvenile arrests for drug-related crimes reached 148,000 in 1998. Drug and alcohol abuse has also been linked with crime and delinquency, with over 40% of the youth incarcerated in long-term juvenile facilities stating they encountered drugs for the first time before the age of twelve.

- ***Physical, psychological, emotional, and sexual abuses or neglect.*** Within the United States, there are over 263,000 reported cases of abuse and neglect to children between the ages of ten and eighteen years old (U.S. Census, 2000). Signs of abuse include bruising, fractures, burns, patterns of injuries, low self-esteem, unexplained aggression, poor hygiene, exhaustion, lethargy, and constant hunger. Neglect is characterized as the failure of the child's parents or care-takers to provide the child with the basic necessities of life, which include shelter, nutrition, supervision, health, education, affection, and protection (Cowen, 1999). Maltreatment or abuse of youth also includes exposure to parents who have substance addictions, psychiatric disorders, and violent tendencies (Atwool, 2000).

- ***Unsafe or unprotected sex, teenage pregnancy, and teenage parenting.*** Research indicates that youth under the age of eighteen years who give birth tend to have academic deficiencies, poorer socioeconomic status, repeat pregnancies, abusive tendencies towards their children, and be single parents (Flanagan, Coll, Andreozzi, & Riggs, 1995). The amount of youth under the age of eighteen that have engaged in sexual intercourse has risen steadily since 1970, and the average age at first intercourse has declined (Caron & Moskey, 2002). In the United States, 24% of females and 27% of males under the age of fifteen years have had sex (Cooksey, Mott, & Neubauer, 2002). Out-of-wedlock birth rates for fifteen to nineteen year olds rose nearly 10% in the early 1990s. According to Miller (2002), there are 900,000 teenage pregnancies a year, and Lowenthal and Lowenthal (1997) indicate those youth ages ten to fourteen comprising the fastest growing group of parents.

- **Delinquency, crime, and violence.** Youth crime increased steadily through 1980s, with nearly fifty thousand people murdered by youths between the ages of twelve and twenty-four years. During this time period, youth accounted for 35.5% of all nontraffic-related arrests in the United States (Simons, Finlay, & Yang, 1991). A result is that many of the incarcerated youth left dependents that were then incorporated into the family structure of relatives or foster homes.

- **Physical fitness.** A third of all high school students fail to meet the current public health recommendations associated with fitness. This includes three or more sessions per week of moderate to vigorous physical activity (Gordon-Larsen, McMurray, & Popkin, 1999, as cited in Hatcher & Scarpa, 2002). An unfortunate combination with the lack of physical activity is that many adolescents have poor diets, consuming too much fat, sodium and sugar with little fiber (Gleason & Suitor, 2001; Munoz, Krebs-Smith, Ballard-Barbash, & Cleveland, 1997, as cited in Hatcher & Scarpa, 2002; Siega-Riz, Carson, & Popkin, 1998;). The importance of exercise, physical fitness, and a healthy diet should be primary components of youth programs and activities.

Educational Attainment

School attendance and success is considered a primary component of a youth's life. School is the place where youth may develop the groundwork for how they will progress through life. It is the opportunity to discover and develop talents in a variety of areas, as well as learn how to interact socially. Teachers guide youth and illustrate the different steps needed to be successful; they are often the first role models that youth encounter in their lives.

There is unfortunately a high number of youth that drop out, underachieve, and fail. About 30% of fourteen to seventeen year olds are behind their modal grade, and each year about 700,000 youth drop out of school, with 25% of eighteen to nineteen year olds failing to complete their high school education (Dryfoos, 1997). Indicators of a youth's possible failure, underachievement or dropout include poor academic performance, lack of social attachment to school, low expectations by the student and the teacher, school discipline problems, low socioeconomic status, and parents' not completing high school (National Center for Education Statistics [NCES], 1995).

The education that youth receive in school is not only academic knowledge, but life skills as well. For example, if we are learning the English language, one of the first things taught in primary school is how to write in English. As we progress through the different grades, we begin to grasp the vowels and con-

Exhibit 1.1
How Could This Happen?

News stories about a teenage girl who went to a party in Des Moines where she was allegedly attacked by teenage boys now charged with sexual abuse should serve as a starting point for a discussion. A serious discussion.

Parents, clergy, and teachers should talk with older youngsters about the horrifying accusations. How could something like this happen?

It's not a theoretical question. Sexual assault is not uncommon. Look at official rape statistics.

The FBI's Uniform Crime Report for 2000 showed the national rate at thirty-two reported rapes per 100,000 population. It's estimated nine of ten such offenses go unreported. Most victims are girls and women, but some are boys and men. Statistics from Iowa State University last year included four reports of forcible sex with men.

Yes, everyone knows sexual assault is abhorrent. Then why isn't it so taboo that it virtually never occurs? What cultural attitudes send the message that this kind of violence is, for too many people, acceptable? The teens involved at the party must have thought it was.

Different societies have different degrees of tolerance for rape. Why in this society, for example, have date rape drugs become something students must guard against on campus? Why didn't other students at the party in Des Moines immediately stop the attack that reportedly continued for thirty to forty-five minutes?

Other boys periodically opened the door to the bathroom and told the alleged attackers to quit, according to police, but the assault continued. Other girls were in the living room while the assault took place. Didn't they hear the victim yelling—as the police report describes—as she fought off the assailants? Was it just a part of the activities at the party?

Youngsters need more guidance than many get regarding sexual assault. Without making them too fearful, they need to know what they can do to protect themselves and others.

And we ask again, why isn't sexual assault so beyond the pale in our culture that it simply doesn't occur?

How could this happen?: Why does our culture, at some level, tolerate sexual assault [Editorial]. (2002, October 28). *The Des Moines Register.*

sonants, how to structure words and sentences to form conversations and write papers. We also learn the appropriateness of language, such as when it is the proper time and place to say something.

The aforementioned example may seem simple, but there are youth that do not have the opportunity to learn such a thing as language. Not every youth has the chance to complete his or her schooling, or in some cases even attend. This absence of educational attainment detrimentally affects the life course of youth. They do not have the opportunity to learn academically or practice their social skills for future endeavors. In the end, a youth may turn to an alternative for education, such as a gang, and become indoctrinated into a culture that can have a fatal conclusion.

Youth and the Economy

Youth culture significantly impacts the market economy, playing a vital role in the production, distribution and sales of goods and services. Each year, advertisements and sales campaigns target the youth culture for potential investment in whatever product is publicized. According to a survey study by Teenage Research Unlimited, American adolescents spend $89 billion per year, or an average of $61 a week each (Teenage Research Unlimited, 1994, as cited in Russell, 1994). Many investments by youth are related to factors associated with the existing social, physical and even political climate of the area they live. Youth may feel the pressure to belong to the "in" crowd or clique, and pur-

chase something believing that it will be a stepping-stone to acceptance. Some youth may have the ability to make these purchases, while other youth may not have the opportunity, thus resulting in disapproval or criticism from their peers.

The spending patterns of youth fluctuate with the trends associated with their culture (Russell, 1994). A favorable style or tendency is labeled a trend. This could be a type of clothing, music, or hairstyle. When something is considered trendy, it is the most appealing product at that time in youth culture. As a product's appeal grows, so does the desire by youth to possess it. Often products will sell out as the wants of youth outweigh the production of goods. As we have witnessed in youth culture, a product's desirability over time will diminish and be replaced with a new fresh product. As the new product moves into the foreground and becomes the trendy thing to own, the other products slip into the background. This cycle continually repeats itself, with the money spent going to the business that can keep up with the trends associated with youth culture.

In some instances, youth become employed to support their spending patterns. There are several industries for youth to gain work—retail, foodservice, and labor are a few examples. Having a job may build important characteristics within youth—resiliency, trust, a sense of responsibility, the ability to share and work together, and loyalty. Many youth are given the opportunity to attend school during the day and work in the evening. This may be an option for youth as long as the job and its requirements do not violate any legal regulations.

The youth population is a budding new group of individuals within the workplace, fresh with new ideas and potential. The naïveté of youth can also be a quality that employers may take advantage of in the workplace. Throughout the twentieth century, there have been instances of overworked, underpaid youth that employers have hired to create products at the cheapest possible prices. The term "child labor" usually refers to youth performing work that is exploitative or detrimental to their development. For the youth, it means less time for an education or, possibly, no education.

Child labor can also be problematic to children's health because they often work in dangerous conditions, exposed to lasting physical and psychological harm (Conley, 2000). Up to seven million children and adolescents in the United States work either part-time or full-time (Ambadekar, Wahab, Zodpey, & Khandait, 1999). The National Safe Workplace Institute reported that there were 5.5 million workers in the United States between the ages of 12 and 17 (as cited in Pignatella, 1995). Within one year of starting their jobs, 70,000 youth had been injured and 300 killed on site. Some of the accidents and fatalities were related to slips, falls, burns, electrical shocks, vehicle accidents, heavy lifting, chemical exposure, and loss of sleep.

Youth may develop into fine young professionals if stable, adequately structured employment programs are built. According to the American News Service (1997), several corporations have established rules delineating the treatment of youth employees. The Kmart Corporation posted placards in all of their stores describing the "Teen Worker's Bill of Rights" and workplace safety for youth. The Whataburger Corporation in the state of Texas developed a computer tracking system monitoring the hours and shifts of youth employees. Wawa convenience stores in four states designed different colored smocks for youth employees so that managers would know on sight who was not allowed to work the electric meat slicer. These acts illustrate the importance of developing strong competent youth workers whose safety and well being is vital to the success of the organization.

CHALLENGES FACED BY YOUTH

Each day a youth encounters multiple challenges that may test their decision-making skills, integrity, and resolve. These challenges manifest themselves in a variety of ways, causing potential anguish, anxiety, and nervousness. Navigating through various social, cognitive, and emotional challenges may require guidance, role modeling, and advice from others around the youth. Collaboration with others allows the youth to experiment and attempt different solutions to dealing with the challenges they encounter.

The Youth Work Press (1994) has identified various social, cognitive, and emotional challenges that youth encounter as they mature in life.

- **Social Isolation.** Inability to relate to others outside their community, few friends and limited relationship building skills, lack of experience and high anxiety levels in a range of unfamiliar social settings, and an inability to share feelings and experiences with others.

- **Limited Mobility.** Difficulty engaging in various activities requiring transportation, difficulty developing distance relationships, time and participation restrictions due to lack of transport that may lead to high risk situations such as hitchhiking or walking alone.

- **Narrow Horizons.** Stigmatizing or labeling according to social expectations of community, a fear of mobility, limitations related to extended learning due to community traditions, and a pressure to conform or fit in.

- **Inequality of Provision.** Low standard of quality related to facilities and supervision, unmet needs due to marginalization of youth, and difficulty challenging local authority structures for improvement.

- **Visibility.** Anonymity in large numbered populations, a feeling of being "lost in the shuffle" of daily activities, close/claustrophobic links to others if community is small, and difficulty in maintaining a level of confidentiality.

- **Negativity.** Perception of mistrust from adults and a feeling of inevitability that adults' needs will be a higher priority.

- **Identity.** Difficulty establishing lifestyle; a feeling of intrusion from unwanted individuals; a sense of entanglement between different roles in life; and dealing with racism, sexism, and other cultural attacks.

As discussed in Chapter 5, the drive behind youth development is to establish a strong, lasting foundation that all stakeholders can build upon in distinct ways that benefit youth. If those stakeholders analyze together the different challenges specific to their community, there may be a focused, precise result involving members of the community, including the youth in question.

Pittman, Irby, and Ferber (2000) discuss two traditional viewpoints regarding youth work and the need to restructure it to address today's youth population. Their discussion of the problem-diagnosis concept and the potential long-lasting effects of collaborative youth work efforts illustrate the importance of combining resources and working together to improve our future generation. Getting on board with these two viewpoints will enable youth and youth workers to become synergetic and create innovative programs beneficial to all whom take part.

Working with youth should include more than just "solving the problem" of the youth; it should include an analysis of all the factors that make up youth's lives. To improve our youth programs, we may want to move beyond a problem-diagnosis concept and into an environmental analysis concept. Piggybacking this environmental analysis is the idea that for effective programs to occur, they should be more than a "quick fix."

Youth development is not a laboratory experiment with all the variables controlled and designed for a specific outcome; it includes spontaneous, often unsuspected factors that are important for understanding. Long-term efforts may be most effective to growth in youth. These efforts may include an extension of services for youth beyond the typical after-school programs that have sprung up in all areas. As the services are extended, the umbrella of resources and programs can encompass more youth than we are currently serving. These different strategic points are part of the dynamic structure of youth development. As we begin to reassess the topic and goals of youth development, our energy will be directed in a more beneficial manner to all involved.

SUMMARY

Youth today are a vibrant portion of our population that will continue to grow and make significant contributions to the overall structure of society. Recognizing the impact of youth includes realizing if they are going to positively affect society, adults are going to need to

provide guidance and role modeling. Youth workers are often the beacon youth turn to when confronted with issues of substance abuse, sexual pressures, and familial problems. Examining the environment of youth gives insight into how to assist them in navigating through instances of confusion and uncertainty so that the result is beneficial to them.

Youth workers who remain ethical in their actions exude the qualities youth need in order to maintain the fortitude to develop their own ethics. Collaborative efforts with youth workers provide youth opportunities to step in and assume leadership roles they may encounter in the future. These roles give youth chances to create and maintain value systems defining who they are. The effectiveness of a youth's value system lies in the nurturing youth workers provide in daily settings. Youth workers who aid in the successful development of youth can take pride and understand that their actions are affecting future generations of society.

REFERENCES

Ambadekar, N. N., Wahab, S. N., Zodpey, S. P., & Khandait, D. W. (1999). Effect of child labor on growth of children. *Public Health, 113*, 303-306.

Atwool, N. (2000). Trauma and children's rights. In A. B. Smith, M. Gollop, K. Marshall, & K. Nairn (Eds.), *Advocating for children: International perspectives on children's rights* (pp. 19-31). Dunedin, New Zealand: University of Otago Press.

Bogenschneider, K. (1996). Family related prevention programs: An ecological risk/protective theory for building prevention programs, policies, and community capacity to support youth, *Family Relations, 45*, 127-138.

Caron, S. L. & Moskey, E. G. (2002). Changes over time in teenage sexual relationships: Comparing the high school class of 1950, 1975, and 2000. *Adolescence, 37*(47), 515-526.

Child Trends Research Brief. (2002, June). *Encouraging teens to adopt a safe, healthy lifestyle: A foundation for improving future adult behaviors* (Issue Brief No. 2). Washington, DC: Juliet L. Hatcher and Juliet Scarpa.

Cooksey, E. C., Mott, F. L., & Neubauer, S. A. (2002). Friendships and early relationships: Links to sexual initiation among American adolescents born to young mothers. *Perspectives on Sexual and Reproductive Health, 34*(3), 118-126.

Cowen, P. S. (1999). Child neglect injuries of omission. *Pediatric Nursing, 25*(4), 401.

Delgado, M. (2002). *New frontiers for youth development in the twenty-first century: Revitalizing and broadening youth development.* New York, NY: Columbia University Press.

Dryfoos, J. G. (1997). Adolescents at risk: Shaping programs to fit the need. *The Journal of Negro Education, 65*(1), 5-19.

Edginton, C. R. (2001). *A profession as one's calling: A personal reflection.* Macau: Revista do Instituto Politécnico de Macau. 4(1). 131-153.

Edginton, C. R. (1997, November/December). Youth development: Enabling the future. *Journal of Physical Education, Recreation and Dance, 68*(9),15-20.

Flanagan, P., Coll, C. G., Andreozzi, L., & Riggs, S. (1995). Predicting maltreatment of children of teenage mothers. *Archives of Pediatrics & Adolescent Medicine, 149*(4), 451-455.

Greenblatt, J. C. (2000, March). *Patterns of alcohol use among adolescents and associations with emotional and behavioral problems.* Rockville, MD: Office of Applied Studies: Substance Abuse and Mental Health Services Administration.

Hahn, A. B., & Raley, G. A. (1998, Summer). Youth development: On the path toward professionalization. *Non-Profit Management & Leadership, 8*(4), 387-401.

Hamilton, S. F., & Hamilton, M. A., & Pittman, K. (2004). Principles for Youth Development. In S.F. Hamilton & M. A. Hamilton (Eds.) *The youth development handbook.* (pp. 3-22). Thousand Oaks, CA: Sage.

Hughes, J. L. (1897). *Fröebel's educational laws for all teachers* (p. 125). New York, NY: D. Appleton and Co.

Johnston, L. D., O'Malley, P. M., & Bachman, J. G. (1996). *National Survey Results on Drug Use from the Monitoring the Future Study, 1975-1994.* Washington, DC: U.S. Department of Health and Human Services.

Kretzmann, J. P., & McKnight, J. L. (1993). *Building communities from the inside out.* Evanston, IL: The Asset Based Community Development Institute.

Lowenthal, B., & Lowenthal, R. (1997). Teenage parenting: Challenges, interventions and programs. *Childhood Education, 74*(1), 29-32.

Miller, K. (2002). Preventing risky sexual behaviors in adolescents. *American Family Physician, 66*(77), 1311.

National Center for Education Statistics. (1995, July). *At-risk eighth graders four years later: Statistics in brief* (Report No. 95-736). Washington, DC: U.S. Department of Education.

Outhwaite, W., & Bottomore, T. (1994). *The Blackwell dictionary of twentieth-century social thought.* Malden, MA: Blackwell Publishers.

Perkins, D. F., Borden, L. M., Keith, J. G., Hoppe-Rooney, T. L., & Villarruel, F. A. (2003). Community youth development. In F. A. Villarruel, D. F. Perkins, L. M. Borden, & J. G. Keith (Eds.), *Community Youth Development.* (pp. 1-23). Thousand Oaks, CA: Sage.

Pignatella, M. A. (1995). The recurring nightmare of child labor abuse: Causes and solutions for the '90s. *Boston College Third World Law Journal, 15,* 171-210.

Pittman, K., Irby, M., & Ferber, T. (2000). *Unfinished business: Further reflections on a decade of promoting youth development.* Takoma Park, MD: Forum for Youth Investment.

Russell, R. (1996). *Pastimes: The context of contemporary leisure.* Dubuque, IA: Times Mirror Higher Education Group, Inc.

Simons, J. M., Finlay, B., & Yang, A. (1991). *The adolescent and young adult fact book.* Washington, DC: Children's Defense Fund.

Statistical Abstract of the United States (2000). Washington, DC: U.S. Bureau of the Census (2000). *Statistical Abstract of the United States: 2000.* Washington, DC.: U.S. Department of Commerce, Economics and Statistics Admin.

Substance Abuse and Mental Health Services Administration. (2000, March). *Patterns of alcohol use among adolescents and associations with emotional and behavioral problems* (OAS Working Paper). Rockville, MD: Janet C. Greenblatt.

Swisher, R., & Whitlock, J. (2004). How neighborhoods matter for youth development. In S. F. Hamilton, M. A. Hamilton, (Eds.), *The youth development handbook* (pp. 216-238). Thousand Oaks, CA: Sage.

Villarruel, F. A., Perkins, D. F., Borden, L. M., & Keith, J. G. (2003). *Community youth development: Programs, policies, and practices.* Thousand Oaks, CA: Sage.

Work safe targets teens nationwide. (1997, July 20). *Omaha World Herald,* p. 1G.

CHAPTER TWO

Adolescence

INTRODUCTION

The fascination with young people in our country runs deep. News headlines, magazine cover pages, multi-million dollar movies, radio airwaves, and even television commercials are packed full with the faces and life stories of young people in America. In fact, in many ways being young reflects our nation's consciousness; we think of ourselves as possessing many of the characteristics that might traditionally be used to describe what it means to be young. We think of ourselves as strong, innovative trendsetters who will provide future leadership throughout the rest of the world.

However, young people are also the targets of much criticism and fear. In many of our communities they are considered to be dangerous, posing risk to individuals, property, and the established social order. They are believed to be at a higher risk than most individuals to commit crimes, abuse drugs and alcohol, drive dangerously, or even commit suicide. They simultaneously represent both our greatest hopes, as well as our deepest fears, and because of this, every hit song, fashion trend, test score, and criminal act that involves a young person hits America's radar screen as an indication of the direction in which our nation is headed.

A testament to this interest in young people and helping them become competent and healthy adults can be found on the shelves of nearly any bookstore or community public library. Shelves upon shelves of books aimed at helping parents understand their teenagers, teachers understand their students, or even to help young people understand themselves are offered by learned experts from a variety of fields. Books with titles such as, *Your Adolescent: What's Normal, What's Not,* and *When to Seek Help* (2000), *Caring for Your Teenager: The Complete and Authoritative Guide* (2003), *Saving Beauty from Beast: How to Protect your Daughters* (2003), and *So You Want to be a Teenager: What Every Pre-teen Must Know* (2002), seek to serve our nation's hunger for both guidance and understanding about the seemingly mysterious young people in our lives.

However, the "mystery" surrounding young people even befuddles the so-called experts at times. Every so often a story about a group of young people, or an individual, is reported by the media that flies in the face of the leading theories or conceptions about the types of behavior we can expect from teenagers. For example, it is popularly accepted in our society that teenage males will at times exhibit aggressive and violent behavior, but when teenage girls exhibit the same type of behavior we wonder what caused the behavior. We wonder whether or not teenage girls in general are changing, or if the incident was a localized misnomer—much like the questions that the hazing situation at Glenbrook North High School in Chicago, Illinois generated in the aftermath of the outrage that the student's actions generated. It seems that our society is continuously asking itself, "What is wrong with young people today and what can be done about them?"

In this chapter, initial definitions of adolescence will be presented. This will be followed by a discussion framing the concept of adolescence. Important in this discussion will be a review of prevailing and related presumptions and concepts regarding adolescence. Following will be a discussion of alternative views of popular thought regarding youth. Presented will be competing views of this period of life. Implications regarding one's chosen view of adolescence for youth workers will be presented. Last, the implications for the use of metaphors and terms used to reflect our thinking about youth will be included.

DEFINING ADOLESCENCE

Without question, adolescence is a period of complexity and challenge. It is a time of great promise, yet also a time fraught with many unforeseen worries and burdens. For youth, adolescence is a period of tremendous freedom, yet also one of increasing responsibility. It is a time of considerable change where youth physically and psychologically are engaged in an extensive metamorphosis. An understanding of adolescence is fundamental to successful youth work. Further, our time is one punctuated by contradictory and competing social representations of youth. Such perspectives must command our attention and also have great influence on our conceptions of youth development.

G. Stanley Hall's two-volume seminal work *Adolescence* (1904) brought attention to this period of development in the lives of individuals. His writings attempted to provide a full survey of the psychological factors that influence youth, including their relationship to physiology, anthropology, sociology, sex, crime, religion, and education. Hall identified puberty as the defining moment of adolescence and suggested that it is a period of "storm and stress" (Roche & Tucker, 1997, p. 19). From this perspective, "adolescence is seen as a potentially distressing time for all young people" due to the biological changes (Roche & Tucker, 1997, p. 19).

Such early definitions gave way to assumptions that youth were in trouble. Initial youth work efforts directed toward adolescents were framed from this perspective which resulted in individuals and organizations attempting to assist youth out of trouble. It also gave way to the notion that youth could be viewed as trouble. This perspective created a sense that youth needed to be controlled or perhaps placated in some fashion so as to maintain the status quo within society.

This perspective continues to permeate the thinking of Americans today. Recently, an article appearing in a midwestern newspaper championed the need for employment for teens. The essence of the editorial found in Exhibit 2.1 is that many youth are impoverished, drop out of school, are living on their own, or are in other desperate situations requiring professional intervention. This perspective perpetuates the notion that youth are in trouble and need to be assisted and that adolescence is a distinct period of time separate from child or adulthood.

We often think of adolescence as the period of time between childhood and adulthood. Most classical definitions of adolescence are similar in their perspective. For example, the *Oxford English Dictionary* defines adolescence as that period which extends childhood to manhood or womanhood and as a process or condition of growing up (1984, p. 31). Similarly, *Webster's New World Dictionary* also defines adolescence as the period of time between puberty and maturity (1988, p. 18). These definitions provide a timeframe for identifying a relative time in one's life in which adolescence occurs. However, the definitions do not provide insight into the processes, whether individual or cultural, that influence this process of development.

No doubt, adolescence is a period of transition, presenting young people with many challenges and opportunities. It is also a time of growth, presenting opportunities for expanding one's horizons, shaping one's self concept, acquiring friendships and peer relationships, and finding one's calling in life. It also provides many opportunities for introspection, reflection, and self-examination. It is a period of great values development, clarification, and testing. Also, adolescence may be a period of serious anxiety, not only for individual youth, but also for their family, friends, peers, and even perhaps society at large. Without question, it is one of the most critical phases of the development of an individual.

Physical development, thinking and reasoning, identity formulation, creation of friendships and peer relationships, reassessment of family relations, sexuality, vocation, and leisure patterns and

Exhibit 2.1
An Editorial Reflecting Youth in Trouble

With all the talk about adult unemployment, it's easy to forget that teenagers are having a tough time finding work, too. The unemployment rate for teens was 18.5% in May, the highest in nine years, according to the U.S. Labor Department. Those kids, ages sixteen to nineteen and generally lacking experience, are on the bottom of the pool of applicants for even minimum-wage jobs.

Maybe this news doesn't seem like such a big deal. The perception, after all, is that American teens, with a roof over their heads and food on the table, work for spending money. A job is just *something extra*.

And that is the case for some lucky teens.

But millions of teens live in impoverished families. New Kids Count data report 17% of kids live in poverty. For every one thousand girls ages fifteen to seventeen, twenty-seven give birth. These girls have children to care for. Nine percent of teens drop out of high school and 8% don't work or go to school.

These young people desperately need job opportunities. Some kids are kicked out of their homes, are in independent living programs for foster youth or have child-support payments.

Even kids in middle- and upper-class families can be responsible for everything from paying for their own necessities to saving for college.

The hope would be that any teen who wanted to work would have the opportunity to do so, but that's not the case in this job market.

How many young Americans are left feeling dejected, wondering what the future holds for them as adults if they can't secure a job fit for a teenager?

Source: Missing opportunities for teens. (2003, June 16). *The Des Moines Register*, p. 6A.

attitudes are greatly influenced during adolescence. As Coleman and Hendry (1996, p. 2) have suggested, adolescence is increasingly recognized as having an important bearing on what happens in later life—equal to the events of an individual's early life. Clearly, life span developmental psychologists have noted that adolescence impacts not only an individual's physical changes but also their emotional, social, and cognitive development. Further, many agents of socialization are present, influencing the development of individuals during this adolescent period. In fact, it may be argued that development of the individual and the social context within which youth exist have a reciprocal influence on each other (Coleman & Hendry, 1996, p. 3).

Extended Adolescence

As indicated above, the concept of adolescence may be shaped and influenced by the social and cultural context of a given society. We have traditionally viewed the process of adolescence as one fixed between childhood and adulthood. However, what constitutes adulthood and when one achieves it is culturally defined and changes from time to time. Today, individuals are extending their adolescence by delaying entry into the work world or by extending the period of time within which they remain in educational institutions. For example, at the turn of the century, adulthood was achieved often by the age of fourteen. However, when child labor laws emerged and secondary schools became more dominant, extending

educational opportunities, the period of adolescence was stretched. The same could be said today as more and more individuals enter colleges and universities, thereby extending adolescence.

What are important steps in achieving adulthood? Irvine (2003, p. 6a) has suggested that some of the important steps in achieving adulthood include: completing an education, working full time, being able to support a family, being financially independent, living independent of parents, marrying, and having a child. She notes that the average age which individuals do the above is changing. For example, she reports that the average age that people should marry is now pegged at 25.7 years and the average age for having children is 26.2. Thus it is apparent that the perception of when an individual should enter adulthood is being extended, and that the period of adolescence is longer.

What are the implications of extended adolescence? Will this period provide greater opportunities for freedom, self-examination, as well as opportunities to bring about different societal and cultural perspectives as youth have been viewed to do in the past? How will educational and other human service institutions be impacted in terms of providing meaningful, relevant, and timely services for an expanded population of adolescents? What will the challenges be of holding individuals out of the labor market? How will this affect our economy? Will this change traditional concepts of self-reliance, independence, and perhaps even family life? How will society's values, norms, and customs be impacted by such changes? All of these elements will have great impact on the way in which society is constructed. All will have impact on how we view youth and how youth work is formulated in the twenty-first century.

FRAMING A CONCEPT OF ADOLESCENCE: PREVAILING ASSUMPTIONS

The concept of adolescence guides much of the popular understandings that our society holds about young people, and represents a central component "to the youth development approach to conceptualizing youth" (Wyn & White, 1997, p. 52). In general, the term "adolescence" refers to the stage in the developmental sequence impacting the cognitive, physical, and psychological maturation of individuals in their second decade of life—the "teen" years. It is during these years of adolescence that an individual is thought to complete the work of moving out of childhood and into adulthood. While a number of competing views exist regarding the notion of adolescence, a few central assumptions appear to dominate the landscape of thought about young people experiencing this period of life.

Assumptions about
Adolescence as a Life Stage
According to Wyn and White (1997) a variety of assumptions appear to take precedence in the

popular conceptualizations of adolescence. The first of these assumptions suggests that the experience of adolescence is universal. That is, everyone experiences a period of life that reflects the life stage adolescence, during which all individuals are actively involved in negotiating their way through a number of developmental tasks. These tasks center around issues involving physical development, thinking and reasoning, identity formulation, creation of friendships and peer relationships, reassessment of family relations, sexuality, vocation, and leisure patterns and attitudes. The ability of an individual to negotiate his or her way through difficulties he or she experiences in these areas as an adolescent, as Coleman and Hendry (1996) have suggested, has an important bearing on what happens in later life—equally important to the events occurring during an individual's early years of life.

A second assumption involves the idea that adolescence is a "dangerous" period in the developmental sequence between childhood and adulthood. As mentioned, this idea originated with G. Stanley Hall's (1904) conception of adolescence as a period of "storm and stress." Hall identified puberty as the defining moment of adolescence and suggested that this experience brought with a great deal of torment, placing and individual's healthy development at risk; and from this perspective, "adolescence is seen as a potentially distressing time for all young people" due to the biological changes taking place (Roche & Tucker, 1997, p. 19).

A last assumption that appears to persist in the common beliefs about adolescence is the idea that, as Wyn and White state, that "a pre-social self exists within the individual, but that it must be found and developed" (1997, p. 53). The belief in the existence of a "pre-social self," a self independent of social relationships or social circumstances, is critical, because it is this notion that youth workers, educators, and other professionals focused on adolescent development use to justify their existence in the lives of young people. From this perspective, young people are qualitatively different from adults in that they have yet to discover who they are. Youth are thought to be actively involved in the process of trying out a variety of different, often competing, selves in the hope of finding their "true" self.

These three assumptions carry with them critical implications for the practice of youth work. They involve thinking about young people in a very specific way, as well as shaping beliefs about what opportunities or supports youth need in order to develop into healthy adults. They impact the way adults legitimize and conceptualize their role in the lives of youth, as well as the role youth are to take in shaping their own developmental paths and opportunities. These practical implications, as well as others, will be discussed later in this chapter, however the key question to consider at this point are which view of adolescence these assumptions tend to align themselves with, and what other conceptions of this period of life may exist.

THINKING OF YOUNG PEOPLE: ALTERNATIVE VIEWS

While the above assumptions tend to dominate popular thought about adolescence, a number of competing views exist about what this period of life involves and how it should be characterized. From a more classical perspective, there are a number of ways to view the concept of adolescence. Seven major views of adolescence have emerged: the psychoanalytical, the biological, the cognitive-developmental, the social learning theory, the ecological, the sociological, anthropological, and the integrated view. These views are very briefly summarized as follows:

Psychoanalytical View of Adolescence

With the psychoanalytical view, influenced by the work of Sigmund Freud (1938), Anna Freud (1974) argues that adolescence is one stage in a series of developmental periods triggered by specific conflicts occurring between natural biological drives and the social expectations young people experience. For the adolescent, the conflict involves puberty and sexual maturation and the prevailing societal views surrounding his or her new found sexual desires and needs. For the psychoanalyst, resolving this conflict is the major task confronting young people; the well adjusted adolescent will have successfully negotiated harmony between their own sexual desires and their society's prevailing beliefs about adolescent sexuality. Erik Erikson (1968) later modified this view, adding that the adolescent also needs to achieve ego identity (i.e., to become one's self). This developmental task coincides with the onset of Freud's psychosexual stage—puberty.

Biological View of Adolescence

The biological point of view, first initiated by G. Stanley Hall (1907), defines adolescence as the final stage of maturation before the child enters adulthood. The primary focus is on the specific body changes, triggered by puberty, which occur during the period of life encompassing the teenage years (ages twelve to twenty). During this developmental stage, young people experience changes in body size, maturation of their reproductive organs, hormonal changes, the emergence of sexual desires, as well as the development of secondary sexual characteristics (i.e., facial hair in males and menarche in females). From this perspective, healthy adolescent development depends on how well a teenager is able to adjust to the biological changes he or she is experiencing, as well as how well he or she is able to control newly forming sexual desires.

Cognitive-Developmental View of Adolescence

The cognitive-developmental view, developed through the work of Piaget and Inhelder (1968), argues that development occurs in a series of distinct stages, each characterized by growth in a variety of areas related to knowledge. These aspects include egocentrism versus objectivity, object permanence (con-servation), symbolic functioning, internalization of action, as well as classes and relationships. For the adolescent (ages eleven to fifteen), the challenge is to overcome lingering egocentrism, develop the ability to recognize unchanged aspects of an object after transformation, negotiate an understanding of complex written and spoken symbols, develop the ability to mentally manipulate objects in the environment, and to recognize the classifications and relationships existing amongst real, as well as perceived, objects and events (e.g., developmental tasks related to Piaget's concept of formal operations).

Social Learning Theory View of Adolescence

The social learning theory perspective on adolescence, developed most significantly by Albert Bandura (1977), is founded on the principles of conditioning and reinforcement—modeling, cognition, personal standards, and a sense of self-efficacy. From this perspective, young people negotiate their transition from childhood to adulthood by actively imitating and modeling the behavior that the adults around them exhibit. Healthy development depends on the extent to which adults in the lives of youth—parents, teachers, youth workers, coaches, and ministers—model healthy adult behavior, as well as the extent which the display of positive behaviors are reinforced. From this perspective, adolescent development is a reflection of the social circumstances surrounding a young person. They literally learn what they live.

Ecological View of Adolescence

From an ecological perspective, a point of view developed by Urie Bronfenbrenner (1979), the social and physical environments within which adolescents reside and participate significantly impacts their development. In general, this point of view suggests that the system of environmental experiences (e.g., school, home, and peer group) that make up the life of a young person develop certain activity, role, and relational patterns that impact who an adolescent later becomes as an adult. It is these patterns that shape the adolescent's conception of self, beliefs about his or her role in society, as well as his or her relational understandings.

Sociological View of Adolescence

Adolescence in the sociological view, influenced by the work of Hans Sebald (1968), is characterized as a period of time within which individuals are socialized and made aware of various expectations and roles. External factors outside family life become great sources of influence during adolescence. For example, the transition from childhood to adulthood can vary according to the social-structural and cultural factors impacting a youth's life. From this perspective, the dominant social structure impacting young people is the division of labor, which creates a period in life where one is no longer considered a child, but has yet to gain the social status and financial freedom shared by adults. Such factors influence the lives of young people, society's perceptions of their social worth, and the opportunities accessible to them for obtaining a meaningful social role, and thus adult social status.

Anthropological View of Adolescence

The anthropological view of adolescence is influenced by the work of several researchers, including Margaret Mead's classic look at young people's experiences in Samoa (1953), the interesting studies carried out by Harold Bernard (1957), Mihaly Csikszentmihalyi, Maria Dubious and R. Doll (1965), as well as those of Elizabeth Douvan and Joseph Adelson (1966). This view presents a conception of adolescence as a period of life significantly impacted by the culture in which one grows up. This view suggests that depending on the cultural values and ideals, as well as the size, of one's community, a young person may become more or less self-assertive, respectful of elders, physically active, or autonomous than his or her peers in other cultures. Here, young people are thought to be experiencing much more than physical body changes, they are also negotiating a whole set of culture values and beliefs about what it means to be a young person approaching adulthood.

Integrated View of Adolescence

This view of adolescence suggests that there is a reciprocal influence between the social environment and the individual. Not only do individuals shape their own development, but they are also influenced by the context of the culture within which they exist. Adolescents not only shape their own development but also are shaped by the environment and, in turn, also influence it. Adolescence is often seen as a metaphor for social change; youth are viewed as "the advance party where innovation and alteration in the values of society are concerned" (Coleman & Hendry, 1996, p. 203).

Each of these views of adolescence suggests a competing view of the experiences of young people as they approach adulthood, as well as differing ideas about the role adults play in the lives of youth. For example, the psychoanalytic view of adolescence suggests that, with the onset of puberty, young people begin to develop adult sexual characteristics, as well as, presumably, the capabilities to negotiate their way through the complex social world within which they live. From this point of view development is a universal experience, occurring roughly around the same period in life for all individuals. Here adults can assist youth by helping them deal with the changes they are experiencing by providing explanations about what is happening, why it is happening, and what one needs to understand in order to deal with one's "new" body.

Within the biological view of adolescence, young people are considered to be experiencing a great deal of life stress, caused by the drastic physical changes they are experiencing as their bodies develop adult physical and sexual characteristics. A young person's developmental path and sense of self can be jeopardized if he or she does not adjust to these changes successfully. Adults, from this perspective, can help youth by explaining to them that the changes associated with puberty are normal, and that their development is not abnormal.

From the cognitive-developmental perspective, adolescents need to confront any "lingering egocentrism" (Thomas, 2000), as well as work to develop more abstract methods for processing information and a sense of self that is differentiated from others. Not accomplishing these tasks can put a youth's cognitive, social, and emotional development at risk. From this view, adults can assist young people by allowing them to actively participate in the environment that surrounds them and by encouraging the development of new understandings about people, objects, and events by challenging existing mental conceptions.

Within the social learning theory framework, adolescents need to experience models of healthy adult behaviors and beliefs. From this point of view, young people who lack opportunities to interact with adults who have successfully negotiated the transition from childhood to adulthood, will also experience difficulty as they approach adulthood. Adults can assist adolescents by modeling socially acceptable behavior, and then reinforcing those behaviors when they are exhibited by youth.

Those suggesting an ecological view of adolescence will express a belief in the notion that "it takes a village a raise a child." They will look to the community as a whole to identify possible areas of risk that might jeopardize a young person's development of adult skills and sensibilities. They will also emphasize the importance of creating quality home, in-school, and out-of-school experiences for youth, and encourage adults to allow youth to take an active role in their communities, as well as to help adolescents establish positive academic and leisure interests and relational patterns with family members and friends.

From the sociological point of view, adolescence is a period of cultural transmission, in which adolescents are explicitly, and implicitly, instructed about what they will be expected to do and know as healthy and competent adults operating in a complex social world. From this point of view, young people are to be considered novices in society, needing to learn the complex inner workings of society itself, as well as their role in it. For example, a young person must learn his or her role as a contributing member or society, one expected to obtain and maintain stable employment in order to earn whatever is necessary to support oneself and one's family. Here adults are viewed as the experts of society, responsible for teaching young people the lessons they must master in order to survive in the "real world."

Lastly, from the integrated point of view, adolescence represents an experience somewhere in the middle of the psychoanalytical view and the sociological view. Adolescence is neither solely a psychological state nor a socially constructed category, rather it is a period in life that represents a little from each point of view. From this point of view, young people are thought to be required to negotiate their ways through a number of universally experienced developmental tasks, but they do so in a social environment within which they are both passive absorbers of a great deal of cultural knowledge, as well as creators and recreators of that social knowledge. Adults are thought to be experts possessing valuable knowledge they need to pass on to youth, but also are to collaborate with young people as they seek to find their own way down the path toward adulthood.

YOUR VIEW OF ADOLESCENCE: IMPLICATIONS FOR YOUTH WORK

It is important to consider competing conceptions of adolescence because they can guide our practice as youth workers, helping us develop developmentally enriching and consistent experiences for young people. However, each of the views of adolescence described in this chapter carries with it very specific implications for the practice of youth work. Depending on the perspective of adolescence that is accepted, there will be significant differences in the ways in which a youth worker thinks about who young people are, what they are capable of doing, as well as what types of supports they need in order to become healthy, competent adults. A program or approach with a cognitive-developmental foundation will be drastically different from a program operating with a social learning theory framework, especially in the area of rewards and punishments for specific types of behavior. These differences are inevitable, because each theory or point view places emphasis on competing developmental tasks, areas, or experiences. It is important to consider the point of view that has explicitly or implicitly shaped your own conceptions of adolescence, as well as the implications that that view has for your approach as a youth worker and for the ways in which youth participate in and interact with the environment and individuals (e.g., adults and peers) within youth programs.

SUMMARY

An awareness of the views of adolescence informing our conceptions of who young people are, what they are capable of being involved in, as well as what kinds of supports they need in order to develop in positive and healthy ways, is important to the practice of youth work. Each competing view answers these questions in differing ways, and thus creates different developmental experiences, as well as social environments, for youth. Each point of view or theory can be thought of as a framework through which youth workers can design programs, create policies, and legitimatize their approach to assisting youth in meeting their developmental needs. However, as this chapter has argued, it is crucial that youth workers examine their beliefs about youth and youth

work, as well as the implications, intended or unintended, that our beliefs create for young people.

REFERENCES

Bandura, A. (1977). *Social learning theory*. Englewood Cliffs, NJ: Prentice-Hall.

Bernard, W. H. (1957). *Adolescent development in American culture*. New York, NY: World Book Company.

Bronfenbrenner, U. (1979). *The ecology of human development*. Cambridge, MA: Harvard University Press.

Coleman, J. D., & Hendry, L. (1996). *The nature of adolescence*. London, England: Routledge.

Crompton, V., & Kessner, E. Z. (2003). *Saving beauty from the beast: How to protect your daughter from an unhealthy relationship*. New York, NY: Little Brown & Company.

Douvan, E., & Adelson, J. (1966). *The adolescent experience*. New York, NY: John Wiley & Sons.

Dubious, E. M. & Doll, R. (1965). *A cross-national study of Buenos Aires and Chicago adolescents*. Switzerland: S. Kager AG.

Erikson, E. (1968). *Identity: Youth and crisis*. New York, NY: Norton.

Freud, A. (1974). *The writings of Anna Freud* (Vols. 1-5). New York, NY: International Universities Press.

Freud, S. (1938). *An outline of psychoanalysis*. London: Hogarth,

Greydanus, D., & Bashe, P. (2003). *American Academy of Pediatrics, Caring for your teenager: The complete and authoritative guide*. New York, NY: Bantam Books.

Grinder, E. R. (1973). *Adolescence.* New York, NY: John Wiley & Sons.

Hall, G. S. (1904). *Adolescence.* New York, NY: D. Appleton & Company.

Irvine, M. (2003, May 11). Adulthood starts at 26, survey says. *Des Moines Register,* p. 6A.

Mead, M. (1953). *Coming of age in Samoa: A psychological study of primitive youth for Western civilization.* New York, NY: Modern Library.

Paul, H. A. (2000). *Is my child ok?: When behavior is a problem, when it's not, and when to seek help.* New York, NY: Bantam Dell Publishing Group.

Piaget, J., & Inhelder, B. (1969). *The psychology of the child.* New York, NY: Basic Books.

Pruitt, D. (1999). *Your adolescent: Emotional, behavioral and cognitive development from early adolescence through the teen years: What's normal, what's not, and when to seek help.* New York, NY: Harper-Collins Publishers.

Rainey, D., & Rainey, B. (2002). *So you want to be a teenager? What every preteen must know about friends, love, sex, dating, and other life issues.* Nashville, TN: Thomas Nelson, Inc.

Roche J., & Tucker, S. (1997). *Youth in society.* London, England: Sage Publications.

Sebald, H. (1968). *Adolescence: A sociological analysis.* New York, NY: Appleton-Century-Crofts.

Thomas, R. M. (2000). *Comparing Theories of Child Development* (5th ed.). Belmont, CA: Wadsworth/Thomas Learning.

Wyn, J., & White, R. (1997). *Rethinking youth.* London, England: Sage Publications.

CHAPTER THREE

A Historical Perspective

INTRODUCTION

Like other social themes, national and global events within the past one hundred years have impacted the evolution of youth work. Events such as World War I, the advent of federal child labor regulations, the Great Depression, and World War II have affected the structure and implementation of organizations aimed at providing a safe haven for youth to grow and mature. Many organizations began as grassroots, community efforts and have since grown considerably with the ever-changing bureaucratic leadership in the United States. The organizations that have succeeded have been able to withstand and forge their way through the hardship of the aforementioned events, developing a policy structure that encourages a focus on the growth of youth and collaboration among community members at various levels.

As early as 1830, youth work in its early stages was a part of the American social fabric. (See Appendix A). Mainly every portion of the American population realized the significance that youth played in the social identity. Their energy, creativity, and vigor were important resources that could benefit the United States. The dilemma that arose was how to incorporate the youth population into the larger societal picture. Initially, the youth population was introduced to the labor force as early as six years of age, creating a cheap and effective working body. As these actions continued, reformers began to realize the energy and creativity they witnessed in youth was being extinguished by their early entrance into the adult working world. Many youth suffered permanent physical, emotional, and psychological scarring. The Industrial Era workplace was devastating the future citizens of the United States, so reformers began a drive to save the children through labor regulations and compulsory schooling. The Progressive movement signaled recognition of what Zelizer (1985) termed "the economically worthless but emotionally priceless child," an understanding that the true value of youth was in the character development and not the amount of backbreaking work they could do.

Following the Progressive movement and enactment of child labor regulations, the concept of youth work incorporated various viewpoints into practice. Developing socially acceptable character traits in youth, assimilating youth to meet the bureaucratic guidelines for systemization, and the fun morality were part of the growth of the field of youth work. This metamorphosis of youth work has seen the creation of several youth work organizations that have established methods of success to this day. This chapter will provide a discussion of the evolution of youth work, especially the past one hundred years and the significant viewpoints that are emerging. We will discuss the different events associated with the transitory stages in youth work and close with a peek into the future of youth work, showing possible trends that could have an impact on youth work. (See Appendix B).

A STARTING POINT FOR YOUTH WORK

Life in the nineteenth century was challenging. "The struggle for existence. . .sometimes leaves ugly marks on character. . .These desperate mothers, they are overworked and harried through a long day, prolonged by the family washing and cooking into the evening. . ." (Addams, as cited in Elshtain, 2002, pp. 69, 185). The average life span was thirty to forty years, and those years consisted of sustaining a family or dodging crime, violence and the allurement of vices such as prostitution and gambling. Youth would start working at a very young age for their parents doing house chores, farming, or other familial duties. The hours were long and at times, the work was dangerous. School for children was not even a consideration for most families; the priority each day was surviving to the next. As youth grew older, they would venture out, start families, acquire jobs in trade, construction or service, and repeat the same cycle with their own children. This was the chain of events for youth until the first types of youth work organizations—clubs, institutes and outreach programs— sprouted up. These organizations began to focus on something nonexistent in social policy—the needs of youth. Youth needed activities and peers to socialize with in order to develop and grow, and these organizations recognized that absence and chose to do something about it. Some of these groups were the forerunners to national organizations such as the Boy Scouts, the YMCA, and Junior Achievement.

The "Special" Needs of Youth

To deal with the rigors of daily life in the mid-1800s, various individuals focused much of their non-work time on religious worship. The constant engagement in activities and duties was a component of the Puritan work ethic. The famous phrase associated with the Puritan work ethic, "Idle hands are the devil's workplace" meant that if a person was not constantly engaging in some form of activity to improve their life, they would fall prey to the vices of society. Religious devotion and worship were preferred non-work activities and were cornerstones for character development at this time. Families would engage in prayer and other forms of worship on a regular basis in church. The Juvenile Missionary Society of Philadelphia (1831) and the Young Men's Missionary Society of New York (1833) were associated with churches and created opportunities for young people to come together and worship with their peers. These outlets provided a brief break to youth engaged in a lifestyle filled with struggles to survive.

Youth had traditionally been assimilated into the working world with their parents, but now there was a growing recognition that their needs were important, or "special" (Erickson, 1994). Working alongside adults as a way to ease into society was being reprimanded and a more formal schooling option was encouraged. Youth were being removed from the work force and displaced into society without a formal alternative, since the idea of schooling was encouraged but not strictly enforced. This displacement unfortunately led to detrimental actions to themselves and society.

Lads from fourteen to twenty-one are the busiest instigators, the most active abettors, and the most daring perpetrators of offenses against the peace and good order of society. In tumults, street fights, and riotous assemblies in resistance to authority and contempt for law, they generally take the lead. (Common School Journal, as cited in Kett, 1977, p. 89)

Without an option for working or an option for leisure time there was a void in youth's lives. Organizations founded at this time, such as the YMCA, set out to fill the void and implement programs that would develop "good character" in youth during the idle hours when dangerous activity could occur. Qualities defining "good character" in a young person's life included determination, a strong will, good physical health, a service-minded mentality, and an appreciation for the natural environment (Erickson, 1994; Kett, 1977).

Unfortunately, many youth were considered "abnormal" due to being orphaned, a vagrant, a runaway, or a juvenile delinquent. The treatment for these youth consisted of moral education through institutionalization (Muncie, 1997). The goal of institutionalization was to deter and prevent offending. The methods used to reach this goal were dehumanizing and brutalizing to youth, often permanently affecting their ability to socialize and interact with their peers. Institutionalization of youth often signaled the end of their participation in mainstream society and entrance into a life filled with little regard for their welfare. These methods were prevalent when reformers such as Jane Addams and Jacob Riis pushed for a national public policy advocating for the welfare of youth. Their efforts would extend to all forms of interaction with youth, including how society handled "abnormal" youth.

THE PROGRESSIVE MOVEMENT—SAVE THE CHILDREN

The first two decades of the twentieth century bore witness to a prevailing notion of human welfare. Reformers proclaimed the need for leisure opportunities for themselves and future generations, urging that the United State's labor-driven mindset would collapse if the population was not given guidelines to follow regarding the welfare of its inhabitants. The idea of reform became so popular that in the 1912 election Theodore Roosevelt established the Bull Moose Party to run against the Democrats and Republicans and based his platform on Progressivism and reform. A main component of Roosevelt's platform and a prevailing notion during the first twenty years of the twentieth century was to improve the welfare

of youth. Working to improve the conditions of youth in society would enable them to prosper and grow into successful adults. Improving the lives of youth would enable them to do the same for future populations, establishing the notion of "civic housekeeping," or taking care of the community (Elshtain, 2002).

Youth Work Reform Movement

The efforts of reformers during the Progressive Era caused a dramatic increase in the amount of youth work organizations. The current conditions of youth included initial employment at the tender age of six, ten to twelve hour workdays, six days a week, and dangerous, life-threatening work conditions. Jane Addams points out the misplacement of priorities in the following quote:

A further difficulty lies in the fact that this industrialism has gathered together multitudes of eager young creatures from all quarters of the earth as a labor supply for the countless factories and workshops, upon which the present industrial city is based. Society cares more for the products they manufacture than for their immemorial ability to reaffirm the charm of existence. (1909, p. 5)

Youth were considered "little adults," losing their innocence and in some cases their lives in the mines and quarries of Industrial America. Reformers, such as Addams, wanted the children to be involved in schooling and to participate in healthy activities run through youth work organizations. Several of these organizations, such as the Hull House, Junior Achievement, Kiwanis Key Clubs, Youth and Children's Ministries, and various youth sports leagues constructed opportunities for youth to gather and practice social interaction. The goals of these organizations were to educate and train youth so that they could sufficiently fulfill their responsibilities as an adult, and to build a strong civic mind in each individual.

Jane Addams and other reformers felt that maneuvering youth onto a path of education and civic-mindedness would enhance their ability to lend to the social claim. The social claim, according to Addams, was developing an attitude of caring not only for our biological family members, but other citizens within society—our social family (Elshtain, 2002). If youth did not learn at an early age to care for their neighbors, it could mean the development of a callous disposition and disregard for the well being of others. Actively engaging in the social claim meant showing concern and respect for peers and elders, and working with those individuals to improve the current conditions of society. Youth did not have much influence at the time, but Progressive reformers believed instilling the desire to help an individual's social family members would translate to fruitful actions once adulthood was reached.

The Idea of "Human Capital"

Youth work organizations realized that developing programs, activities and areas for youth to grow would increase the "human capital" within the United States. Human capital theory is similar to the concept of financial capital. Within an economic sense, a person wants to invest in their assets so that they will appreciate, increasing their value and yielding a high return. If the asset is property, this could mean upkeep and maintenance over time to the point of sale. If it is intangible, such as a bond or stock, it could mean continually investing money so that it will appreciate in financial value and yield a subsequent return when sold. Human capital theory follows the same steps as the concept of financial capital, except it pertains to the properties of individuals within a workplace or community (Putnam, 2000). The asset in this case is the youth, and the appreciation in value is the overall positive maturation of the youth so that he or she is a viable member of the community. The investment in the youth originates during their formative years and continues into adulthood.

Compulsory Schooling

Combined with the efforts to develop human capital and the welfare of youth was the importance of compulsory schooling and laws to mandate attendance. School attendance was a new concept, and many citizens questioned the purpose of schooling, stating that youth could learn what they needed to survive in the workplace. Many parents scolded individuals who pushed for compulsory schooling, stating that in order to survive all capable family members needed to work to build the family income. Compulsory schooling required youth to attend school, and state governments instituted inspections to verify that businesses were adhering to these laws. Compulsory schooling also helped set parameters for youth work organizations when interacting and guiding young people (James, 1993). Schools mandated the knowledge and skills that a youth needed to be a civic-minded person. These regulations were the results of studies done and the subsequent literature related to human growth and development. A by-product of these rules and regulations of interaction and youth work was the acknowledgment of a pivotal culture within society— the culture of youth.

Youth Culture

In Chapter 8, the term culture is defined as an organized system of shared meanings that are attributed to a certain group of individuals. The members who make up the culture give the meanings to that culture, and pass those meanings on to subsequent generations (Peregoy & Dieser, 1997; Smith & Bond, as cited in Imam, 1999). Youth culture is the conglomeration of characteristics that define the time between childhood and adulthood (Garratt, 1997). As indicated in chapter one, these characteristics may include clothing style, music taste, and leisure activities. The culture of youth witnessed in the early twentieth century included several specific characteristics, such as milk bars, colorful clothing forbidden at work and school, and the hero worship of sports and entertainment figures through games (Cross, 1990). Youth created language habits, rituals, strategies for resistance to authority figures, and forms of consumption unique to their portion of the population. Youth work organizations initially regarded youth culture as a form of anti-socialization, a problem, instead of a vital component in the formation of identity by youth. Subsequent research indicated that youth culture plays an integral role in the identity development of youth.

A robust youth culture has been identified as essential to the creation of an effective youth work organization (Fine & Mechling, 1993). The difficulty with allowing the formation of a strong youth culture for youth workers is not relinquishing too much of their authority. Opportunities to examine and develop friendships and play with others are central to the formation of a youth culture. Youth may "create their own world" within an organization by developing traditions, labels, and identity markers signifying who they are. Many of these cultural traits may make a youth worker uncomfortable, but it is an opportunity for youth to experiment and learn about themselves. Youth may perceive their culture as a form of resistance to adults, but it can serve as a form of unification for members of the group, strengthening their identity and building their self-esteem, which is what youth workers want to see occur in youth.

Character Building within Youth

Youth work organizations functioned as a tool for building a strong character in youth during the early decades of the twentieth century. Many organizations emerged during this time, emphasizing the importance of character building, such as Boy Scouts of America (1910), Camp Fire Girls (1910), Girl Scouts (1912), and Junior Achievement (1919). For example, the Boy Scouts of America and the Girl Scouts of the USA were founded on the premise that youth of strong moral character would be the individuals to carry the United States through the middle and later years of the twentieth century. From their inception, the Boy Scouts were involved in acts designed to serve the community and to develop interaction with diverse populations, developing sound young men with good morals. Boy Scouts mobilized together for national civic Good Turns promoting safe methods of patriotism throughout the year, provided service for the influenza epidemic in 1918, and aided the Department of Labor in its Americanization program in 1919 (About the Boy Scouts of America, 2003). During both World War I and World War II, Girl Scouts served their country on the home front collecting scrap iron, growing Victory Gardens, and selling defense bonds (Girl Scouts of the USA, 2003). The Girl Scout movement gave girls of all ages the opportunity to develop self-reliance and resourcefulness. Preparation through the Girl Scouts was not only for traditional homemaking roles, but also for possible future roles as professional women, in the arts, sciences and business, and for active citizenship outside the home. Robert Baden-Powell and Juliette Gordon Lowe, founders of the Boy Scouts and Girl Scouts, believed their programs would enhance youth through activities designed to build upon the various qualities associated with a person's character.

Federal Involvement in Youth Work

From 1900 to 1930, youth work took several steps forward in developing the "emotionally priceless" child. At the state and local levels, governments were abolishing child labor, regulating school attendance, and striving for an attitude of civic-mindedness in all citizens. Establishment of federal regulations governing the treatment of youth proved difficult. A significant victory occurred when federal politicians and activists lobbied and were successful in establishing the Children's Bureau (Lindenmeyer, 1997). The Children's Bureau was a part of the Department of Commerce and focused on constructing a healthy child welfare policy. The Bureau was an extension of the Progressive movement (Muncy, 1991). The idea behind the Bureau was to harvest the "child crop," to inject a component of social justice into a portion of the population that was being abused by the industrial-era working conditions. The Children's Bureau identified injustices within American society affecting youth and labored for laws monitoring their health and well being. Youth work organizations grew tremendously at this time due to the explosion in the youth population, resulting from the actions of the Children's Bureau.

YOUTH WORK IN THE MID-1900s

By the middle of the twentieth century, the United States was out of the Great Depression and World War II, and parents were creating a distinctly "American" way of life. Youth were reaping the rewards of their parents' earlier hardships in life, benefiting from the mentality of most parents that their children were going to receive all the opportunities that they did not have during the Great Depression. All of this pointed to a new direction regarding youth work, a time when expertism moved to the forefront of youth work. Parents were steadily ingesting the research on youth work to which they were exposed through radio and television, and this research would aid in raising their children. Youth workers also listened intently to the experts discuss how to work with youth and their various personalities. The experts were the gatekeepers on how to develop strong civic-minded patriotic youth who would eventually be the future citizens of the United States.

The "Fun Morality"

The abundance of benefits youth received was a by-product of the "fun morality" (Wolfenstein,

1955, as cited in Fine & Mechling, 1993) noted earlier in the chapter. Children were no longer needed in the workplace, and the compulsory schooling laws created an arena for learning and growth. School was the laboratory for the social experiment—to educate and develop youth that would be viable members of their community and society. Organizations and programs such as Young Life, Big Brothers of America, The President's Council on Physical Fitness, the Girls' Brigades of America, and Awana Clubs International cropped up, encouraging youth to develop their own identities yet still remain part of the larger social body. Workers were advised to maintain a playful attitude when guiding youth during this era, to allow youth to express themselves and enjoy doing it, but to always keep in mind that youth were to be molded to fit into societal expectations.

The Importance of Individualism

As the United States' involvement in World War II ended, Americans were ignited with the desire to maintain a sense of individualism, even within youth work (Fine & Mechling, 1993). The population was saturated with images of conformity when our opponents in the global conflicts—the Japanese and the Nazis—were discussed. The devastation to humanity associated with the swastika armbands and uniform marching in pictures and descriptions created a stereotype from which Americans wanted to deviate as far as possible. Youth workers also became immersed in this drive, emphasizing the importance of uniqueness among youth and development of individual personalities. The opportunity to conform was good, as long as it was in a manner that adhered to the societal expectations of the government and its leaders.

A consequence of the "American" way of life was that pockets of the population had to work harder to achieve their goals of individualism and national growth. The decade of the 1950s was the springboard for many ethnic groups to push for civil rights in America. The ideal lifestyle was a white, European-American, middle-class way of life, and the structuring of youth work was to maintain social behaviors that conformed to these characteristics. For those individuals who were not part of this population, recognition and acceptance proved difficult. Integration into various youth programs and activities was impossible at times, based upon the notion that certain youth did not have the qualities to fit in (James, 1993). Incorporation of youth who did not fit the preferred characteristics was interpreted as a potential threat to the well being of the preferred youth and they were subsequently excluded from programs and activities. For many youth, there were no alternatives for positive social interaction. This exclusion was a form of the national dilemma of segregation that would eventually explode like a cannon during the 1960s.

YOUTH WORK IN THE 1980s

The latter part of the twentieth century saw an awakening to the potential threats to the development of youth. Statistics illustrating drug and alcohol abuse, teen sexual activity, and delinquency introduced the general population to behaviors with life-altering effects. "At-risk" became the buzzword to describe youth of the last two decades. As shown in Chapter 10, the motive behind youth work was to fix the youth, to solve the problem that was engulfing them in life at that point. Jarvis, Shear, and Hughes (1997) describe the model for youth work in the last two decades imitating a doctor-patient dynamic in medicine. The premise behind this model of youth work was that healthy individuals would create healthy families and communities. For youth to participate in programs, there needed to be an identifiable problem that workers could solve. A program was deemed successful if there was a quantifiable change within the youth.

The Clinical Model of Youth Work

Following a doctor-patient, or clinical, model for youth work provided little opportunity for interaction between other individuals involved with youth outside of the worker. The goal of youth work was to eliminate unwelcome behaviors based upon what the worker observed in the youth work setting.

The dilemma with this critique and analyzation is that there are multiple factors outside of the worker's control that can affect youth. Youth visit friends, hang out in various areas, and engage in behaviors outside of the youth work organization, and these interactions profoundly affect their personality and actions. Focusing only on the problem limited the range of understanding by the worker as to what might cause youth to act in certain ways.

The structure of youth work organizations included a hierarchy based upon expertise and research. Usually the administrators and directors of organizations were empowered based upon their previous quantitative research and analysis of youth. Workers would consult their supervisors for methods of dealing with youth and how to correct unwanted behaviors, and the supervisors would respond with answers based upon staged-environment studies. The flaw with expertise was the notion that the worker had all the answers, and somehow among all those answers was the solution for every youth's problems. Unfortunately, this was not the case, and the knowledge needed to help youth came from the various community members the youth encountered daily, not staged studies. Workers began to realize the idea of being an expert in youth work was not possible, considering the continual evolvement of youth and their surroundings—nothing ever remained the same. Interactions and connections with family, friends, and other role models were what youth workers needed to observe and understand in order to guide youth down the path of maturity and growth.

YOUTH WORK IN THE TWENTY-FIRST CENTURY

Currently, youth work organizations are focusing on a collaborative effort between all stakeholders who are associated with youth. The concept of expertism is being replaced with an understanding that there may not be a ceiling on the quantity of knowledge associated with youth work, and that everyone involved continues to learn and grow. Peters describes programs of this nature as having a central principle of participation by all that interact with youth (1993). Youth and Shelter Services of Ames, Iowa outlines goals that include community youth development and asset building, increased awareness of needs and problems of troubled youth and their families, promotion of family life enrichment and self-sufficiency, reduction of the number of teens in institutions and who are runaways, and to divert youth from the juvenile courts back into the community (Youth and Shelter Services, 2001). These organizations are emphasizing the importance of working with individuals who influence youth in various capacities. Due to the amount of influence a youth receives from various environments, it is important to work with everyone, including parents, youth workers, coaches, and teachers.

Collaborative Efforts in Present Day Youth Work

Several efforts in youth work today constitute a collaborative effort with participation in varying degrees from stakeholders who care about the well being of youth. Two examples of collaboration on a national level are America's Promise and the 21st Century Community Learning Centers. America's Promise was established in 1997 and its purpose is for citizens to come together in a collaborative effort to strengthen the character and competence of youth (Powell, as cited in America's Promise, 2003). Founding Chairman Colin Powell states, "Character, at the end of the day, is the foundation block for our society—foundation block for a happy childhood" (*America's Promise: The Alliance for Youth*, 2003, p. 1).

The mission of America's Promise is a collaborative network that builds upon the communities to address the "Five Promises" for every youth in America. In essence, America's Promise is attempting to create a nation of neighborhoods, uniting citizens of all nationalities, religious faiths, and political parties in a common goal—meeting the needs of our children and youth (America's Promise, 2003).

The "Five Promises" are 1) caring adults, 2) safe places, 3) a healthy start, 4) marketable skills, and 5) opportunities to serve. Members in various communities may give to America's Promise in different capacities to ensure that the Five Promises are met. Examples include mentoring, coaching, protecting youth from violent situations, edu-cating, vocational counseling, and becoming a youth worker. America's Promise offers the chance for individuals to participate in youth work through incorporation of their abilities and knowledge into areas where they can make a difference.

The 21st Century Community Learning Centers Program is a key component of President George W. Bush's No Child Left Behind Act of 2001. Congress has supported the 21st Century Community Learning Centers Program by appropriating $1 billion, providing opportunities for youth and their families to learn and grow after the school day has ended, (Programs in Western MA/ 21st Century Learning Centers, 2003). The Learning Centers are located throughout the United States and emphasize the development of trusting relationships between youth. The different Learning Centers provide youth with an environment in which to work with guidance counselors, social workers, and mentors. Discussions revolving around alcohol and substance usage, handling stress and pressure from peers, are relevant topics that youth have the prerogative to discuss with workers in the Learning Centers. Students are encouraged to take leadership roles in various Learning Centers, organizing activities and working with other youth to facilitate fun and educational ventures. The Hampshire Educational Collaborative Learning Centers' goals include providing a safe, drug-free environment where social and emotional development may occur, a location for youth and families to freely and enjoyably engage in activities together, and to work with school staff, parents, and community organizations to provide services to youth of all ages (Programs in Western MA/21st Century Learning Centers, 2003).

The 21st Century Community Learning Centers address the concept of youth work by initiating programs in communities around the country. These programs focus on three critical needs related to youth work: temporary adult supervision until parents or guardians are available from work or other obligations, avenues for enrichment, and a "field" to practice social skills and avoid the seamy dark side of society (21st Century Learning Centers After-school Programs, 2003). The Community Learning Centers, or CLCs, provide alternatives to unstructured and unsupervised activities that inhibit social interaction and growth. One example from the Lane County, Oregon CLC was an art program that included a rock and funk musician from Louisiana giving fiddle lessons to youth on a weekly basis (21st Century Learning Centers After-school Programs, 2003).

The efforts of America's Promise and the 21st Century Community Learning Centers echo the ideas the reformers of the 1920s envisioned when conceptualizing youth work. The "Five Promises" that form America's Promise mirror the efforts of Robert Baden-Powell, Luther Gulick, and Jane Addams. The Second Promise, to provide safe places for youth, parallels the desires of Frederick James Olmstead, the designer of Central Park, and Joseph Lee, the father of the playground movement. A footnote associated

with the "Fifth Promise" is to give children and adolescents opportunities to serve others, shaping the character of America's future population into a socially responsible group of citizens. Social responsibility to others is the same as taking care of the social claim that Addams theorized through her efforts. The establishment of 21st Century Community Learning Centers and their individual goals and mission statements remind us of how community members in the early 1900s wanted to do the same for their youth. Those individuals wanted to remove youth from the streets and to educate them and enrich their lives so they could do the same for future generations. The organizations then and now understand the importance of the "emotionally priceless" child and how influential youth work is to society.

Current Funding Strategies for Youth Work Organizations

America's Promise, 21st Century Community Learning Centers, and other youth work organizations have a common trait that affects their ability to function—monetary resources. Accessibility to such resources may make or break a youth work organization. Non-profit and public youth work organizations, such as the Boys and Girls Clubs and local recreation agencies are feeling the pinch of budget cuts to programs. These cuts can affect the continuation of programs designed for youth. Many organizations are turning to alternative strategies of funding, including writing grants, soliciting private donations, and levying bonds to raise the dollars needed to sustain programs. Reception of these types of funding includes criteria to which the organization may be required to adhere. If the organization does not comply with the guidelines for the funding, there is a distinct possibility of loss of funds.

Another strategy includes raising the cost of youth participation in activities at the organization. Raising fees can create an ethical dilemma with the mission of the organization. The Boys and Girls Clubs' mission is to develop programs for kids who cannot afford to or do not have the opportunities to interact with their peers. Many of these Clubs are constructed in areas of lower socioeconomic status, and the cost to use the Club is minimal, providing a positive place for kids to attend and play. Raising fees may exclude portions of the population for which the Club was designed, limiting the number of children that may use the Club. The result is that the Club may become fiscally secure, but at the cost of youth's involvement. This option may be the simplest to enact, but it can have devastating consequences.

To maintain a collaborative effort with community members, youth work organizations solicit donations from all members in the community. Not every youth work organization receives funding from the larger bureaucratic sector, and those organizations are forced to fend for themselves. Self-preservation of the organization and its programs includes active involvement of stakeholders in the community. Many of these individu-

als are asked to give what they can, and often that includes in-kind donations. In-kind donations include equipment, space for activities, and time.

THE EVOLUTION OF VOLUNTEERISM IN YOUTH WORK

Of the various in-kind options, time may be the most important. James (1993) suggests that returning to the small-scale, grassroots, voluntary style of youth work from the 1950s may be the most significant move that organizations can make. Youth workers are realizing that it may be easier to function on a small-scale level than to try to work in the massive bureaucratic structure of youth work. Grassroots volunteerism has its and advantages and disadvantages.

One advantage is that a youth work organization can develop its mission and goals to meet the needs of the youth, specific to that community. Workers are familiar with the youth in the community and can tailor the programs so that the youth who participate get the most out of their experience. Grassroots volunteerism also allows workers and stakeholders to witness the positive effect their donation of time has on the youth. Coaching a peewee football team, leading an outdoor excursion to a local park, or facilitating a cultural awareness day gives individuals the opportunity to actively participate in shaping and molding the future generation. Former President Clinton encouraged all people regardless of their age to give something back to their community, and Vineyard (1993) calls this the "Social Compact of Responsibility." The "Social Compact of Responsibility" calls all citizens to bear the responsibility of the needs of their community. Many youth work programs engage in the "Social Compact of Responsibility" through intergenerational activities, environmental awareness programs, and services for disadvantaged or at-risk youth. Volunteers often participate in these programs and activities, lending their expertise or guidance so that youth may learn and grow from the experience. These efforts allow volunteers to visualize how they would like the future to look in their corner of the world and to actively do something about it.

A disadvantage to maintaining a small-scale grassroots organization is that there may be an elimination of funding streams from parent organizations. Many national organizations are financially maintained through a network and when funding is needed by the different satellite agencies, they can solicit the funds from the headquarters. Becoming a part of a larger parent organization may provide the opportunity for funding that may not exist if the organization remains small and locally run. Local establishment and maintenance requires extra effort for resources that may involve capital campaigns or time-consuming fundraisers.

Transitioning from a small-scale organization to a member of a national organization includes an adherence to national guidelines and the possibility of a favorable repu-tation through association. National youth work organizations may have accredited operating procedures that are time tested, therefore establishing a credible reputation to the general population. Becoming a member of a national youth work organization may boost attendance in activities and create an aura of success with youth that can favorably influence families, community members, and potential funding sources. Inclusion into national organizations offers training opportunities, conferences, and networking opportunities for its workers.

SUMMARY

Since the middle of the nineteenth century, youth work has been a focus in society. Youth have experienced an array of attitudes and beliefs regarding how and why they should receive guidance and direction from members of their community. Moral character building, civic housekeeping, and the social claim are causes to which youth workers adhere when working with youth.

The philosophy of youth work has undergone a transformation since its inception. Originally designed as a tool for religious worship, youth work has grown into a field of national significance, with stakeholders in all communities understanding that for the future population to be viable members in society, collaboration is a fundamental ingredient. We have acknowledged that youth have rights and needs, and as we enter the twenty-first century, we are recognizing that we are not experts due to the dynamic evolutionary nature of youth work. Youth workers may continually learn long into their careers, and the current method of collaboration with youth and community stakeholders affords the opportunity for learning.

References

21st Century Learning Centers After-School Programs (April, 2001). *Events/news: After-school programs help solve vexing problem* [On-line]. Available: http://www.lane.k12.or.us/CM/News/news_afterschool41301.html

Addams, J. (1909). *The spirit of youth and the city streets*. Chicago, IL: MacMillan Company.

America's Promise—The Alliance for Youth. (2003). *America's Promise* [On-line]. Available: http://www.americaspromise.org

Boy Scout Troop 168. (June ,2003). Available: http://www2.powercom.net/stolerd/about/history.html

Cross, G. (1990). *A social history of leisure since 1600*. State College, PA: Venture Publishing.

Elshtain, J. B. (2002). *The Jane Addams reader*. New York, NY: Basic Books.

Erickson, J. B. (1994). 1994-1995 *Directory of American youth organizations* (5th ed.). Minneapolis, MN: Free Spirit Publishing Inc.

Fine, G. A., & Mechling, J. (1993). Child saving and children's cultures at century's end. In S. B. Heath & M. W. McLaughlin (Eds.), *Identity and inner city youth: Be-*

yond ethnicity and gender (pp. 120-146). New York, NY: Columbia University.

Garratt, D. (1997). Youth cultures and sub-cultures. In J. Roche & S. Tucker (Eds.), *Youth in society* (pp. 143-150). London, England: Sage Publications.

Girl Scouts of the USA. (June 3, 2003). Available: http://www.qas-church.org/qas_gs.html

Imam, U. (1999). Youth workers as mediators and interpreters: Ethical issues in work with black young people. In S. Banks' (Ed.) *Ethical issues in youth work* (pp. 125-144). London, England: Routledge.

James, T. (1993). The winnowing of organizations. In S. B. Heath & M. W. McLaughlin (Eds.), *Identity and inner city youth: Beyond ethnicity and gender* (pp. 176-195). New York, NY: Columbia University.

Jarvis, S. V., Shear, L., & Hughes, D. M. (1997). *Community youth development: Learning the new story*. Child Welfare, 76(5), 719-741.

Kett, J. F. (1977). *Rites of passage: Adolescence in America, 1790-present*. New York, NY: Basic Books.

Lindenmeyer, K. (1997). *A right to childhood: The U.S. Children's Bureau and child welfare, 1912-46*. Urbana and Chicago, IL: University of Illinois Press.

Muncie, J. (1997). Shifting sands: Care, community and custody in youth justice discourse. In J. Roche & S. Tucker (Eds.), *Youth in Society* (pp. 133-142). London, England: Sage Publications.

Muncy, R. (1991). *Creating a female dominion in American reform 1890-1935.* New York, NY: Oxford University Press.

National Child Labor Committee. (1911). *Uniform child labor laws.* New York, NY: American Academy of Political and Social Sciences.

Peregoy, J. J., & Dieser, R. B. (1997). Multicultural awareness in therapeutic recreation: Hamlet Living, *Therapeutic Recreation Journal, 31*(3), 174-188.

Peters, S. J. (1993). A new citizenship in the making? *Social Policy, 24*(1), 44-50.

Programs in Western MA/21st Century Community Learning Centers. (March 13, 2003). *21st Century Community Learning Centers: Soaring beyond expectations* [On-line]. Available: http://www.collaborative.org/21stCenturySite/index.html

Putnam, R. (2000). *Bowling alone: The collapse and revival of American community.* New York, NY: Simon & Schuster.

Vineyard, S. (1993). *Megatrends and volunteerism.* Downers Grove, IL: Heritage Arts Publishing.

Youth and Shelter Services. (June 2, 2003). *About youth and shelter services* [On-line]. Available: http://www.yss.ames.ia.us/contact.html

Zelizer, V. A. (1985). *Pricing the priceless child: The changing social value of children.* New York, NY: Basic Books.

CHAPTER FOUR

THE LANGUAGE OF YOUTH WORK AND YOUTH DEVELOPMENT

INTRODUCTION

There is a language of youth work, a way of communicating to others concerned with youth and/or involved in the delivery of services to and with youth. Professionals, part-time/seasonal staff, and volunteers all use various symbols to communicate meaning to one another. Also, commonly understood and subscribed terms provide a way for professionals to explain with greater understanding their intentions to policy makers, consumers, and others—through the use of language we convey our ideas, values, and meanings to others, increasing the power and precision of our efforts.

Edginton and de Oliveira (1995) have suggested that the youth field has been lacking in the development of commonly agreed upon definitions, theories, and models. Why does the profession need to develop such definitions, theories, and models? Without commonly agreed upon terms, concepts, and definitions, the power of professional practice is diminished. Edginton and Rossman (1988) explain that our body of knowledge helps the profession "explain, control, and ultimately predict the consequences of our interventions." As Jeffs and Smith note, a key weakness of the youth work field remains the appalling lack of scholarship, rigor and commitment to literature and research. They write, ". . .students and field workers alike struggle to make sense of their practice and career on a diet of ill-digested material culled from the *vox-pop* end or sociology, social policy and psychology and a host of practical guides' based on folk wisdom and often little else" (1995, p. 5).

Furthermore, as Murphy (1995) has stated, it is important to seek to define the field of youth work in comparison to the other major professions focused on work with young people. "If youth work is to be considered a field, youth development workers will have to (define) youth development work as exclusive related but distinct from teaching, child care, counseling, (and the) social services." Without clearly defined boundaries within the field, youth work runs the risk of becoming irrelevant, a simple "add-on" to other more established professions and approaches to working with the young (Delgado, 2002). Youth development can occur in a variety of different settings, but without a clear idea of what youth work is, as well as what youth work looks like, we run the risk of applying the terms 'youth development' and 'youth work' to every youth development or after-school program (McKenna, 2000).

This chapter is focused on providing a framework for youth development, youth work, and youth work organizations. In the next chapter we will focus our discussion on theories and models of youth work and youth development.

EARLY PERSPECTIVES OF YOUTH DEVELOPMENT

It is difficult if not impossible to precisely delineate the origins of the application of the term youth development to youth work. Clearly the work of individuals and institutions including government agencies, religious groups, schools, and adult-sponsored youth associations resulted in the need for common terms and definitions related to their efforts. In preindustrial America, Kett reports that "the language of age had a nebulous quality" (1997, p. 11). In other words, there were no common terms for defining youth, let alone the concept of youth development. Most early youth work efforts were centered around religious institutions and the individuals involved "exhibited the putative qualities of youth—vigor, energy, and idealism" (Kett, 1977, p. 74). Such efforts by religious institutions and later adult-sponsored youth organizations focused on "saving youth" and thus the language of youth work was influenced. It became similar to the language found in religious settings, with strong moral overtones, often focused on soul saving or character building. It wasn't until the turn of the twentieth century that the efforts of youth workers to begin to define basic concepts emerged. In fact, as was previously indicated, most individuals attribute the beginning of the serious study of youth to the work of American psychologists Edwin D.

Starbuck and G. Stanley Hall (Kett, 1962). For the first half of the twentieth century, there was a general merging of philosophical concepts that focused on the moral development of youth with what we learned from early scientific inquiry related to the development of youth.

In the latter half of the twentieth century, new concepts, terms, and definitions for youth work emerged. Such concepts were reflected in the work of individuals, such as Bruno Bettelheim, Fritz Redl, and Gisela Konopka, who influenced youth development. For example, Bettelheim's (1950) approach incorporated Freudian psychoanalytical thinking, coupled with the educational philosophy of John Dewey, Johann Pestalozzi, and Jean Piaget. Redl (1966) and Konopka (1973), discussed the importance of analyzing or viewing the "life-space" of youth in relation to their overall development. Thus the language of youth began to incorporate and emphasize terms such as environment, deviance, group work, and the connections between practice and theory. Delgado (2002) has suggested that Werner (1989) and his colleagues (Werner & Smith, 1982, 1992) influenced the language of youth work through their research and inclusion of resiliency and environmental protective factors.

From this brief review, we can see that the language of youth work and youth development have often reflected the thinking and perspectives of the prevailing times. "In the 1990s, the term youth development came to be applied to a set of principles, a philosophy or approach emphasizing active support for the growing capacity of young peoples by individuals, organizations, and institutions, especially at the community level" (Hamilton, Hamilton & Pittman, 2004, p. 4). Recent attention focused on the performance and success of youth, including their social health and especially in non-school hours, had brought increased interest and greater study of this area. Such a focus, especially by philanthropic organizations and foundations with interest in youth, has brought forth many new ideas, definitions, concepts, and perspectives influencing youth work and youth development. In fact, one could argue that this is a very vibrant time in the thinking of youth workers, academics, policy makers, and others with interest in advancing ways of engaging and assisting in the development of youth.

YOUTH DEVELOPMENT: TOWARD A DEFINITION

There is no universally accepted definition of youth development (Delgado, 2002). It is a difficult term to define because the term itself is broad and has been used in a multiplicity of disciplines and professional areas, work spanning back to Havinghurst (1952), Beker and Alejandra (1970), and Werner (1989). As Edginton and de Oliveira (1995, p. 3) have pointed out, youth development is multi-dimensional, embracing 1) a process of human growth and development, 2) a philosophical orientation to social development and community, and 3) a programmatic framework of youth services. The term youth development is unevenly applied to the efforts of youth workers as a way of defining their professional efforts. Further, all the myriad of youth organizations that exist in North America have not embraced the term as a way of describing their professional focus. However, the term "youth development" is increasingly accepted as a way of describing the professional efforts of youth workers.

The term youth development can be used to describe a goal, a process, activities, and/or an approach to programming. As a process, youth development is a progressive process in which youth attempt to meet their needs and build their lives in a positive progression toward adulthood. As noted in *Contract with America's Youth: Toward a National Youth Development Agenda* (1995), ". . .youth development is an ongoing process in which young people are engaged and invested." Throughout this process, young people seek ways to meet their basic physical and social needs and to build the competencies and connections they need for survival and success. The acquisition of a broad range of competencies and the demonstration of a full complement of connections to self, others and the larger community (Halperin, Cusack, & O'Brien, 1995). As Nixon (1997, p. 71) has written, "youth development can be defined as the process in which all youths engage over time in order to meet their needs and build their confidence. Perhaps the most complete definition of youth

development is offered by the National Collaboration for Youth. They have suggested that youth development is ". . .a process which prepares young people to meet the challenges of adolescence and adulthood through a coordinated, progressive series of activities and experiences which help them to become socially, morally, emotionally, physically, and cognitively competent" (National Collaboration for Youth, 2001, p. 1). More recently, Witt (2002) also suggests that youth development ". . .is a process which prepares young people to meet the challenges of adolescence and adulthood."

Another perspective for defining youth development is to view the definition in the context of community life. From this perspective, youth are viewed as active and contributing members of a community. As Perkins, Borden, Keith, Hoppe-Rooney, and Villarruel (2003, p. 6) have suggested, ". . .community youth development is defined as purposely creating environments that provide constructive, affirmative and encouraging relationships that are sustained over time with adults and peers, while concurrently providing an array of opportunities that enable youth to build their competencies and become engaged as partners in their own development as well as the development of their communities." These authors go on to point out that "...youth development, either positive or negative, occurs as youth interact with all levels of their surroundings, including other people in the environment such as family, peers, other adults, and members of their communities."

In support of this proposition, Hamilton, Hamilton, and Pittman (2004, p. 16) have suggested that ". . .youth development entails attempts to make communities healthier places for youth to live and grow. . . ." Confirming this perspective, the United Nations has defined youth development as an effective strategy for achieving both youth and community potentials (1999).

Still another perspective of youth development is to view youth as being marginalized or disenfranchised members of society. From this perspective, youth development is seen as a way of combating social injustice and assisting youth in becoming fully participating members of society. Youth development often involves examining and exposing power relationships and equipping youth with the knowledge and skills required for meaningful participation in community life. Youth culture often represents the opportunity for creative alternatives to traditional thoughts as generated by adults, hence the opportunity for change. However, at the same time, society often considers young people a threat to the status quo, perceived as lacking wisdom, maturity, and life experience. The dominant discourse of society often leaves youth and their ideas for change at the margins. Learning to negotiate, communicate, and dialogue enables youth to more fully participate in community life and be viewed as contributing members to society.

Increasingly, youth development is being framed as a positive way to work with adolescents. In fact, the term "positive youth de-velopment" is found frequently in the literature (NCY, 2001, Nixon, 1997, Robertson, 1997). The concept of positive youth development is one that suggests that attention should be paid to the broader developmental needs of youth rather than focusing on at-risk youth or what is defined as a deficit-based model. In support of this concept, the National Collaboration for Youth (2001) has suggested that ". . .positive youth development addresses the broader developmental needs of youth, in contrast to a deficit-based model that focuses solely on youth problems." Nixon (1997, p. 573) has suggested that ". . .the best way to help young people who are considered to be at-risk is to provide them with the same supports and services that all youth need." Further, this author suggests that the ". . .emphasis on youth problems has contributed to a persuasive negativity toward youth as a collectively group (Nixon, 1997, p. 571). "Positive youth development is a strength-based microconcept that directs the programs and services available in communities to all young people rather than targeting only those with defined problems or those in high-risk situations (Robertson, 1997, p. 579). A positive youth development philosophy and approach reflects, according to Nixon, a "desire for positive outcomes in the development process and. . .[results in] purposeful efforts to design services that will continue outcomes" (1997, p. 571).

The U.S. Department of Health and Human Services' Administration for Children and Families has suggested that "positive youth development is a policy perspective that emphasizes providing services and opportunities to support all young people in developing a sense of competence, usefulness, belonging, and empowerment." (U.S. Department of Health and Human Services, 2002). This agency suggests that positive youth development works best when entire communities are involved in creating a continuum that enable youth to grow into happy and healthy adults. They note "...youth development is a youth process that everyone goes through. The goal of the positive youth development approach is to ensure that all adolescents experience this life state positively" (U.S. Department of Health and Human Services, 2002).

Another perspective of youth development is that it ". . .is the process through which adolescents actively seek, and are assisted, to meet their basic needs and build individual assets or competencies" (Carnegie Council on Adolescent Development, 1992). They further note that youth development "...strives to help young people develop the inner resources and skills they need to cope with pressure that might lead them into unhealthy and antisocial behaviors. It aims to promote and prevent, not to treat or remediate. Prevention of undesirable behaviors is one outcome of healthy youth development, but there are others: the production of a self-reliant, self-confident adult who can take their place as responsible members of society" (Carnegie Council on Adolescent Development, 1992).

Still further, youth development has been described as a means toward the end of promoting and nurturing our democratic society. Youth development, encourages young people to become autonomous, critical decision-makers. As Lakes (1996, p. 134) states, "youth development practices. . .work best when kids and adults engage in participatory decision making and practical democratic actions. . . strengthen[ing] democratic foundations of citizenship. . .rooted in problem solving. Through the process of nurturing an active participatory role for young people, youth development workers are able to encourage the development of a democratic belief system in the young."

Many definitions of youth development suggest that youth workers should work to build competencies that enable youth to be successful adults. Confirming this prospective, Witt (2000) recommends that youth development is a ". . .coordinated progressive series of support and opportunities which help[s] them to become socially, morally, emotionally, physically and cognitively competent." He compares youth development to building scaffolding, suggesting that ". . .youth, like an emerging building, need support during construction development. Eventually, when ready to stand on their own, the scaffolding can be lessened and eventually withdrawn" (Witt, 2000). Politz (1996) has suggested that:

Through youth development, young people attempt to meet their basic personal and social needs and to build competencies necessary for successful adolescent and adult life. It is an approach, framework, a way to think about young people that focuses on their capacities, strengths, and developmental needs and not on their weaknesses and problems. All young people have basic needs that are critical to survival and healthy development. They include a sense of safety and structure; belonging and membership; self worth and an ability to contribute; independence and control over one's life, closeness and several good relationships; and competency and mastery.

Youth Development Competencies

Hamilton, Hamilton, and Pittman (2004, p. 6) have noted that there are five critical elements that lead to youth development including character, connections, confidence, contribution (caring/compassion), and competence. Competence may be thought of as including ". . .knowledge and skills that enable a person to function more effectively to understand and act on the environment. Competence enables a person to accomplish what he or she intends, provided external circumstances are favorable, or to adapt to circumstances to achieve as much as possible" (Hamilton,

Hamilton, & Pittman 2004, p. 6). Edginton and Edginton (1994, p. 85), drawing from the work of Pittman (1991), have identified and defined five basic youth competencies as being important in assisting youth to become successful adults. The five areas are 1) health/physical, 2) personal/social, 3) cognitive/creative, 4) vocational, and 5) citizenship.

Health/Physical Competence. Youth need to have good current health status and appropriate knowledge, attitudes, and behaviors to ensure future health (e.g., exercise, good diet, nutrition).

Personal/Social Competence. It is important that youth gain: intrapersonal skills (ability to understand personal emotions and exercise self-discipline), interpersonal skills (ability to work with others to develop friendships and relationships through communicating, cooperating, empathizing, and negotiating), coping system skills (ability to adapt, assume responsibility), and judgment skills (play, make decisions, solve problems).

Cognitive/Creative Competence. Youth need to develop a broad base of knowledge; the ability to appreciate and participate in areas of creative expression; good oral and written language skills; problem-solving and analytical skills; and the ability to learn and interest in learning and achieving.

Vocational Competence. It is important for youth to develop a broad understanding/awareness of vocational (and avocational) options and of the steps needed to act on choices; adequate preparation for career, understanding of value and function.

Citizenship Competencies (ethics and preparation). Youth need to understand their nations' and communities' histories and values and have the desire to contribute to their nations and communities.

These five competencies are similar to the Pittman model of competencies offered by the Carnegie Commission (1989). The model included in the Carnegie Commission include such competencies as cognitive, social, physical, emotional, and moral development. They are:

Cognitive Development. Expand knowledge, develop ethical thinking and reasoning skills, and experience competence through academic achievement.

Social Development. Increase communication and negotiation skills, increase capacity for meaningful relationships with peers and adults, and explore adult rights and responsibilities.

Physical Development. Begin to mature physically and to understand changes that come with puberty, increase movement skills through physical activity, develop habits that promote lifelong physical fitness, and learn to take and manage appropriate physical risks.

Emotional Development. Develop a sense of personal identity; develop a sense of personal autonomy and control; and develop coping, decision-making, and stress-management skills.

Moral Development. Develop personal values, develop a sense of accountability and responsibility in relation to the larger society, and apply values and beliefs in meaningful ways.

In 2004, Hamilton, Hamilton, and Pittman (pp. 7-8) have refined those personal and social assets that they believe facilitate positive youth development. They include:

Physical Development. This competency refers to good health habits and good health risk-management skills.

Intellectual Development. This competency area refers to knowledge of life skills, vocational skills, critical thinking and reasoning, and good decision making. In addition, it involves knowledge of how to operate in multicultural environments.

Psychological and Emotional Development. This refers to good mental health, positive self-regard, knowledge of conflict resolution, motivation and personal achievement, personal efficacy, optimism, spiritual awareness, moral character, good use of time, effective coping, and self-regulation skills.

Social Development. This refers to building relationships of trust with others, a sense of social place, social networking, attachment to positive institutions, and a commitment to civic engagement.

Building competencies within youth are also sometimes referred to as building resilience or assets. Such competencies or assets can serve as the basis for program objects. The Boys and Girls Clubs of America provide an excellent example of the outcomes, expectations and goals for youth participating in their youth development programs and services. See Figure 4.1.

Figure 4.1
Example of Agency Competency Statements

WHAT KIDS NEED TO SUCCEED
Outcomes, expectations and goals for young people in Clubs

- **POSITIVE SELF-IDENTITY:** Youth have a healthy self-concept, a strong belief in their own self-worth, and a sense of hope about their future. They are adept at setting and attaining goals, confidently making the necessary decisions to achieve their life plans.

- **COMPETENCIES:** Youth have the knowledge, skills, strategies, and attitudes necessary to have a positive foundation for success. Youth become competent by mastering tasks, demonstrating to themselves that they can do things well. They develop competence in the following areas:

    Educational: Youth are proficient in basic educational disciplines and have the capacity to utilize technology. Having graduated from high school, they are motivated to pursue learning opportunities throughout their lives.

    Employment: Youth have the skills and attributes to be successful in the work force. They are motivated to constantly develop new abilities and hone existing skills to maintain a competitive edge.

    Social: Youth are able to develop and sustain positive relationships with others.

    Emotional: Youth are able to recognize, reflect on, and appropriately express their emotions, manage stress, and cope with positive and adverse situations.

    Cultural: Youth have an understanding and respect for their own cultural identity and for the cultures of others; they are able to contribute in a multicultural society and demonstrate tolerance for differences among people.

- **COMMUNITY AND CIVIC INVOLVEMENT:** Youth have a sense of belonging to their community, family, and/or group, and are willing to take civic responsibility. They work closely with others to contribute to the greater good.

(continued)

Figure 4.1 (continued)

- **HEALTH AND WELL-BEING:** Youth live healthy lives, take part in regular fitness activities, are able to access health care resources, and engage in positive behaviors. They use sound judgment about personal safety, nutrition and avoidance of alcohol, drugs and premature sexual activity.
- **MORAL COMPASS:** Youth have values enabling them to develop positive relationships with others. These values include honesty, a sense of justice and fairness, respect, caring and spirituality.

The Boys & Girls Club Movement must engage youth in activities that are fun and enjoyable while supporting development of the capacities described above. This is accomplished through Club programs and in discussions between staff and Club members. Clubs cannot achieve without caring, capable staff who forge relationships with youth people and influence their ability to succeed in life.

Source: Boy's & Girl's Club of America (1998). *Youth development: The foundation for the future.* Atlanta, GA: Boy's & Girl's Clubs of America.

Witt (2002) has suggested that assets can be divided into two categories: external and internal. He suggests that there are four major external asset categories. They are:

Support. Young people need to experience support, care, and love from their families, neighbors, and many others. They need organizations and institutions that provide positive, supportive environments.

Empowerment. Young people need to be valued by their community and have opportunities to contribute to others. For this to occur, they must be safe and feel secure.

Boundaries and Expectations. Young people need to know what is expected of them and whether activities and behaviors are "in bounds" and "out of bounds."

Constructive Use of Time. Young people need constructive, enriching opportunities for growth through creative activities, youth programs, congregational involvement, and quality time at home.

The internal asset categories defined by Witt (2002) are as follows:

Commitment to Learning. Young people need to develop a lifelong commitment to education and learning.

Positive Values. Youth need to develop strong values that guide their choices.

Social Competencies. Young people need skills and competencies that equip them to make positive choices, to build relationships, and to succeed in life.

Positive Identity. Young people need a strong sense of their own power, purpose, worth, and promise.

Competency frameworks such as the one identified above can be used to build a youth organization's program and service strategy. However, the idea of using a competency approach has been criticized in the literature. Bulgarelli and Almeida (1987) suggest that providing com-

Exhibit 4.1
Principles of Youth Development

Key Principles of Youth Development Practice

- Youth development must strive to enhance individual and community capacities. One is not possible without the other.

- Youth development is predicated on youth exercising meaningful decision making over their programs.

- Youth development must break down racial/ethnic, gender, disability, sexual orientation, and class barriers and stereotypes.

- Youth development builds bridges between community-based organizations (formal and informal).

- Youth-development activities must transform the environment in which youth live in the process of transforming the lives of participants.

- Youth development must provide participants with an opportunity to learn and at the same time to have fun.

- Youth-developement activities must provide youth with opportunities to serve their community.

- Youth development must provide youth with the necessary knowledge and skills that can be converted into meaningful, lifelong employment.

- Youth development must actively integrate as many core elements as possible into all activities.

Source: Delgado, M. (2002). *New frontiers for youth development in the twenty-first century.* New York: Columbia University Press, 164.

petencies to serve the available market is not an end in itself. Discussing this matter, Edginton and de Oliveira (1995) have reported that society should encourage its youth to think and promote social change, rather than focus on a set of specific competencies. The focus of youth work according to these authors should be to embrace youth as an important component of cultural transformation. Pittman, Irby, and Ferber (2000, p. 4) have written, "competence alone, while critical, is not enough." As they note, "skills may go unused or even be used in unproductive, antisocial ways if not anchored by confidence, character and connections (Pittman et al., 2000, p. 4)."

Adding to the above perspective, competency frameworks are often viewed as being attractive because they describe a variety of desirable traits and characteristics that our society wishes for its young people to possess. Such theories appear to make clear the ways in which youth workers and agencies can "build competent, successful, and healthy youth" (Benson & Pittman, 2001, p. vii), and they do so in a seemingly scientific manner. While these ways of thinking are useful for attracting support for the youth development movement, they are problematic, as Magnuson (1999) has argued, because: 1) they do not identify a normative moral criterion; 2) they make effectiveness a moral criterion; 3) they conflate moral commitment into obedience to rules; 4) they use lists of positive competencies, processes, and pathways that are arbitrary and relative; and

5) the skills, traits, and competencies they list present conceptual difficulties.

Building Resilience in Youth

In recent years, there has been a great deal of discussion regarding building resilience in youth, families, and even communities. Resilience refers to an individual's ability to recover after being challenged. "A resilient individual is one who has the capacity to effectively cope, adjust, and respond to the problems, issues, and circumstances that face him or her in everyday life" (Edginton & O'Neill, 1999, p. 204). In other words, an individual's resilience can be thought of as those qualities that enable him to recover and bounce back with good humor in a quick fashion, "in a variety of ways depending on context or local circumstances. . . influenced by sociocultural influences" (Delgado, 2002, p. 30).

Youth are challenged throughout their adolescence with many stressful life situations. Youth are often in situations where they are alienated, lonely, and sometimes depressed. Still further, youth often live in dysfunctional family situations lacking consistent value structure, patterns, or discipline. An inconsistent family life can place youth in very stressful situations. Peer pressure, as well as the demand for success in school and non-school activities, also are sources of challenge for youth. There are environmental circumstances that impact youth such as their social-economic status, exposure to drugs and other forms of substance abuse, as well as the constant bombardment of images in the media encouraging conformity to risky health behaviors such as smoking and drinking. The media encourages youth to see themselves in ways that often affect their self-concept in a negative fashion. For some, the media encourages unhealthy and unobtainable body images. Building resilience in youth enables them to cope with these and other challenging life situations.

Some youth are in situations where they are at greater risk than others. Risk factors can be thought of as those individual or environmental circumstances or characteristics that can lead to a negative or undesirable behavior (Delgado, 2002, p. 30). Youth workers and youth work organizations direct their energies toward minimizing both the individual and environmental factors that may impact the well being of youth. The Search Institute of Minneapolis, Minnesota, has developed a widely used strategy of identifying assets and deficits that impact youth. The idea of this strategy is to work toward enhancing the assets available in a community to support healthy youth development and to minimize the deficits that may exist. This strategy has gained favor in many communities throughout the United States, although additional research is required to validate this approach.

Benard (1991) has suggested that there are three characteristics in environmental systems that support growth and development. The first of these is the presence of caring relations, second is the establishment of high expectations,

and third the creation of opportunities for participation. It is evident that creating a caring environment for youth may be one of the most important ways of helping youth—basically, creating a protective shield to enable youth through the journey of adolescence. Obviously, these characteristics are necessary throughout the entire lifespan. They constitute one of the most powerful factors in assisting youth as they build resilient behaviors.

There are a number of elements that can assist in promoting resilience in youth. First is the home/family environment. Parental standards, discipline, family support, and the social resources that are provided by parents are elements within the home/family environment that can build resilience. The school and other learning environments also contribute to building resilience. The climate of the school (is it safe and supportive?), the quantity and quality of extracurricular activities, and the educational aspirations of the school as a whole as translated to youth, can promote resiliency. In a more personal sense, an individual's values/commitment can be a reflection of their resilience. Individuals with compassion and concern for others and who have been steered to avoid smoking, inappropriate sexual activity, and drug use often will be more resilient than those who have not developed such qualities. Still further, an individual youth's motivation, quest, or vision for life can have a dramatic impact on his ability to cope. A youth's calling, motivation to achieve, and educational aspirations are all factors that can influence whether or not a person is resilient.

Resiliency is enhanced within youth when several life components are strengthened. These characteristics are as follows:

- Insight.
- Interdependence.
- Relationships.
- Initiative.
- Creativity (Delgado, 2002).
- Humor.
- Values Orientation. (Wolin & Wolin, 1993)

When these life components are present, an individual may be more resilient. Youth workers can help strengthen these personal characteristics in youth.

YOUTH WORK

Youth work, like youth development is difficult to define. Smith has noted that definitions of youth work are problematic. He writes that the "aims, character of the organization, processes utilized, client group, nature of the provider, and the form of the relationship between user and provider could separately or collectively be used to form a definition" (1988, p. 51). In their discussion of youth work, Jeffs and Smith (1995, pg.11) speak to the challenges of the definitional problems of youth work. They argue that there is no underlying universally accepted body of knowledge to build "consensus regarding the role, function, and raison détre for youth work." Thus, there is tension, ambiguity, and a lack of clarity regarding youth work.

De Oliveira and Edginton (1999, pg. 260) have suggested that youth work can be viewed from two perspectives:

First, it has been used to define those professionals who work directly with youth, especially in the context of outreach work. Usually, outreach youth work is directed toward disenfranchised youth. Youth workers are found working with youth in streets, shelters, and other unusual places where the youth congregate. Because of their geographical and sometimes philosophical and ideological distance from central bureaucracies and supervision, the detached youth work has emerged to describe professional, philosophical and ideological stances.
Second, the term youth work has been applied to those working with youth inside character-building organizations, usually in the context of offering recreation and leisure programs. In that sense, youth workers are found in organizations such as Boy Scouts, Girl Scouts, 4-H, Camp Fire, YWCAs, and other similar organizations. Still, some have suggested that the term youth work should be used for all people who work with youth.

This discussion helps illustrate where youth work may occur and helps to define that youth work primarily involves working with youth. However, it is lacking in its clarity for definitional purposes. Obviously, there is a need for greater clarity when defining the term youth work.

We offer the following definition as a way of further the discussion. We believe that youth work is in fact, a professional field. "Youth work" is focused on promoting ". . .the personal and social development of young people. Youth work aims to insure that each individual has equal opportunity to fulfill their potential as an individual and as a member of their community" (NCY, 2001). Jeffs and Smith (1999, p. 120) have suggested that youth work involves ". . .work with young people that is committed to furthering their well being." Youth workers engage youth in both structured and informal environments encouraging their participation in and reflection on life events.

There is an emerging body of knowledge in reference to the efforts of youth workers—a set of common understandings regarding the values, theories, and methods used which guide professional practice. We believe that youth work can be thought of as a professional field comprised of a set of related occupations with common purpose, philosophy, and practice principles. Youth workers are those individuals who have selected careers in direct service, program development, or management within this field. Youth workers often have a focus or specialty area, such as sports, recreation, education, after-

school care, health, counseling, the arts, environmental education, vocational skills training, group work, social work, or casework/assessment. Youth workers can be employed to work with youth in structured, semi-structured, or unstructured (outreach/street work) settings, as well as in groups or individually.

Perhaps one of the most salient elements found in the practice of youth work is in the application of its educational methods. Youth workers primarily use informal educational strategies built upon democratic principles in their professional practice. Banks (1999, p. 8) suggests "what defines youth work is that it is informal educational work with young people." According to the Center for Youth Development and Policy Research (1993) youth work is a field defined by the following:

> The purpose of youth work is to nurture lives, foster self-direction, and generate skills and commitments, which enable young people to make positive contributions to society. As a compliment to the emphasis on the development of academic and vocational knowledge, skills and attainment found in other systems (e.g., formal education), the primary focus of youth development work is on the development of personal, social, and citizenship competencies and

the development of youth's connections and commitments to individuals, family, and community.

What Are the Values of Youth Workers?

Values can be thought of as the underlying beliefs or intentions with which a profession frames its practice. In other words, values are the principles, goals, or standards that are held or accepted by the profession, which guides its effort and serves as the underpinning for its efforts. Banks (1999) has suggested that the values that underline youth work are as follows:

- Respect for basic human rights (e.g. justice, freedom).
- Respect for the individual rights to self-determination.
- Respect for the different cultures and religions in society.
- A commitment to empowerment and participatory democracy.
- Collaborative working relationships and collective action.
- An acknowledgment that all relationships and activities with young people and adults are based on their consent.

These broad guidelines serve as a starting point grounding the work of youth workers. Such values provide a framework against which decisions, which influence professional practice, can be made. Such values are rooted in the values of our culture and society, especially in our beliefs in democracy, freedom, social justice, self-determination, and respect for others. Many are drawn from the principals found in Judeo Christian scriptures, the United Nations Declaration of Human Rights, the United States Declaration of Independence, and the Bill of Rights.

Youth work is diverse and multifaceted in nature. Youth work is an expression of many different values. Such values guide the efforts of youth workers. Values provide a framework that provides direction for both individual youth workers as well as for agencies, organizations, and associations that engage and practice youth work. Some of the more common values that are associated with youth work include:

Democratic Participation. Democratic participation implies that youth are recognized as contributing members in their communities. Democracy is a social condition that leads to equity, respect, and tolerance for the individual and his or her views. Youth workers encourage youth to join or share with others while promoting equity, respect, and tolerance. Democratic learning as a foundation will be discussed further in chapter five.

Informal Education. Learning occurs in many different settings and venues. This approach employs conversation as it's major form of pedagogy, the focus of youth work practice. Conversations with youth in a myriad of settings can provide great insight for youth and assist them in gaining knowledge, skills, and competence for living their lives. Conversation, often spontaneous, unexpected, and informal, can result in a pivotal moment of learning and insight for a youth. Meeting youth in their own settings is an important element of youth work.

Relationship Building. Youth work is about relationship building. It involves building relationships of trust, confidence, respect, equity, and feelings of well being between all parties involved in the process of youth work. Relationship building as a cornerstone to youth work places emphasis on building positive interactions between individuals. It is not about the content of an activity or even the activity itself. It's about the connections made between people regardless of one's characteristics.

Empowerment. Youth work is involved in empowering individuals to have control of the decisions that influence their lives and well-being. A goal of youth work is to give youth a voice, to give them the opportunity to have influence in the affairs related to their lives. Empowering individuals often involves assisting youth in developing a sense of ownership, as well as giving credence to their ideas, values, opinions, and interests.

Collaboration and Partnership Building. Youth work is often about assisting individuals in linking their ideas, interests, needs, and values with others. In this sense, youth work is a process of networking, of building collaborative relationships and partnerships with others. Youth work involves linking others, especially those who have been marginalized, in ways that assist them in influencing community life.

Holistic Functioning. Youth work involves viewing an individual from a holistic perspective. In other words, youth workers are concerned with the total functioning of an individual. A youth's social, physical, spiritual, and creative growth is as important as their intellectual development. In this sense, youth work is multifaceted with a focus on enhancing the total functioning of an individual.

The Center for Youth Development and Policy Research (1994) has offered values and a number of principals impacting youth work practices. Such underlying principals of practice support the role of youth workers and, in fact, serve as guiding values similar to the above-mentioned values. They are:

Learning and Engagement. Activities are not seen as ends in themselves, but as vehicles for building skills and competencies (learning) and solidifying relationships and commitments (engagement). The creation of safe, nonthreatening, nurturing environments (formal or informal) is essential to learning and engagement.

Equality of Outcome. All youth have the right to the assistance and support needed to help them achieve positive outcomes. Youth with "problems" have the right to and can benefit from the same type of assistance as those without. The goal is always development, never just problem remediation. All youth have the right to be accepted, respected, and valued by others and the responsibility to welcome others in the same manner.

Participation and Choice. Youth need opportunities to be active participants in the design, management, implementation, and assessment of the activities, structures, institutions, and environments which affect their lives. Youth need opportunities to choose how, when, in what, and with whom to be engaged.

Responsibility and Empowerment (Self-Direction). Youth need to be given opportunities to develop their own beliefs and action plans and to implement them, even if it involves failure. Youth need to feel that there are clear expectations, that they will act on their own beliefs and take responsibility for their own actions.

Partnership. The relationship between youth and adults is one partnership. The relationships en-

couraged among youth are based on partnership and reinforced through teamwork and shared opportunities for leadership.

The practice of youth work often hinges on the creation of settings where informal education is practiced and youth come voluntarily to participate. In these settings, youth and adults form relationships that build upon these principles of professional practice. Obviously, a key element in youth work is the noncoercive nature of the involvement of youth. That is, youth voluntarily participate in experiences and/or programs, services, and activities. The noncoercive, voluntary nature of youth work places a high level of importance on such factors as youth involvement, ownership, empowerment, being

Exhibit 4.2
Settings that Promote Youth Development

- Physical and Psychological Safety
- Appropriate Structure
- Supportive Relationships
- Opportunities to Belong
- Positive Social Norms
- Support for Efficacy and Mattering
- Opportunities for Skill Building
- Integration of Family, School, and Community Efforts

Source: Hamilton, S. F, Hamilton, M. G., & Pittman, K. (2002). Principles for youth development. In S. F. Hamilton & M. G. Hamilton (Eds.), *The youth development handbook*. Twin Oaks, CA: Sage.

responsive to the needs of youth, and treating them in a manner which demonstrates dignity, respect, and an understanding of their individuality. Youth "vote with their feet" when it comes to making decisions about how to invest their time, money, energy, and effort. As Smith (1988) has noted, central to youth work practice is the principal of self-determination, the nondirective enabling of young people to make decisions and choices in their lives leading to self-emancipation."

Youth Worker Roles

The roles that youth workers play are varied and dynamic in nature. We find youth workers involved in a variety of roles carrying many different job titles. There is no established nomenclature or consistency in the titles that are assigned to individuals engaging in youth work. Many titles are agency specific. Table 4.1 provides a list of occupational titles used in the United States for individuals associated with organizations that are involved in youth development. Individuals occupying such roles are often engaged in a myriad of functions. Table 4.2 provides a list of functions with which youth workers may be involved. Obviously, the functions that an individual assumes will be dependent on their position within an organization. Those involved in direct service delivery will focus on different functions when compared with individuals involved in supervisory or management type positions.

Banks (1999) has provided an interesting framework to describe the work of youth workers. She suggests that there are numerous functions which youth workers are involved. These are as follows:

Youth Worker as Guide, Philosopher, and Friend. Youth workers have long been involved in promoting moral education, character education, and/or values development. Youth workers as guides, philosophers, and friends provide opportunities for individuals to explore questions dealing with a major focus of adolescence—the search for identity. Youth workers assist individuals as they transition into adulthood by promoting moral thinking and reflection, learning, empowerment, and power sharing. The building of "reciprocal relationships with morally good persons, engagement with young peoples' real lives and conversations, which enable them to think critically" is a major focus of youth workers (Young, 1999, p. 89).

Youth Worker as Controller. Youth workers have historically been involved in efforts at shaping or controlling the behavior of youth. In recent years, "the sense of diverting or preventing young people from activities considered harmful, should be regarded, and indeed promoted as a core purpose of the work" (Jeffs & Banks, 1999, p. 93). From a historical perspective, youth work often focused on building discipline, turning youth away from delinquent or harmful activities, or even to encourage individuals to participate in "fun, wholesome" activities as an alternative to other behaviors. In a sense, youth workers were working

Table 4.1
Typical Youth Worker Titles

Activity Specialist	Group Worker
Before/After-School Child-Care Worker	Health Promotion Director
Case Worker	Housing (Shelter) Director
Case Work Supervisor	Human Resource Director
Center Director	Juvenile Justice Worker
Child-Care Assistant	Mentor
Child-Care Worker	Outreach Worker
Child/Youth-Care Worker	Physical Education Director
Clinical Director	Prevention Specialist
Community Organizer	Program Aid/Assistant
Coach	Program Administrator
Counselor	Program Director
Cultural Enrichment Director	Program Manager/Supervisor
Day Care/Preschool Teacher	Public Relations Director
Detached Youth Worker	Recreation Director
Director of Before/After-School Care	School-Based Programs Director
Director of Day Care	Social Worker
Director of Membership/Marketing	Social Educator
Director of Product/Sales	Street Youth Worker
Direct Service Worker	Therapist
Educational Director	Volunteer Coordinator
Educational Specialist	Volunteer Development Director
Employment Counselor	Youth Advisor
Environmental Educator	Youth Center Director
Environmental Education Director	Youth Minister
Event Manager	Youth Spiritual Leader
Field Director	Youth Trainer
Fund Development Director	Youth Work Supervisor
Group Leader/Worker	Youth Worker

to control the behavior of youth as they were promoting desirable behavior from an adult perspective.

Youth Worker as Converter. Youth workers have worked to transmit the norms, customs and values from one generation to another. In this sense, youth workers attempt to convert youth by passing on their generations' values to the next. We often think of the process of conversion as associated with religious organizations; however, conversion is not only limited to religious ideas and values, but may be found across the spectrum of our social, cultural, political, and economic institutions. For example, Junior Achievement, Inc. attempts to convert youth to capitalistic values through its edu-

Table 4.2
Typical Youth Worker Functions

Administrative support	Management/administration
Advising	Mediating
Canvassing	Mediator
Character building	Membership and marketing
Community organizing/builder	Mentor
Confidante	Mentoring
Controller	Modeling positive behaviors
Converting	Negotiating
Consciousness	Networking
Counseling	Philosopher
Direct service delivery	Program development
Educating	Problem solving
Empowering	Public relations
Environmental guide	Rehabilitating
Facilitating	Rights advocating
Fact finding	Skill building
Financial support	Social education
Fostering political power structures	Teaching
Friend	Team building
Fundraising	Therapy
Guiding	Training
Intervention activities	Vocational school training
Lobbying	

cational and experiential learning programs. "Because youth come to informal educational environments voluntarily the prospects for meeting the needs of youth especially those associated with identity, the need to belong, and opportunities for ownership makes this function of youth workers very powerful" (Green, 1999, p. 110).

Youth Workers as Mediators and Interpreters. America is a diverse and pluralistic society. The intersecting boundaries between social and cultural groups, have from a historical perspective, created friction in American societies. The relationships between ethnic groups, races, and socioeconomic clusters provide rich opportunities for youth workers to serve as mediators and interpreters. In American society, we increasingly view our diversity as strength, however, this interpretation often requires youth workers to mediate and interpret the value and importance of these broader social and cultural factors with youth. On an individual basis, youth workers work to assist youth in resolving conflicts, clarifying differences in values, problem solving, and in effect, understanding each other.

Youth Worker as Confidante. "Youth workers often form close relationships with young people and are sought out as adults who can help with personal problems" (Morgan & Banks, 1999, p. 145). In other words, youth workers are building relationships of caring and trust; and therefore, confidentiality is central to their efforts. Confidential relationships occur between individuals when something is shared with another person in trust. Usually, the youth worker is entrusted by the youth with private or secret matters. Bond (1995, p. 6) provides four interpretations of how the principle of confidentiality may be applied when working with youth. They are: 1) secrecy—everything disclosed is secret to the people present; 2) confidential disclosures remain the property of the person who made the disclosure who must therefore be consulted before that information is communicated to others; 3) confidential disclosures are given on trust to be used in the best interests of the person who made the disclosure to someone who needs to know that information in order to further the best interests; and 4) confidentiality entails following the practice laid down in agency policy and by the appropriate professional body. Obviously, confidential relationships require a great deal of trust and understanding between the youth worker and the individual confiding. If confidential relationships did not exist, people would not share information. As a result, their needs, concerns, problems, and issues may not be fully addressed.

Youth Worker as a Rights Advocate. Youth workers often are involved in advocating for the rights of others, especially for those who have been marginalized in society. In the main stream, youth are often viewed as individuals whose needs, interests, and concerns are underrepresented, ignored or seen as being "out of whack" with those of the main stream of society. As Franklin (1995, p. 7) has written,

> Societies tend to divide their members' life cycles into two broad age states; childhood and adulthood. The transfer from one to the other is often associated with the acquisition of distinctive rights, privileges and obligations and is usually celebrated to confirm the significance of this *rite de passage*. The age of 18 signals the age of majority, when individuals become formally adult, but this age boundary creates a number of anomalies.

Crimmens and Whalen (1999, p. 164) have suggested that a major value to be pursued by youth workers and youth organizations is that of inclusion. This suggests that youth workers should strive to involve youth as a part of our society and culture. As it is evident from the above statement by Franklin, that rights, privileges, and obligations are often divided. Therefore, it becomes necessary for youth workers to bridge the gap for adolescents, ensuring their needs, interests, and concerns are reflected in mainstream society. Youth have rights that often require youth workers to advocate on their behalf. In fact, at the turn of the century much of the child saving movement in the United States was focused on protecting children and youth through the creation of social policies leading to laws that protected youth from those elements in society that preyed on their vulnerability.

Further, the efforts of youth workers are present in many settings and locations—from the street corner to the youth center, in schools and at home, in parks and on the playground, and at business and other places where youth gather. Wherever we find youth, there is an opportunity for the youth worker to apply their professional knowledge and skills.

YOUTH WORK ORGANIZATIONS

In North America, there is a wide variety of youth work organizations. Youth work organizations are found in public, nonprofit, and commercial sectors and are primarily focused in mission, programs, and services on children and youth. However, the goals and focus of these

Exhibit 4.3
Big Brothers Big Sisters

Big Brothers Big Sisters

Roots: Irvin Westheimer of Cincinnati is credited with creating the Big Brothers Big Sisters concept in 1903 in response to media exposure of child abuse, labor problems, crime, and absent parents. Westheimer went on to found Big Brothers of Cincinnati in 1910.

First: Ernest Coulter, a court clerk from New York City, started New York Big Brothers in 1904, which would eventually become Big Brothers Big Sisters of America. Coulter was influenced by the work of Jude Julius Mayer, who recruited influential men to mentor delinquent boys.

Screened: Each volunteer gets a background check, training, and supervision. The only requirement is a willingness to make a new friend and share some fun with a young person.

Success: A recent study found that 46% of children in the program were less likely to use drugs, and 52% were less likely to skip school.

Information: www.biglink.org"

Source: Big brothers big sisters. (2003, December 27). *The Des Moines Register.* p. 1B.

organizations vary greatly. They may focus their efforts on youth with a high degree of need who are at high risk on skill development, on spiritual development, on personal and social development or what has been termed "character-building," a combination of these goals or others. Pittman (1991) notes that the Carnegie Council on Adolescent Development Task Force on Youth Development and Community Programs, has compiled six groups of youth work organizations. They include the following:

1. National youth organizations.
2. Multipurpose national organization that provides some youth services.
3. Grassroots youth development organizations.
4. Religious youth groups.
5. Youth groups operated by adult service clubs and other similar organizations.
6. Public service organizations.

These types of organizations are more fully described in Table 4.3.

Judith Erickson offers another conceptualization of youth organizations. She suggests that there are "more than 500 adult-sponsored organizations enrolling millions of America children and youth in groups, troops, teams and clubs. These young people are lead by a veritable army of volunteers, and the programs are administered by some 50,000 staff members" (Erickson, 1994, p. 3). Erickson goes on to suggest that youth organizations share the following similar characteristics:

- They serve children and youths of high school age and under
- The foster groups, troops, or teams of young peers that are conducted under adult supervision.
- They are nonprofit (although a few are associated with profit-making corporations).
- They are national in scope, members are drawn from more than one state, and there is a central coordinating office. (Erickson, 1994, p. 3)

Table 4.3
Types of Youth Service Organizations

Type of Organization	Description	Examples
National youth organizations	Membership organizations; organizations character-education-oriented; nationally developed programs; voluntary and professional leadership, often supported by dues, charitable giving/donations, and/or local fundraising activities.	Girls, Inc., Boy Scouts of America, Big Brothers/Big Sisters, Boys and Girls Clubs, Campfire Boys and Girls, Child Welfare League, 4-H for Youth of America, Girl Scouts of the USA, Junior Achievement, ASPIRA, WAVE, Inc.
Multipurpose national organizations with services for youth	Membership organizations; disaster relief; multiple target populations including youths, dependent on voluntary and professional leadership, often supported by dues, charitable giving; nationally developed programs often with local control.	American Red Cross, Salvation Army, YWCA of the USA, YMCA of the USA.
Grassroots youth development organizations	Local focus, may be affiliated with broader-based organizations, but often emerge as a result of community action and/or individual initiative of youth and adults.	Youth sport groups, outreach programs, centers, shelters, camps.
Religious youth groups	Spiritual growth and development, affiliated with religious order groups, supported by charitable gifts, donations, fees, membership dues. Usually locates activities in conjunction with community religious institutions.	Athletes in Action, Awana Clubs International, Boys' and Girls' Brigades of America, Campus Crusade for Christ International, Christian Service Brigade, Fellowship of Christian Athletes, government supported sports bodies, public libraries, public museums, park and recreation departments, Pioneer Clubs, Royal Rangers, Young Life, youth bureaus.
Youth programs conducted by adult service clubs and other similar type organizations	Often aligned with fraternal/sorority/service clubs. Membership based; character development and civic organizations supported by dues, fees, donations, institutions.	Anchor Clubs, Excel Clubs, Junior Civitan International, Junior Optimist, Octagon International, Key Club International, S Clubs.
Public sector youth groups	Tax supported, focused on character building, diversion/entertainment; organized with a broad conception of "public good" including equal opportunity access; promotes democratic principles.	Park and recreation departments, youth bureaus, government supported sports bodies, public libraries, public museums.

The classifications established by Erickson are described in Table 4.4.

SUMMARY

Developing a framework for understanding youth development, youth work, and youth organizations is an important element in the professional practice of youth work. Definitions, concepts and terms provide a way of focusing the efforts of professional youth workers. By defining the nature of professional youth work, a common framework for professional action is established. This has been a challenge in youth work as there have been no universally accepted definitions to guide the efforts of youth workers. However, there are increasingly consistent ideas as to how the terms of youth development, youth work, and youth organizations should be framed. As a result, a body of knowledge is beginning to emerge and be accepted and applied to the efforts of youth workers.

Essentially, youth development is focused on preparing young people to build the competencies necessary for adult life. Youth work and youth workers are focused primarily on promoting the development of youth. To do so, youth workers craft environments, both structured and informal, which provide opportunities for youth to develop competencies for adult life and in large measure provide opportunities for them to embrace the major challenge of adolescence, that of forming one's self identity. Through conversation, dialogue, action with reflection (praxis), and other learning strategies, youth workers assist youth and promote self-reliant, adult-like behaviors. There are myriad of youth organizations within which youth workers practice. Such organizations provide a host of programs and services aimed at meeting the needs of youth and building competencies for a successful life.

REFERENCES

Banks, S. (1999). *Ethical issues in youth work* London, England: Routledge.

Beker, J., & Alejandra, L. A. (1970). *Critical incidents in institutional child care: A case book for child care workers.* New York, NY: Human Sciences Press.

Bernard, B. (1991). *Fostering resiliency in kids: Protective factors in the family, school, and community.* Portland, OR: Western Regional Centre for Drug-Free Schools and Communities.

Benson, P. L., & Pittman, K. J. (2001). *Trends in youth development: Visions, realities, and challenges.* New York, NY: Kluwer Academic Publishers.

Bettelheim, B. (1952). *Love is not enough: The treatment of emotionally disturbed children.* Glencoe, IL: The Free Press.

Bond, T. (1995). *Confidentiality about HIV in multidisciplinary teams.* Newcastle, England: Northern and Yorkshire Regional Health Authority.

Bulgarelli, R., & Almeida, S. (1987). *E possivel educar na rua?* (Is it possible to educate in the street?) Brasfia: UNICEP/MPAS.

Table 4.4
Erickson's Classification of Types of Youth Organizations

Type of Organization	Description	Examples
Hobby and special interest groups, school subject matter clubs, and honor societies	Narrowly focused on single area of interest.	American Checker Federation, Bands of America, Inc., Drum Corps International, Junior Fire Marshal Program, Junior Philatelists of America, Magical Youths International, Mensa, National Junior Honor Society, Omega Gamma Delta.
Career education and vocational student groups	Linked to career and vocational interests of youth. Youth learn about various occupations.	Civil Air Patrol, Future Homemakers of America, Future Business Leaders of America, Junior Achievement, WAVE, Inc, Young Actors Guild, Naval Sea Cadet Corps, Future Farmers of America, Young Marine of the Marine Corps League.
Science, math, and technology	Supports career explorations, activities, and areas of study in math, science, technology, and engineering.	Academy of Model Aeronomics, American Junior Academy of Science, Inent Associety, JETS, Inc., Mu Alpha Theta, Odyssey of the Mind, The Planetary Society, Society of Physics Society.
Sport organizations	Sports organization for young people, including youth with disabilities that teaches related skills, encourages competition, promotes organized play, and focuses on development.	AAU/USA Youth Sports Program, Direction Sports, IronKids Health and Fitness Program, National Council of Youth Sports, National Youth Sports Program, The President's Council on Physical Fitness and Sports, All American Baseball Association, Amateur Softball Association, American Legion Baseball, USA Volleyball, Hoop-It-Up, USA Basketball, Youth Basketball of America, Inc., American Bicycle Association, Young American Bowling Alliance, U.S. Junior National Cycling Program, USA Boxing, American Canoe Association, NSA

(continued)

Table 4.4 (continued)
Erickson's Classification of Types of Youth Organizations

Type of Organization	Description	Examples
Sport organizations Continued		Field Hockey, USA Field Hockey Association, Pop Warner Football, American Gymnastics, American Golf Association, USA Hockey, Inc., Ice Skating Institute of America, USA Karate Federation, All American Youth, American Youth Soccer Organization (AYSO), Soccer Association for Youth, USA Cup, National Junior Tennis League, USA Track and Field, USA Youth Volleyball Program, U.S. Olympic Committee, National Handicapped Sports, Special Olympics, Inc.
Peace and global understanding groups	Groups promoting nonviolence, world peace, and other efforts to promote cultural awareness and understanding	AFS International Intercultural Programs, American Friends Service Committee Youth Programs, Amigos de las Americas, Amnesty International Youth Program, Anti-Defamation League of B'nai Brith, Children's Campaign for Nuclear Disarmament, Children's Edition, Council on International Education Exchange, Creative Response, Fellowship of Reconciliation, Grace Contrino Abrams Peace Education Foundation, Heifer Project International, International Christian Youth Exchange, Legacy International, Little Friends for Peace, MADRE, Open Door Student Exchange, The National Student Campaign Against Hunger and Homelessness, World Federalist Association, World Learning, World Vision, Youth Exchange Program, Youth for Understanding International Exchange.
Civic education and political organizations	Aims to socialize and familiarize youth with political issues and responsibility or a political party.	FRONLASH, National Traditionalist Caucus, Spartacus Youth League, Young Communist League of the United States of America, Young Democrats of America, Young Republican National Federation, Young Socialist Alliance, Boys State, Boys Nation, Girls State, Girls Nation, American Student Council Association, Junior Statesmen of America, NAACP Youth and College Division, National Association of Student Councils, YMCA Teen Leadership Programs, The Center for Democracy and Citizenship, Close Up Foundation.

(continued)

Table 4.4 (continued)
Erickson's Classification of Types of Youth Organizations

Type of Organization	Description	Examples
Social welfare and community betterment	Aims to provide services to assist youth experiencing difficult life experiences; intently focused on helping youth learn how to help themselves and others.	American Red Cross, Big Brothers/Big Sisters of America, Guardian Angels, Junior Guardian Angels, National Network of Runaway and Youth Services, Inc., Volunteers of America, Inc., YouthBuild USA, YouthBuild Coalition.
Religious organizations Protestant Catholic Jewish Other religious organizations	Organizations, denominational and nondenominational, that provide a wide range of activities for youth and others.	Athletes in Action, Awana Clubs International, Boys' and Girls' Brigades of America, Campus Crusade for Christ International, Center for Youth Ministry, Youth Quest Ministries, Child Evangelism Fellowship, Christian Endeavor International, Christian Service Brigade, Coalition for Christian Outreach, Fellowship of Christian Athletes, High School Evangelism Fellowship, The International Order of the Kings Daughters and Sons, Pro-Teens, Teen Missions International, Inc., Success with Youth, World of Life Fellowship, Young Life, Youth for Christ/U.S.A., Inc., Alliance Youth Fellowship, Berean Youth Fellowship, Christian Life Clubs, Free Methodist Youth Ministries, Free Church Student Ministries, Girl Guards, Adventure Corps, Girls in Action/Acteens, Lutheran Pioneers, Lutheran Youth Fellowship, National Youth Ministry Organization, Pentecostal Young People's Association, Presbyterian Youth Ministry, O-Teens, Teen World Outreach, Young Religious Unitarian Universalists, Youth and Children's Ministries, Catholic Big Brothers of New York, Inc., National Christ Child Society, Inc., National Federation for Catholic Youth Ministry, American Zionist Youth Foundation, Ezrah Youth Movement, Lubavitch Youth

(continued)

Table 4.4 (continued)
Erickson's Classification of Types of Youth Organizations

Type of Organization	Description	Examples
Religious organizations Continued		Organizations, National Council of Young Israeli Youth, Moslem Youth of North America, Western Young Buddhist League, Youth Leadership, Inc., Programs of Religious Activities with Youth (P.R.A.Y.).
Conservation and humane education groups	Promotes human treatment of animals and others, as well as preservation of natural environment.	American Society for the Prevention of Cruelty to Animals, Children's Action for Animals, Children's Alliance for the Protection of the Environment, EARTHWATCH, Inner City Outings, Kids for a Clean Environment, Kids for Saving Earth, Kids in Bloom, National Audubon Society, National Association for Humane and Environmental Education, National Wildlife Federation, PETA Kids, Student Action Corps for Animals, The Student Conservation Association, Inc., Student Environmental Action Coalition, Youth for Environmental Sanity.
Service organization youth program	Programs that promote youth involvement in providing service to community and schools.	Anchor Clubs, Pilot International, C.L.A.S.S. Program, Excel Clubs, Interact, Junior Optimist Octagon International, Junior Civitan International, S Clubs, Leo Club Program, Key Club International, School Safety Patrols, Serteen Clubs.
Self-help organizations	National groups that dedicate time and skills to help youth cope with problems.	Alateen, Cocaine Anonymous World Services, Daughters and Sons United, Gay/Lesbian Youth Hotline, Hug-a-Tree and Survive, Narcotics Anonymous, RAINBOWS, Youth Suicide National Center.

(continued)

Table 4.4 (continued)
Erickson's Classification of Types of Youth Organizations

Type of Organization	Description	Examples
Substance abuse prevention and temperance organization	Provides education and programs geared to preventing substance abuse, such as of drugs and alcohol.	America's PRIDE Program, International Good Templars Youth Fellowship, "Just Say No" International, Loyal Temperance Legion, National Association of Teen Institutes, National Family Partnership, Students Against Driving Drunk, Youth to Youth International, Students to Offset Peer Pressure, CompDrug.
Hereditary, veterans, military, and patriotic groups	Membership organizations or organizations that are associated with adult sponsoring organizations that provide programs for youth.	Junior Members, American Legion Auxiliary, Sons of the American Legion, Veterans of Foreign Wars and Ladies Auxiliary Youth Programs, Sons of the Veterans of Foreign Wars, Children of the Confederacy, Children of the Republic of Texas, Devil Pups, Inc., Junior American Citizens Committee, Junior Sons of America, National Organization, Sons of Union Veterans of the Civil War, National Society, Children of the American Revolution.
Ethnic heritage groups	Linked to preserve and promote ethnic and cultural heritage. Some linked to members of a specific ethnic background or open to all youth.	American Carpatho-Russian Youth, American Romanian Orthodox Youth, American Sokol Organizations, ARCAYD, Armenian Church Youth, ASPIRA Association, Inc., Association of American Youth of Ukrainian Descent, Byelorussian-American Youth Organization, Cherokee Nation Youth Leadership Program, Greek Orthodox Young Adult League, Indian Youth of America, Junior Cultural Federation of America, Knights of Lithuania Juniors, Maids of Athena, National Indian Youth Council, National Indian Youth Leadership Project, National Urban League Incentives to Excel and Succeed, Sokol USA, Sons of Norway Youth Club, SPJST Youth Clubs, United National Indian Tribal Youth, Inc. (UNITY), Young Vikings of the Danish Brotherhood of America, Youth of Evrytania.

(continued)

Table 4.4 (continued)
Erickson's Classification of Types of Youth Organizations

Type of Organization	Description	Examples
Youth lodges and orders	Junior divisions of adult sororal or fraternal organization often requiring membership.	Constellation of Junior Stars, Inc., Degree of Anona, Degree of Hiawatha, Degree of Honor Protective Association Junior Clubs, Junior Lodge, Independent Order of Odd Fellows, Junior Service Club, Teen Clubs, National Grange Youth and Young Adults, Pithead Sunshine Girls, Theta Rho Girl's Club, William Penn Association, Supreme Assembly, International Order of Rainbow for Girls, Order of Pythagorans, Order of DeMolay.
Agricultural and livestock	Encourages youth to be engaged in activities devoted to agriculture, raising livestock, and agricultural breeding.	American Cavy Breeders Association, American–International Junior Charolais Association, American Junior Hereford Association, American Junior Paint Horse Association, American Junior Quarterhorse Association, American Junior Shorthorn Association, American Junior Simmental Association, American Milking Shorthorn Junior Society, American Rabbit Breeders Association, Inc., The Holstein Junior Program, International Arabian House Youth Association, National Hampshire Junior Association, National Junior Polled Hereford Council, Pony of the Americas, Inc.

Carnegie Council on Adolescent Development (1989). *Turning points: Preparing American youth for the 21st century.* New York, NY: Carnegie Corporation.

Carnegie Council on Adolescent Development. (1992). *A matter of time: Risk and Opportunity in the Nonschool Hours.* Report of the Task Force of Youth Development and Community Programs. New York, NY: Carnegie Corporation.

Center for Youth Development and Policy Research. (1993). *Achieving positive outcomes for youth: Changing the goal from problem reduction to promoting development.* Washington, DC: Academy for Educational Development.

Crimmens, D., & Whalen, A. (1999). Rights-based approaches to work with young people. In S. Banks (Ed.), *Ethical issues in youth work* (pp. 164-180). London, England: Routledge.

Delgado, M. (2002). *New frontiers for youth development in the twenty-first century: Revitalizing and broadening youth development.* New York, NY: Columbia University Press.

De Oliveira, W., & Edginton. C. R. (1999). Youth and human services. In H. S. Harris & D. D. Maloney (Eds.), *Human services: Contemporary issues and trends* (pp. 255-268). Boston, MA: Allyn and Bacon.

Edginton, C. R., & de Oliveira, W. (1995, Spring). A model of youth work orientations. Humanics: The *Journal of Leadership for Youth and Human Service, 4*(2), 3-7.

Edginton, C. R., & de Oliveira, W. (1995). Youth development: A program framework. *PERS Review Hong Kong, 1*(2), 22-27. Refereed.

Edginton, C. R., & O'Neill, J. P. (1999). Program, services, and event management. In B. van der Smissen, M. Moiseichik, V. J. Hartenburg, & L. F. Twardzik (Eds.), *Management of park and recreation agencies* (pp. 175-240). Ashburn, VA: The National Recreation and Park Association.

Edginton, C. R., & Rossman, J. R. (1988). Leisure programming: Building a theoretical base. *Journal of Park and Recreation Administration, 6*(4), viii-x.

Edginton, S. R., & Edginton. C. R. (1994). *Youth programs: Promoting quality services.* Champaign, IL: Sagamore Publishing.

Erickson, J. B. (1994). *Directory of American youth organizations 1996-1997.* Minneapolis, MN: Free Spirit Publishing.

Franklin, B. (1995). *The handbook of children's rights.* London, England: Routledge.

Green. M. (1999). The youth worker as converter. In S. Banks (Ed.), *Ethical issues in youth work* (pp. 110-124). London, England: Routledge.

Halperin, S., Cusack, J. & O'Brien, R. (1995). Contract with America's Youth: Toward a National Youth Development Agenda. Washington, D.C.: American Youth Policy Forum.

Hamilton, S. F., Hamilton, M. G., & Pittman, K. (2004). Principles for youth development. In S.F. Hamilton & M.G. Hamilton (Eds.),

The youth development handbook (pp. 3-22). Thousand Oaks, CA: Sage.

Havinghurst, R. J. (1952). *Developmental tasks and education.* Toronto, Canada: Longmans, Green and Company.

Jeffs, T., & Banks, S. (1999). Youth workers as controllers. In S. Banks (Ed.), *Ethical issues in youth work* (pp. 93-109). London, England: Routledge.

Jeffs, T., & Smith, M. K. (1995). Getting the dirtbags off the streets. *Youth and Policy, 53,* 1-14.

Jeffs, T., & Smith, M. K. (1999). *Informal education.* Ticknall, Derbyshire: Education Now.

Kett, J. F. (1977). *Rite of passage: Adolescence in America 1790 to the present.* New York, NY: Basic Books.

Konopka, G. (1973). *Requirements for the Healthy Development of Adolescent Youth.* Adolescence, VIII, 31, Fall.

Lakes, R. (1996). *Youth development and critical education: The promise of democratic action.* New York, NY: SUNY.

Magnuson, D. (1999). *Social interdependence: The goal structure of moral experience.* Unpublished doctoral dissertation, University of Minnesota, Minneapolis.

McKenna, T. (2000, June). Imbedding positive youth development. *Youth Today, 52.*

Morgan, S., & Banks, S. (1999). The youth worker as confidante. In S. Banks (Ed.), *Ethical issues in youth work* (pp. 145-163). London, England: Routledge.

Murphy, J. (1995). *Training for youth workers: An assessment guide for community-based organizations to promote youth development.* Washington, DC: Academy for Educational Development, Center for Youth Development and Policy Research.

National Collaboration for Youth. (2001). *A national youth development agenda.* Washington, DC: National Assembly of Health and Human Service Organizations.

Nixon, R. (1997, September/October). Introduction. *Child Welfare, 76*(5), 571-575.

Perkins, D. F., Borden, L. M., Keith, J. G., Hoppe-Rooney, T. L., & Villarruel, F. A. (2003). Community youth development. In F. A. Villarruel, Perkins, D. F., Borden, L. M. & Keith, J. G. (Eds.), *Community youth development* (pp. 1-24). Thousand Oaks, CA: Sage.

Pittman, K. J. (1991). *Promoting youth development: Strengthening the role of youth serving and community organizations.* New York, NY: Center for Youth Development and Policy Research.

Pittman, K. J., Irby, M., & Ferber, T. (2000). *Unfinished business: Further reflections on a decade of promoting youth development.* Takoma Park, MD: The Forum for Youth Investment.

Politz, B. (1996). *Making the case: Community foundations and youth development.* Center for Youth Development & Policy Research, Foundations for Change.

Redl, F. (1966). *When we deal with children: Selected writings.* New York, NY: The Free Press.

Redl, F., & Wineman, D. (1957). *The aggressive child.* Glencoe, IL: The Free Press.

Robertson, R. M. (1997, September/October). Walking the talk: Organizational modeling and commitment to youth and staff development. *Child Welfare 76*(5), 577-589.

Rossman, J. R. (1988). Development of leisure programming theory. *Journal of Park & Recreation Administration, 6*(4), 1-13.

Smith, M. (1988). *Developing youth work: Informal education mutual aid and popular practice,* Milton Keynes: Open University Press.

U.S. Department of Health and Human Services. (2002). Positive youth development [On-line]. Available: http://www.acf.dhhs.gov/programs/fysb/positve.htm

Werner, E. E. (1989). High-risk children in young adulthood: A longitudinal study from birth to 32 years. *American Journal of Orthopsychiatry, 59,* 72-81.

Werner, E. E., & Smith, R. S. (1982). *Overcoming the odds: High risk children from birth to adulthood.* Ithaca, NY: Cornell University Press.

Werner, E. E., & Smith, R. S. (1992). *Vulnerable but invincible: A longitudinal study of resilient children and youth.* New York, NY: McGraw-Hill.

Wolin, S. J., & Wolin, S. (1993). *The resilient self: How survivors of troubled families rise above adversity.* New York, NY: Villard Books.

Witt, P. A. (2002, October). *Youth development: The importance of intentionality.* Paper presented at the meeting of the National Recreation and Park Association, Tampa Bay, FL.

Young, K. (1999). The youth worker as a guide, philosopher, and friend. In S. Banks (Ed.), *Ethical issues in youth work* (pp. 77-92). London, England: Routledge.

CHAPTER FIVE

Approaches to Youth Work

INTRODUCTION

A review of a number of approaches, philosophies, and models employed in youth work and youth development can be useful in creating a framework for professional practice. In this chapter, we identify democratic learning as a central philosophical underpinning for youth work. Such a philosophy provides us with an understanding of the general principles that are used to guide professional practice. A focus on democratic learning helps us establish a system of thinking and knowledge to guide our professional efforts. Models are usually thought of as an abstract representation or even hypothetical description of some phenomena. Models can help

us explain and often provide a visual representation of some concept or idea. In this chapter, we will present several philosophical ideas and models that we believe may be useful in the practice of youth work.

Most youth programs and services are often built on conceptions of how youth learn and develop, as well as other considerations. Such approaches and the establishment of a philosophical underpinning provide a conceptual framework to guide the activities of youth workers. For example, What is the purpose of youth development? What approaches do youth workers employ in framing experiences for youth? How is freedom and democracy associated with such factors as youth ownership, involvement, and issues of control? What is the function of education within the context of youth work and youth development? What models may be available to guide the professional practice of youth work? In this chapter, some of the underlying philosophical ideas and models for the professional practice of youth work will be presented.

PHILOSOPHICAL APPROACHES TO YOUTH WORK

Youth work involves assisting youth in discovering themselves through the process identified as adolescence. In a sense, youth work is focused on helping individuals in their transformational journey to adulthood. In every society, there are organizations and institutions that have been established to facilitate this process. Such organizations offer programs and services that are built upon a set of assumptions or what could be referred to as a philosophical foundation. Such a philosophical underpinning provides guidance for the vision and mission of an organization, its goals and objectives, strategies of intervention, assumptions regarding the way that youth learn and grow, and the roles that individuals within these organizations assume to serve youth.

One's philosophical orientation provides a guide for their actions; it can be thought of as a framework for professional practice. Individual and organizational philosophies are value laden. A philosophy reflects one's beliefs, ideals, and assumptions. Every organization has a core set of beliefs that serve to clarify its

basic values, principles, and strategies that guide actions. Further, the philosophy that an organization adopts serves as the foundation upon which an individual youth worker builds his interactions with individual youth.

This is especially true regarding the assumptions that youth workers make concerning how youth learn and grow. Such basic philosophical assumptions have a significant impact on the developmental aims of the programs and services provided by youth service organizations. Further, one's philosophical assumptions impact the way that one "thinks about" or frames youth and their development. (See Table 5.1 below.) For example, if we believe that adolescence is a natural process, then we would strive to eliminate the barriers or obstacles towards healthy development. On the other hand, if we believe that maturing involves acquiring social knowledge or cultural norms, than youth workers would seek to provide information regarding society's expectations and existing values.

Wiles and Bondi (1979) have developed a number of primary questions for applying philosophical thought to curriculum strategies. We have adapted these questions and applied them to youth work. In developing a philosophical approach to youth work, some of the more useful questions that may be framed include the following:

1. Is the purpose of youth work to change, to adapt, or to accept societal order?

Table 5.1
Philosophical Approaches to Youth Work

	Classical	Romanticist	Progressivist	Constructivist
Purpose of Youth Programs	Provide educational opportunities focused on knowledge and cultural rules, norms, and values.	Provide educational programs devoted to promoting the development of youth as freethinking individuals.	Provide educational programs where youth, being social beings, have the opportunity to actively engage with and learn from others.	Create youth-centered learning environments that offer positive learning opportunities, encourage individual growth, and promote positive social interactions.
Focus of Programming Content	Explicit social rules and norms examples of proper social behavior.	Civil liberty and individual freedom; encourage the expression of the "inner good."	Promotion of critical thinking, reflection, and mature problem-solving skills.	Construction of individual knowledge and meaning.
Role of the Youth Worker	Promote the transmission of cultural rules, norms, values, and social knowledge to young people.	Work toward opening up a young person's individual personality; leading them toward success and achievement.	Engage youth in educational activity that is meaningful, interesting, and challenging within a context of democratic values.	Encourage the development of autonomy, natural curiosity, initiative, cooperation, and reflection in youth.

(continued)

Table 5.1
Philosophical Approaches to Youth Work
(continued)

	Classical	Romanticist	Progressivist	Constructivist
Role of Youth	Passive; expected to learn and conform to the estab-lished social order.	Active; learn to partici-pate in a free and civil society.	Active; must become reflective thinkers, applying acquired knowledge to social experience.	Active; must work toward the ability to self-regulate learning and personal development activity.
Attitude Toward Change and Devel-opment	Transmission of cultural values and norms leads to the development of desired personalities in young people.	Expression of self pro-motes the development of well-rounded, freethinking individuals.	Values of democracy and freedom have to be applied to educational endeavors.	Opportunities for young people to apply knowledge, challenging personal conceptions and miscon-ceptions, promotes development.

2. What unique contributions, in terms of learning and growth opportunities, can a given youth organization provide for young people?
3. What common goals and objectives should be pursued by individuals within the context of a given youth service organization?
4. What program strategies can be adopted that support the unique learning and growth opportunities to be provided (e.g., should values be transmitted, skills taught, or prob-lem-solving strategies pursued)?
5. What strategies should be employed by the youth worker when interacting with youth?
6. What types of pedagogy should be employed by youth workers (e.g., how should a youth worker frame their conversation and dialogue with each individual youth)?
7. Should we emphasize constructed activity or should we seek to connect youth to the experience that comes from living one's life?

8. Should youth services reflect the expressed or felt needs of youth or should they project a given community's desires for young people or society's broader constructs?

9. Should the structure of youth programs emphasize individualistic goals or pursue more cooperative strategies? In addition, should program strategies be framed in a fashion that seeks definitive outcomes that can be defined in a specific time frame or meet individual developmental needs that may vary among youth?

10. Should youth workers expose and involve youth in controversial themes, or should youth be sheltered and exposed to a more limited perspective?

There are a number of ways to frame an exploration of philosophical approaches to youth work. In this book, we have chosen to identify what could be thought of as four distinct educational philosophies that can be applied to frame youth work. Why educational philosophies? What does linking philosophy with education imply? Education is a process of learning whereby young people are actively engaged in the process of their own personal growth. It may involve acquiring values, attitudes, knowledge, or skills that may assist them in their journey toward adulthood. So one's educational philosophy as applied to youth work involves establishing a set of values, beliefs, or assumptions about how youth learn and grow.

In their classic article, Kohlberg and Mayer (1972) have outlined three educational philosophies that have been used in guiding the development of educational programs. They have identified these as romanticism, cultural transmission, and the cognitive-development or interactional schools of philosophical thought. We have adapted these so that they may be applied to youth work and added a fourth, constructivist education, that is built upon cognitive-development philosophical thought. We have renamed cultural transmission as the classical approach and cognitive-development as the progressive approach. Thus the four philosophical approaches which can be applied to youth work are 1) the classical approach, 2) romanticism, 3) progressivism, and 4) constructivist education. The following is a brief discussion of each of these philosophical orientations.

The Classical Approach to Youth Work

The primary objective of the classical approach to youth work involves cultural transmission. It is primarily concerned with promoting common virtues and wisdom that support the existence of a common human nature. It assumes that "young people could be socialized through a firm instructional regiment consisting of explicit rules or examples for proper behavior" (Linkona, 1993, p. 38). These rules or cultural norms, customs, and values were thought to be eternal and the foundation of the established social order of the day. Such cultural traditions can be transmitted from one generation to the next and serve as a basis for defining one's role in society. The classical approach is more concerned with maintaining the established social order rather than allowing young people to challenge, add to, and/or reinvent the prevailing norms, customs, and values. Summing up this approach, Kohlberg and Mayer (1972, p. 162) have written:

> Traditional educators believe that their primary task is the transmission to the present generation of bodies of information and of rules or values collected in the past; they believe that the educator's job is the direct instruction of such information and rules. The important emphasis, however is not on the sanctity of the past, but on the view that education consists of transmitting knowledge, skills, and social and moral rules of the culture. Knowledge and rules of the culture may be rapidly changing or they may be static. In either case, however, it is assumed that education is the transmission of the culturally given.

Youth work reflecting a classical philosophical approach involves the transmission of norms, customs, and values of the prevailing societal order. Many youth work organizations are predicated upon the transmission of such values to young people. For example, the Boy Scouts of America have historically focused their efforts on the transmission of such virtues as trustworthiness, loyalty, helpfulness, friendliness, courtesy, kindness, obedience, cheerfulness, thriftiness, bravery, cleanliness, and reverence. Thus, the legacy of the classical philosophical approach is one of character forming. In this case, the youth worker interprets and teaches desired virtues that are received passively by youth and incorporated into their personality. Such values serve as external guidelines to measure one's success in life.

Romanticism and Youth Work

Romanticism rejected the classical approach to education. This concept emerged toward the end of the eighteen century as a result of the works of Jean Jacques Rousseau. Rousseau emphasized the importance of expression rather than repression to produce a well-balanced, freethinking individual. In his famous political treatise *The Social Contract* written in 1762 he developed a case for civil liberty and individual freedom as opposed to the absolutism of the times.

Romanticism represented a significant form of cultural rebellion which influenced prevailing social, cultural, political, and economic structures and emphasized individual freedoms rather than collective ends. Romanticism sought to promote the value of the subjective experience and escape classical forms of goodness and virtue. Romanticism promoted the concept of liberal individualism. It was not focused on assisting individuals acquire wisdom or virtue in the classical sense, but rather was focused on promoting individual success and achievement. Romanticism was in conflict with the character-forming legacy of the classical approach to education. Romanticism promoted and encouraged freedom, more expansive expression, and the opening of one's personality. In a sense, romanticism promoted greater self-awareness and a focus on one's internal feelings and thoughts rather than external expressions of right or wrong. As Kohlberg and Meyer have written:

> Romantics hold that what comes from within the [youth] is the most important aspect of development; therefore the pedagogical environment should be permissive enough to allow the inner "good" (abilities and social virtues) to unfold and the inner "bad" to come under control. Thus teaching the [youth] the ideas and attitudes of others through rote or drill would result in meaningless learning and the suppression of inner spontaneous tendencies of positive value. Romantics stress the biological metaphors of "health" and "growth" in equating optimal physical development with bodily health and optimal mental development with mental health. (1972, p. 161)

Youth work using romanticism as a philosophical framework involves providing a nurturing context in which the natural process of development could occur. Such a philosophy encourages an open framework for the expression of one's personality. Programs encourage individuals to be intellectually curious and to find their inner-self, in addition to promoting mental health. Youth programs encourage youth to seek satisfaction and happiness intrinsically, rather than conforming to extrinsic models of goodness or virtue. For example, youth workers operating from the romantic tradition seek to protect young people from a host of harmful experiences (e.g., drug use) that places natural developmental processes at risk.

Progressivism and Youth Work

The idea of progressivism was advanced by John Dewey in the late 1800s and early 1900s. Dewey (1938) had a deep respect for the individual and his or her ability to initiate change through the experiential learning process. However, in order for change to occur, Dewey believed that the values of democracy and freedom had to be applied to the educational experience. He believed that people are social beings who learn and grow while actively engaging in meaningful experiences with others. In order to learn, Dewey would say, one must be actively involved in the process of "doing." For Dewey, learning involved people gaining problem-solving skills that they could apply throughout their lives, rather than filling them with facts. The educated person was a reflective thinker, applying one's acquired knowledge in a thoughtful and analytical fashion to life's circumstances.

As an educational ideollogy, progressivism holds that education should nourish the child's natural interaction with a developing society or environment. Unlike the romantics, the progressives do not assume that development is the unfolding of an innate pattern of which the primary aim is to create an unconflicted environment able to foster healthy development. Instead, they define development as a progression through invariant ordered sequential states. The educational goal is the eventual attainment of a higher level or stage of development in adulthood, not merely the healthy functioning of the . . .[youth] . . . at a present level. (Kohlberg & Mayer, 1972, p. 163)

Youth work employing progressivism as a philosophical approach equips youth with problem-solving and reflective thinking skills. The progressivist youth worker engages young people in activity that is both interesting and personally meaningful to a young person, but that also challenges him to move beyond present personal understandings. Such activity also promotes youth development by having young people learn while doing, or experientially, nurturing the natural interaction between the individual and his or her environment.

Constructivist Education and Youth Work

Youth work reflecting constructivist education principles focuses on the construction of individual knowledge and meaning by providing opportunities for young people to apply their reasoning in a variety of contexts. Based on the principles of Jean Piaget (Duckworth, 1964), who advocated that interest and intellectual curiosity were linked, constructivist education has been advanced by American educators Lawrence Kohlberg and Rheta De Vries. Linked to progressivism, constructivist education encourages autonomy, natural curiosity, initiative, dialogue, cooperative learning, and reflection. Within this philosophy, the goal of learning is to construct knowledge and meaning while interacting with the environment. Its focus is on *con*struction of the individual rather than the *in*struction of the individual. Constructivist education focuses on building the individual and being attentive to his or her individual developmental needs, rather than some predetermined normative guidelines.

Constructivism is not a theory about teaching. It's a theory about knowledge and learning. Drawing on a synthesis of current work in cognitive psychology, philosophy, and anthropology, the theory defines knowledge as temporary, developmental, socially and culturally mediated, and thus, nonobjective. Learning from this perspective is understood as a self-regulated process of resolving inner cognitive conflicts that often become apparent through concrete experience, collaborative discourse, and reflection. (Brooks & Brooks, 1993, p. vii).

Youth work from a constructivist educational philosophy seeks to promote individual development by helping the individual construct meaning by providing opportunities to explore, analyze, and interact with his or her physical and social environment. Youth workers would seek to create environments that support individual curiosity, rather than seeking to control. The goal is to create, a learning environment that offers rich learning opportunities, stimulation, and meaningful interactions between youth and their peers and between youth and adults. The youth worker seeks to assist young people to construct more mature understandings by raising their awareness of the consequences of their actions.

PROMOTING DEMOCRATIC LEARNING

A worthy pursuit of youth work is that of democratic learning. Democratic learning provides a philosophical foundation upon which the work of the youth worker can be focused or directed. The goal of the youth worker is to craft informal and structured learning opportunities where youth understand, embrace, and practice democratic learning. By engaging in democratic learning youth workers "support, perpetuate, enlarge, and strengthen the democratic way of life" (Mursell, 1955).

Democracy is a way of life. It is built on the ideal that each individual should be treated with dignity and respect. Each individual in a democratic society is viewed as being equal, especially in the eyes of the law. "In a true democracy, the rights of all levels of maturity should be equally respected and protected, irrespective of sex, race, creed, or class, with no favoritism or prejudice" (Hill, 1933: p. 6). Democratic learning is essential in promoting and preserving human rights and providing equal opportunities. Further, an important goal of democratic living is to ensure that individuals are provided with opportunities to reach their maximum potential. A key element of democratic living is that of freedom and self-determination. In other words, individuals are vested with the responsibility to make decisions about their own lives, rather than others. They are free to choose, to voluntarily participate, to express themselves, and to exercise self-direction and free will in decisions which impact their lives.

For youth, democratic learning creates the opportunity for an individual to acquire and practice the skills necessary to be a responsible decision maker. Democratic environments empower and often liberate individuals to pursue those interests that contribute to their development in meaningful ways. Often youth programs promote opportunities for active involvement on the part of individuals by providing them with a strong sense of ownership in the planning, development, and implementation of programs and activities which meet their needs.

Democratic learning promotes a respect for others. As such, youth workers often assist youth in understanding strategies to make decisions, engage in reflective thinking, communicate effectively, think creatively, solve problems, resolve conflicts, and respond ethically and sensitively in such a way as to ensure that the rights of others are respected. Youth workers assist youth in learning how to collaborate, cooperate, and dialogue with others to support a democratic way of life.

Basis for Democratic Learning

The ideals of a democratic life are rooted in our cultural traditions. From a historical perspective, England's King John approved the Magna Carta in 1612 establishing laws that applied to all and led to the establishment of Parliament. In particular, the Magna Carta placed a check on the arbitrariness of the application of the law. In 1689, Parliament established the English Bill of Rights. English philosopher, John Locke (1632-1704) writing in *Two Treatise of Government* (1689) argued for the natural rights of individuals, especially for the right to life, property rights, freedom of religion, speech, and opinion. As noted, the French philosopher, Jean Jacques Rousseau (1712-1778), provided additional support to individual rights and freedom. In his famous political treatise *The Social Contract* (1762) Rousseau developed a case for civil liberty. Also, Rousseau proposed a new theory of education emphasizing the importance of expression rather than repression in the development of children. Documents such as the United States Declaration of Independence, United States Constitution, and the United Nations Declaration of Human Rights draw their inspiration from these and other documents. For example, the Declaration of Independence notes that "all men are created equal, that they are endowed by their Creator with certain unalienable Rights, that among these are Life, Liberty, and the Pursuit of Happiness." The UN Declaration of Human Rights expresses that "all human beings are born free and equal in dignity and rights" and that "everyone has to right to life, liberty, and security of persons." These documents provide a basis upon which democratic principles have been built and provide a basis for the efforts of youth work.

Educational Philosophies and Democratic Learning

We draw more contemporary notions of democratic learning from a variety of educational philosophers. Some of the more prominent individuals include Johann Heinrich Petalozzi, Fredrick Fröebel, Jean Piaget, John Dewey, Lev Vygotsky, and Rheta De Vries. For example, Fröebel, a German educator known worldwide as the inventor of kindergarten, spoke eloquently about the harmony between spontaneity and control. According to Hughes (1896, p. 125):

Fröebel's work in undertaking to systematic play and direct it so as to make it most effective as an educational force was a difficult and delicate task. He knew that spontaneity must not be sacrificed to system, as the great value of play intellectually and morally depends on the freedom of the child in expressing its own purposes and carrying out its own decisions . . . Fröebel's task was the systematizing of play under the leadership of adults, without robbing play of its freedom or the child of its perfect spontaneity and independence of action.

Fröebel emphasized the importance of individuals living their lives with self-determination and freedom in accordance with their own individuality and personalities, which provided foundational support for democratic learning principles. Table 5.2 presents information regarding some of several educational theorists and philosophers who have provided

a foundation for incorporating democratic principles into youth work. In addition, our ideals of democratic learning are drawn from a number of individuals involved in the child saving movement of the late 1800s and 1900s. The child saving movement manifested itself in many innovations, including playgrounds, settlement houses, fresh air camps, field houses, recreation centers, and youth organizations focused on moral education.

APPROACHES TO YOUTH WORK

There are a number of approaches that can be applied to the field of youth work. By approaches we refer to the means by which youth workers organize their efforts in providing programs and/or services. Generally speaking, the approaches that are used by a youth worker will reflect the mission of the organization within which they are employed. It is important to remember the context must often be seen from the work of a larger organization as well as from the individual involved in providing services. Every youth organization has a defined (or sometimes implied) vision and/or mission statement to guide the work and efforts of its employees. Such statements provide the basis upon which youth workers apply their professional value, knowledge, and skills to practice.

De Oliviera and Edginton (1999) have identified several approaches that can be employed by youth workers. They are the remedial approach, the prosocial ap-

Table 5.2
Educational Philosophers and Democratic Learning

Educational Philosophers	Background	Contribution	Ideas on Democracy	Ideas on Learning
Johann Heinrich Petalozzi (1746–1827)	Swiss educator, founder of modern pedagogy	Advocated educational opportunities for all children; education of the whole child; Laws of Human Unfolding —"hand, heart, and head" represents the body, one's moral, and one's intellect.	Promoted the democratic ideal of enabling all individuals to reach their full potential.	Discovery vs. rote learning; use of manipulatives.
Fredrick Fröbel (1782–1852)	German educator	Inventor of kindergarten.	Emphasized self-determination and freedom providing foundational support for democratic learning principles.	Promoted individualism, cooperation, nature study, objective work, manual training play, and self-directed activity; emphasized critical thinking rather than memorization.
John Dewey (1859–1952)	American philosopher and educational theorist	Promoted pragmatism, instrumentalism.	Authored *Democracy and Education*; suggested that democracy, as a form of life, was essential for human advancement.	Self-directed learning, learning tied to practical consequences.

(continued)

Table 5.2 (continued)

Educational Philosophers	Background	Contribution	Ideas on Democracy	Ideas on Learning
Jean Piaget (1896-1980)	Swiss psychologist & educator	Learning theories based on cognitive stages of development.	Self-constructed principles build ownership, self-determination, choice, freedom, and free expression.	Create men who can do new things, not simply repeat what others have done; form minds which can be critical not accept everything offered.
Lev Vygotsky (1897-1934)	Russian psychologist	Humans create material and psychological cultural tools, known as mediation.	Evolutionary progression of civilization provides a prism of new ideas and concepts.	Humans restructure themselves through the creation of cultural tools.
Rheta De Vries (1936-)	American educator	Coined the term "Constructivist Education."	Encourages autonomy, natural curiosity, initiative, dialogue, cooperative learning, and reflection.	Goal of learning is to construct knowledge and meaning in interaction with environment; focus on the construction of the individual rather than the instruction.

proach, and the integrative approach.

Remedial Approach

The application of the remedial approach to youth work basically finds youth as a problem. In other words, youth are viewed as under stress, in turmoil, and in need of the intervention of adults. At the turn of the twentieth century, this was often viewed in light of the "idleness of youth" and the perceived propensity of youth to misuse their time and energies. The thought was that if the time available to youth could be filled with meaningful activity, they would not engage in destructive behaviors. Youth programs were seen as attempts as "remediating" undesirable behaviors. Such behaviors often resulted in delinquency. Further, youth who were seen as being exposed to societal ills were often viewed as being "at risk" and, in a sense, the victims of social and/or economic turmoil.

As de Oliviera and Edginton note, "youth are to be treated, and their behavior is the focus of the treatment. The basis for intervention is the medical model, and the forms of intervening are mainly counseling, therapy, or corrections." (1999, p. 261). They further note that intervention strategies often were aimed at isolating youth from one another. The assumption in many intervention strategies was that "the bad can contaminate the good and so must be isolated and treated, not left unsupervised" (De Oliviera & Edgington, 1999, p. 261)

Another perspective on the remedial approach is the creation of environments to fill youth time with wholesome activities. The thought is that youth can not get into trouble if their time is filled with activity. Parallel to this concept is the idea of attempting to keep youth happy, perhaps even entertained, in fun play environments. This has led to what was previously mentioned as the "fun morality." In other words, if you can keep youth happy by providing fun, wholesome activities, problems will be fixed and even perhaps, youth will stay out of trouble.

Prosocial Approach

This approach to youth work starts with the assumption that youth are inherently good and the work of youth workers and youth organizations is to assist them in their further positive development. The focus of the prosocial approach is to build assets within youth that strengthen them against the ills of society. In other words, if youth today are prone to engage in premarital sex, act violently, take drugs, drink alcoholic beverages, steal, lie, cheat, or engage in other delinquent behaviors, it is the role of youth workers "to guide or even steer" youth with appropriate values so that they may make decisions that result in desirable behaviors. In this sense, youth workers were involved at the turn of the twentieth century with what was known as moral education, just as today the focus is on what is called character building.

Character-building programs are focused on providing positive alternatives for youth. The assumption is, according to de Oliviera and Edginton (1999, p. 262), that this "philosophical approach proposes youth as competent individuals who, given proper assistance, will naturally become responsible adults ready to assume their roles in a complex society." The task is in building competencies within individuals to assist them in their journey from adolescence to adulthood. In the previous chapter, youth development competencies were identified as health/fitness, personal/social, cognitive/creative, vocational, and citizenship. Work of the Search Institute in Minneapolis, Minnesota has led to the creation of a framework to identify assets/deficits of youth. The assumption is that communities can build their base of assets and diminish the deficits by building programs and services for youth that help strengthen their ability to operate successfully.

Integrative Approach

This approach to youth work is built on the assumption that youth can contribute dramatically to help frame, shape, and influence community life. In this context, youth should be viewed as a valuable asset to any community. As is the case with other community members, their opinions, interests, and values should be sought and integrated into the community as a whole. The views of youth are to be encouraged, welcomed, and valued by community members. Youth are seen as important contributors to community life, problematic, and in need of intervention and control on the part of adults. The integrative approach encourages the full participation of youth in community life.

As de Oliviera and Edginton (1999, p. 262) have stated:

> Youth are, in themselves, a transformational force in society. In the integrative paradigm, youth activities and idiosyncrasies are therefore not to be feared but mostly welcomed. Like all human beings, youth are in the process of becoming. We are all unfinished uncompleted beings in and with a likewise unfinished reality. We must be conscious of being unfinished, and aware of our incompleteness. Risk taking and other forms of youth expression must be seen as a natural part of health development and therefore not to be "treated" but discussed within a framework of collective social support.

As de Oliveira and Edginton (1999, p. 262) further note, "accepting the above principles makes the mission of youth services organizations truly transformational" and the work of youth workers "becomes one of learning about and supporting and enabling this transformational force."

ORIENTATIONS TO YOUTH WORK AND YOUTH DEVELOPMENT

De Oliveira and Edginton (1999) have provided a useful perspective to help understand the varying orientations to youth work.

They have classified different orientations that may be employed by different types of youth organizations. They have suggested that most youth organizations can be defined or referred to as using one or more of the following orientations: 1) leisure, 2) sports fitness, 3) social services, 4) character-building, 5) religious, 6) vocational/career, 7) advocacy/social policy, and 8) social pedagogy. Each of these types of orientations is predicated upon a different set of goals, assumptions, perceptions of youth, and concepts of development. In addition, the typical types of settings where programs are offered may vary according to the orientation employed and may result in differing program formats and professional roles. Table 5.3 provides an outline of the different orientations and how the characteristics vary for each of the aforementioned elements.

THEORETICAL PERSPECTIVES AND THEIR APPLICATION TO YOUTH WORK AND YOUTH DEVELOPMENT

Still another perspective for viewing youth work and youth development is to conceptualize various theoretical orientations including: 1) key understandings regarding what youth need to be successful; 2) how youth are viewed; and 3) what the dominant methods of professional practice that emerge as a result of the application of these orientations. Table 5.4 identifies five major theoretical orientations that may be applied to youth work and youth development.

Glanz, Lewis, and Piner (1997) have advanced the concept of promoting youth health from a problem behavior theoretical orientation. The problem behavior theory suggests that all behaviors, whether positive or negative, are functional and assumes that susceptibility to problem behavior results from interaction of the person and the environment. From this perspective, problem behaviors can be linked to a series of life choices that can be detrimental to youth health. From this perspective, youth workers intervene to increase youth awareness of positive health related issues and to promote healthy environments.

Another perspective is to address problem behaviors through the use of a social learning/social cognitive theoretical perspective. Here youth are thought to be affected by environmental influences, personal factors, and the attribute of negative behavior itself. In order to prevent problem behaviors from occurring, or to intervene when they have occurred, youth workers focus on increasing the self-efficacy of youth. In order to avoid the developmental difficulties that are sometimes associated with risky behaviors (i.e., drugs, alcohol, sex), intervention strategies from this perspective typically include helping young people build skills or providing training in areas that they are developmentally deficient. From this perspective, youth are viewed as lacking critical skills in order to make a successful transition into adulthood.

Table 5.3
Orientations to Youth Work and Youth Development

	Leisure Orientation	Sports/Fitness Orientation	Social Services Orientation	Character Building Orientation	Religious Orientation	Vocation/Career Orientation	Advocacy/Social Policy Orientation	Social Orientation Pedagogy Orientation
1. Goals	Constructive use of motor skill development; free time; enhancement/development of lifetime leisure skills; promotion of quality of life.	Motor skill development; competition; fair play; social interaction.	Promote youth welfare through provision of social services.	Moral/character building; positive socialization friendship development; civic education; strengthening	Spiritual fulfillment through practicing charity; moral education character building.	Career exploration work habits/attitudes; career skills; opportunities for cooperative work.	Fostering debate on youth concerns and problems; defending a youth's rights before public institutions.	Bringing youth and adults together to build stronger sense of community; providing youth services based on social pedagogy philosophies and principles,
2. Assumptions/perceptions of youth	Participants, customers.	Participants, team members.	Clients.	Participants, customers, members.	Receivers/deliverers of charity services, disciples, learners.	Clients, partners.	Constituents, clients.	Partners, learners.

(continued)

Table 5.3 (continued)

	Leisure Orientation	Sports/Fitness Orientation	Social Services Orientation	Character Building Orientation	Religious Orientation	Vocation/Career Orientation	Advocacy/Social Policy Orientation	Social Pedagogy Orientation
3. Basic values and concepts of development	Leisure as a social instrument, pursued as an end in itself; enabling/expanding the human potential.	Sports teaches competition and cooperation; skill development; promotes fun, fitness, and friend making.	Welfare as community's right; welfare as community's benefit; helping; caring.	Promotion of civic spirit; promotion of democratic values through moral education.	Search of spiritual elevation and fulfillment; helping the disadvantaged, the destitute, and the oppressed.	Fitting youth into the job market; revealing youth's personal inclinations; facilitating youth's realization as worker and/or human being.	State responsibility for protection of youth; equality; rights of citizenship.	Phenomeno-logical understand-ing of youth emphasis on impact of encounters and relationships.
4. Typical settings (examples)	Local park and recreation departments; nonprofit clubs and associations; commercial leisure organizations; schools; camps.	Local park and recreation departments; AAU; AYSO; Hershey Track & Field; Police Athletic League Pony Baseball; Pop Warner Football; YABA.	Rehabilitation center; juvenile system; government social welfare agencies; treatment centers.	Boy Scouts of America; Girl Scouts of the U.S.A.; Boys & Girls Clubs of America; Camp Fire Boys and Girls; Girls Inc; YMCA of the USA; YWCA of the USA	Young Life; Salvation Army; Athletes in Action; Youth for Christ; church youth groups.	4-H; WAVE, Inc.; Job Corps; governmental agencies.	Child Welfare League of America; National Coalition of Hispanics; Health & Human Services; National Network of Runaways and Youth Services.	Youths agencies; street corners; govern-mental agencies

(continued)

Table 5.3 (continued)

	Leisure Orientation	Sports/Fitness Orientation	Social Services Orientation	Character Building Orientation	Religious Orientation	Vocation/Career Orientation	Advocacy/Social Policy Orientation	Social Pedagogy Orientation
5. Program formats	Classes/instruction; drop-in; special events; contests; clubs; leagues.	Leagues; clinics; tournaments; clubs; special events.	Counseling; training; rehabilitation programs; mentoring.	Clubs; classes/instructional; social recreation; special events; outdoor/adventure activities.	Charity; spiritual education; social recreation; special events; service projects; encounters.	Vocational programs; job training; job seeking support; skills building.	Lobbying; community organization; public education; fostering political power structures.	Encounters; social education.
6. Professional roles	Instructor, event manager, camp counselor, program leader.	Coach, official; volunteer, manager, fund raising coordinator.	Social worker, therapist; counselor; trainer/instructor; psychologist, mentor.	Counselor, instructor, fund raiser, volunteer coordinator, program leader.	Spiritual leader, program leader.	Instructor, trainer, counselor, placement advisor, mentor.	Lobbyist, community organizer, fact finder, public relations canvasser.	Outreach worker; detached youth worker social educator.

Source: from De Oliveira, W. & Edginton, C. R. (1999). Youth and Human Services. In H. D. Harris & D. D. Maloney. (Eds.), *Human Services: Contemporary Issues and Trends.* Boston, MA: Allyn and Bacon.

Table 5.4
Selected Theoretical Perspectives and Their Application to Youth Development

	Theoretical Orientation	Key Understandings	View of Young People	Dominant Methods of Youth Work
Health Promotion Glanz, Lewis & Pimer, 1997	<u>Problem Behavior Theory</u>: All behaviors whether positive or negative are functional and assumes that susceptibility to problem behavior results from interaction of the person and the environment.	Lifestyle choices and chronic diseases are linked; lifestyle change	Youth exhibit a host of unhealthy behaviors (i.e., drug and alcohol use, unprotected sexual interactions, poor dietary habits) which impact their developmental trajectories.	<u>Intervention</u>: Aimed at increasing awareness of health related issues; promotion of healthy environments.
Problem Behavior Prevention Bandura, 1986	<u>Social Learning/Social Cognitive Theory</u>: Behavior change is believed to be affected by environmental influences, personal factors, and attributes of the behavior itself.	Self-efficacy is critically important to behavior change; a youth must believe in his or her capability to perform certain behaviors and must perceive an incentive to do so.	Youth who experience developmental difficulties do so because they lack the abilities needed to overcome the environmental, personal, and/or motivational factors nurturing those factors.	<u>Intervention</u>: Focused on increasing the self-efficacy of youth; seeks to help young people build skills or training in needed areas, as well as providing youth with opportunities to witness modeled positive behaviors.
Ecological Model of Youth Development Bronfenbrenner, 1979; 1986	<u>Ecological/Contextual Developmental Theory</u>: Emphasizes the importance of the social context in which the individual's life trajectory unfolds; as well as the complex system of interlaced and interdependent relationships that exist between the individual and the social/physical setting which shapes the individual.	The individual is embedded within multiple contexts. Thus their development occurs within a complex system of relationships that are affected by multiple surrounding environments.	Youth are members a variety of social contexts and cultures (e.g., they are members of families, ethnic groups, religious groups, classrooms, youth organizations, peer groups, intimate relationships, as well as places of employment); young people are developmentally impacted by each of these social contexts.	<u>Intervention</u>: Need to occur on multiple levels (i.e., individual, communal, organizational); interventions that simultaneously influence these multiple levels and multiple settings may be expected to lead to greater and longer-lasting changes and maintenance of existing health-promoting habits.

(continued)

Table 5.4 (continued)

Theoretical Orientation	Key Understandings	View of Young People	Dominant Methods of Youth Work
Positive Youth Development Benson, 1997; Benson, Leffert, Scales & Blyth, 1998	Developmental Assets: This framework consists of two groups of 20 assets. First, external assets are defined as the positive experiences young people encounter in the community, culture, and society around them; and recognize the crucial roles that families, schools, congregations, neighborhoods, and youth organizations can play in promoting healthy adolescent development. Internal assets include those characteristics and behaviors that reflect healthy growth and development within young people. These assets are about positive values and identities, social competencies, and commitment to learning that promote inner strength and confidence (Benson, 1997; Benson et al., 1998)...	All youth need access to positive developmental opportunities; focused on the positive, rather than youth problems; requires a community-wide effort.	Youth are resources to be developed rather than problems to be managed; the majority of young people are lacking in sufficient developmental assets needed for healthy development.	Intervention: Conducted through providing social support for youth to bring about developmental change; social support may be instrumental (i.e., providing safe places for youth to gather), informational (i.e., explaining the negative consequences of drug use); or emotional (i.e., providing care for neglected youth).
Informal Education as Youth Work Smith, 1988	Informal Education: Learning which takes place in the context of doing (i.e., inventing, producing, researching), and which is not formally structured into a program or curriculum (Jeffs and Smith, 1990).	Voluntary participation, relationships, association, and informal educational practices are key for effective youth work.	Youth are individuals in need of opportunities to participate in activity that is meaningful, socially valuable, and interesting; such opportunities promote development through encouraging self-initiated continued learning, individual self-efficacy, as well as a positive social conception of the value of youth.	Education: Educational and relational experiences for youth in a variety of settings (i.e., street corners, skateboard parks, libraries).

A third perspective employs the ecological theory of development, emphasizing the importance of the social context in which an individual's life trajectory unfolds. From this perspective, it is believed that a young person is embedded within multiple contexts, and that their development occurs within a complex system of relationships that are affected by multiple surrounding environments. In other words, youth are members of a variety of social settings and cultures—families, ethnic groups, religious groups, classrooms, youth organizations, peer groups, intimate relationships, and places of employment—and are developmentally impacted by each of these contexts. In order to promote healthy development, youth workers strive, from the ecological perspective, to influence the lives of youth at multiple levels and in multiple settings. Doing so allows youth workers to have more success in creating longer lasting changes in the developmental life of young people.

A fourth perspective includes the positive youth development model of youth work based on the theory of developmental assets. This framework consists of two groups of 20 assets. First, external assets are defined as the positive experiences young people encounter in the community, culture, and society around them; thus recognition is given to the crucial roles that families, schools, congregations, neighborhoods, and youth organizations can play in promoting healthy adolescent development. Internal assets include those characteristics and behaviors that reflect healthy growth and de-

velopment within young people. These assets are about positive values and identities, social competencies, and commitment to learning that promote inner strength and confidence (Benson, et al., 1998; Benson, 1997).

From this perspective all youth need access to positive developmental opportunities—assets—in order to achieve healthy development. Young people are viewed as resources to be developed rather than problems to be managed. Intervention strategies seek to provide social supports, both external and internal, for youth to bring about developmental change.

A final perspective includes conducting youth work from an informal educational standpoint. This perspective is described in detail below.

INFORMAL EDUCATION

Learning takes place in many locations—such as school, home, and in the community. We often think of environments such as schools as being the major focal point for what might be termed "formal education." In other words, formal education is that which takes place in the schools and is planned by subject with a syllabus and lesson plans, and is usually organized in a comprehensive fashion into a curriculum promoting the acquisition of basic skills. We also know that learning occurs outside of the school and that is the focus of the efforts of youth workers. It might be suggested that youth workers are involved in what could be defined as "informal education."

The term informal education follows a tradition of efforts aimed at providing learning opportunities beyond the school environment. Smith (1994, p. 2) has noted that there are efforts world wide aimed at extending education into unconventional settings. In the United Kingdom, Smith (1994, p. 2) suggests that informal education is similar to what is referred to as local education and that educators seek to "meet people where they are." Freire (1968), writing in the *Pedagogy of the Oppressed*, suggests that learning is most powerful when it begins within the context of the individual. In Latin American countries, liberation theology encourages popular education and seeks meaning from the lessons that come from living and reflecting on one's life events, experiences, or circumstances (phenomenological pedagogy). In the United States, informal education follows traditions established in social work, community organization, and community education. It also is embedded in the work of early play leaders advocating learning from involvement in spontaneous play environments. In Germany, the term *sozialpädagogik,*—or social pedagogy, captures the essence of this type of effort. The terms animation and social cultural work in Belgium also reflect this notion of informal education.

Informal and Formal Education: Areas of Differentiation

What is informal education? Can it be differentiated from formal education? Perhaps the best way to start this discussion is to provide a definition of informal education. Education is about learning and learning is about changing one's behavior. Educators are involved in the process of assisting individuals to develop their cognitive, social, physical, and spiritual knowledge, skills, abilities, attitudes, and character. What is most relevant in understanding informal education is the setting and the process in which it occurs. The setting and interaction between youth and youth workers is not fixed or controlled, but rather consists of spontaneous interaction/conversation in which the potential for learning occurs. As Jeffs and Smith (1999, p. 16) have written, ". . . informal educators supposedly offer choice not compulsion; freedom not order; empowerment not indoctrination." Therefore, we can think of informal education as a process which encourages learning in hospitable environments where youth gather.

Jeffs and Smith (1999, p. 15) suggests that it is important to differentiate between education and indoctrination. In fact, education is values-driven in that it is established around several key values. Informal educators should, according to these authors and others, build their efforts around the following values:

- Respect for process.
- The promotion of well-being.
- Truth.
- Democracy.
- Fairness and equality.

These values guide the work of youth workers as informal educators. They serve as a framework for dialogue and social encounters. Youth workers, without a grounding moral framework, are rudderless. Their actions and behavior often are driven by situational imperatives rather than a firm understanding of the moral precepts upon which the practice of one's profession occurs.

Table 5.5 presents a way of comparing and contrasting informal and formal education according to goals, settings, curricular organization, pedagogy, subject matter, roles, focus of youth workers/teachers, conceptions of youth, reasons for participation, and learning environments. In reviewing this table, what may be more striking than the differences are the similarities between formal and informal education. When viewing the goals of either of these two concepts, one can see that both are focused on democratic learning. Formal educators are concerned with assisting youth in acquiring knowledge, skills, and attitudes for effective living in a democratic society, and informal educators are involved in promoting life skills that encourage an awareness of self and an understanding of community life, as well as promoting democratic learning. The settings in which each of these is practiced is different. Formal educators mainly practice in the schools, whereas informal educators work with youth where they find them. The focus of informal education is to create meaningful conversation, social discourse, or encounters to facilitate education. On the other hand, teachers organize their work by subject, syllabus, or lesson plan. They are involved in

the crafting of controlled exchanges ranging from direct instruction to free inquiry. Informal educators seek conversation and in doing so encourage youth to reflect on their actions as a way of learning (praxis).

The subject matter employed in formal educational environments usually focuses on basic skills seen as being necessary for living. Reading, writing, speaking, and acquiring other knowledge in subject matter such as mathematics, science, the arts, and social studies are often emphasized. Informal educators work to promote life skills and awareness of self. They are interested in helping youth in their search for meaning in life and the process of becoming who they will be as they enter adulthood. Teachers often are viewed as "the" primary source of knowledge and information. Youth workers engage in a process of facilitation, encouraging introspection and reflection as well as mastery of selected knowledge, skills, and competencies. Youth workers are concerned with the formation of a youth's character and as such, often model positive behaviors. Both teachers and youth workers often view youth as valuable community assets and work to assist them in their life's journey. The nature of formal education is such that law mandates it, and as a result, participation is obligatory, involuntary and compelled. Learning environments are prescribed, driven by standards, and closely controlled and monitored. On the other hand, participation in informal learning environments is voluntary, spontaneous, and freely chosen. Such

Table 5.5
Formal and Informal Education

	Formal Education	Informal Education
Goals	Acquiring knowledge, skills, and attitudes for effective living in a democratic society.	Focused on promoting life skills that encourage an awareness of self, community life; promotion of democratic learning.
Typical Settings	Public schools, parochial schools, private academics, profit and nonprofit learning centers.	Parks, youth centers, street corners, camps, homes, public meeting areas (e.g., shopping malls).
Curricular organization	Organized by subject, syllabus, or lesson; crafting of social and physical environments with focus on content.	Focus on social discourse, encounters, promotion of hospitable settings for learning.
Pedagological strategies	Crafting of controlled exchanges ranging from direct instruction to free inquiry; generally guided by inquiry with some identified knowledge base.	Conversation, reflection, use of praxis, collaboration, and participation in activities that are self-directed, enjoyable, and meaningful to the individual.
Typical subject matter content	Basic skills necessary for effective living (reading, writing, speaking) and knowledge deemed important from subject matter areas (math, science, social studies, etc.).	Life skills, health, behaviors, leadership development, career/vocational, spirituality, sports fitness and recreation, academic enrichment, service learning.
Roles of youth workers/ teachers	Teachers supported by aids/ assistants, coaches, guidance counselors, curriculum specialists, technology consultants.	Youth workers serve as activity leaders, advisors, center directors, community organizers, coaches, counselors, group workers, mentors, outreach workers, program supervisors, social workers, therapists.

(continued)

Table 5.5 (continued)

	Formal Education	Informal Education
Focus of youth workers/ teachers	Teacher serves as a knowledgeable source of information on skill development/ information and guide how best to acquire that skill/ knowledge.	Leaders serve as guides, confidants, and counselors, facilitating the development of youth as well as modeling positive behaviors
Conception of youth	Valuable assets to society if properly educated and socialized into a democratic society.	Viewed as community resources/assets; at times viewed as under siege and at risk.
Reasons for participation	Mandated by law, involuntary/compelled participation.	Voluntary, freely chosen, done of one's own free will, spontaneous participation.
Learning environments	Controlled, monitored, prescribed, criterion referenced, driven by standards.	Open, eclectic, organic, interfaced with community life.

Jeffs, T. & Smith, M. K. (1999). *Informal Education*. Ticknall, Derbyshire: Education Now Publishing

environments tend to be more open, eclectic, and infused into community life.

Formal and informal learning environments are complementary to one another. Teachers and youth workers should work hand in hand to facilitate the development of youth. Figure 5.1 presents the informal/formal education continuum. As one can see from viewing this figure, youth workers and teachers are involved in a mix of informal and formal education. Youth workers may work to promote learning in settings through more spontaneous interactions where the exchanges are not prescribed, controlled, or even predictable. The outcomes of such exchanges may vary depending on the youth's interpretation of his or her interactions with youth workers. On the other hand, teachers often are involved in controlled exchanges with desirable outcomes as a basis for their interaction with youth.

It is important to note that in the settings that either youth workers or teachers engage youth, there are opportunities for both formal and informal exchanges. The degree to which formal or informal strategies are employed will depend on the goals of the program as well the needs of individual youth. Youth workers mainly work in venues where informal education is the major strategy employed. However, youth leaders are involved in the creation of structured, formal learning environments where skills, knowledge, and competencies are sought and outcomes prescribed. For example, a youth leader may establish a class focusing on an area of health promotion such as understanding one's sexuality. There may be a time, a place and a very specific curriculum that guides information disseminated in this format. From the standpoint of the work of a teacher in the classroom, often opportunities are provided for free inquiry where the student is able to pursue those learning elements of particular interest to him, thereby promoting greater intellectual curiosity.

The point of the above is that the work of youth workers and teachers will vary and the mixture of informal and formal learning will vary according to the needs of the situation. As the continuum in Figure 5.1 suggests, youth workers have a greater focus on informal education versus formal education. The reverse is the case for teachers. One is not more important than the other; what is important is to recognize that these two components of education may exist side-by-side in support of the development of youth. Both youth workers and teachers must be capable of moving back and forth on this continuum modifying their strategies in meeting the needs of youth.

Bruner's Models of the Mind and Models of Pedagogy

In order to identify effective pedagogies for youth work, it is important to have some notion of the way in which youth may learn. Bruner (1996, pp. 53-63) suggests that there are several models that

Figure 5.1
A Continuum of Formal and Informal Education

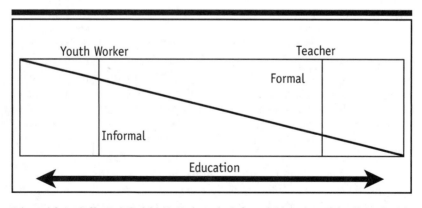

Adapted from Jeffs, T. & Smith, M. K. (1999). *Informal Education*. Ticknall, Derbyshire: Education Now Publishing. p. 18.

help us understand how youth may learn. As one reviews each of these models, it is important to note that an effective set of learning strategies may involve all of these concepts. As youth workers build a strategy to work with youth, several of these models of the mind and of pedagogy may be brought into play. It is not a question of one or the other, but rather the fact that all may be appropriate strategies, depending upon the predisposition of youth for learning and their development.

Of great importance in using Bruner's models of the mind and models of pedagogy is to understand that leading (teaching, in some cases) and learning are linked. How we conceive of each youth and how they learn will influence our choice of pedagogies employed. As Bruner has written ". . . a choice of pedagogy inevitably communicates a perception of the learning process and the learner." As Bruner notes, and we paraphrase, explaining what youth do is not enough; today's task is one of determining what youth think they are doing and what their reasons are for doing it (1996, p. 49). Bruner defines this as a cultural approach, which emphasizes that youth only gradually come to appreciate that they are acting not directly on "the world" but on beliefs they hold about the world. In this approach, youth have more of the responsibility and ownership for their own learning and thinking (Bruner, 1996, p. 49). "They can begin to think about their thinking, as well as about the world." To understand how youth learn, we must

attempt to understand how they think and provide them with the tools they need in constructing or reconstructing or even inventing new meanings in a changing world.

Further, Bruner notes that different models emphasize different goals. And, the goals of various youth programs often reflect the culture of a society and its priorities and concerns at any given time. For example, discussing the function of education, Bruner (1996, pp. 67-68) reminds us that there are at least three chief approaches that may be considered. First, he notes ". . . it is unquestionably the function of education to enable people, individual human beings, to operate at their fullest potential, to equip them with the tools and the sense of opportunity to use their wits, skills, and passions to the fullest" (1996, p. 67). Second, ". . . the function of education is to reproduce the culture that supports it—not only reproduce it, but further its economic, political and cultural ends" (1996, p. 68). And the third function of education ". . .is about ways of thinking, ways of constructing meaning, and ways of experiencing the world are to be judged, by what standards and by whom?" Each of these reasonable approaches to the function of education provides a different set of philosophical underpinnings to guide the efforts of youth workers.

Table 5.6 applies Bruner's conception of human development and learning to youth work. In his model, there are four propositions for understanding how youth learn. The first of these is imitation. In this construct, youth learn by imitating

Table 5.6
Conceptions of Youth Development and Learning

| | | Models of Learning | | |
	Imitation	Instruction	Collaborative Learning	Reconstructional Discovery
Goals	To teach youth how to do something skillfully.	To help youth acquire knowledge and skills.	To aid youth constructing their own experience.	To assist youth in grasping the distinction between personal knowledge and cultural knowledge.
Methods of Pedagogy	Demonstrations, modeling, role playing, apprenticeship.	Didactic exposure; presentation of facts, principles, and rules of action.	Praxis, reflection, mutual dialogue, discussion, problem solving, collaboration, and negotiation.	Linking the discourse and ideas of the past with those currently held through discourse and interpretation. *(going meta)*
Outcomes	Demonstrative actions transformed into performances.	Ability to learn, remember, and apply facts, principles, and rules of action.	The ability to visualize oneself as well as recognize different views.	The ability to reach beyond one's own impressions to join a past world of ideas.
Assumptions of Youth	Consists of talent, skills, abilities, and the capacity to imitate the youth worker's action.	Focused on knowledge and understanding; the mind is a *tabula rasa*, a clean slate; presumes that youth are interested in the subject matter.	Youth have the ability to reason, to make sense of their own ideas and those of others through discourse.	Youth have the ability to link with the past through reflection, reason, and mutual dialogue with others and reconcile these with current thinking.

(continued)

Table 5.6 (continued)

	Imitation	Instruction	Models of Learning Collaborative Learning	Reconstructional Discovery
Ways of Knowing	Knowing "how to" to do something.	Knowing "that" and how to apply.	Knowledge is what is shared within discourse.	Knowledge is that which is linked between the past and the present and what may be constructed in the future.
How Youth Demonstrate	Performance comes through repeated practice.	The ability to acquire new knowledge via the aid of facts, principles and rules of action.	The ability to grasp another's beliefs, promises, intentions or desires; to know what others are thinking or feeling (*innersubjectivity*); to think about one's own cognitive operations (*metacognition*).	Linking what is known of the past, with what is currently known, and what may be constructed in the future.
Roles of Youth Workers	Provider of skilled performance.	Repository and dispenser of facts, principles, and rules of action.	Builder of exchanges focused on interpretation and understanding	Promoter of discourse and interpretation, linking the past with the present and the future.

Source: Adapted from Bruner, J. (1996). *The culture of education.* Cambridge, MA: Harvard University Press. pp. 53-65.

the skillful displays, demonstrations, or performances of youth workers. The focus is on knowing how to perform in a skillful way. The second of these is what we have referred to as instruction. In this model of learning, the focus is on the ability of youth to grasp facts, principles, and rules of action. The role of the youth worker is to present through didactic instruction the knowledge that one is to acquire. In this case, the interaction is one way and does not necessarily involve the creation of dialogue between the youth worker and those instructed. The next model is what we have defined as collaborative learning. The aim of this approach is to assist youth in constructing their own experience through reflection, mutual dialogue, discussion, problem solving, and negotiation. It involves shared discourse. At the heart of the work of a youth worker is the ability to craft meaningful conversation with youth. The fourth model of learning is what we have viewed as reconstructional discovery. In this model, the youth worker assists youth in linking ideas of the past with those of the present through reflection and mutual dialogue. Further, youth are assisted in reconciling ideas of the past with the present and even perhaps constructing new scenarios of what may occur in the future.

The Intime Learning Model Applied to Informal Education

A useful model that has been adapted to informal education is known as the Intime Learning Model (see Figure 5.2). Placing youth at the center of their development, this model proposes that youth are active participants as opposed to passive recipients in the learning process (Callahan & Switzer, 2001). The model includes different principles of learning, information processing, youth program areas, and the various tenants of democratic learning sought by youth service organizations. These principles provide a way for youth workers to integrate various elements of learning, program development, and the democratic values sought within youth development programs.

The model proposes that to enhance learning a variety of strategies have been identified from contemporary, cognitive research. These have been proposed by Peter Euwell (1997) and adapted for use in the Intime Learning Model. These elements include active involvement, patterns and connections, incidental learning, direct experience, reflection, compelling situation, frequent feedback, and hospitable setting. These are the elements that we know that enhance opportunities for youth to learn. By assuring as many of these elements are present in the environment, you increase the probability of learning.

The next circle contains the elements of information processing that are typically used in library and media studies, but can also be applied to other learning situations. These elements help youth organize and process information from their environment. The elements of this model were originally identified by Marjorie Pappas and Ann Tepe (1997). The elements included are appreciation (understanding the per-

Figure 5.2
A Model for Youth Development as Informal Education

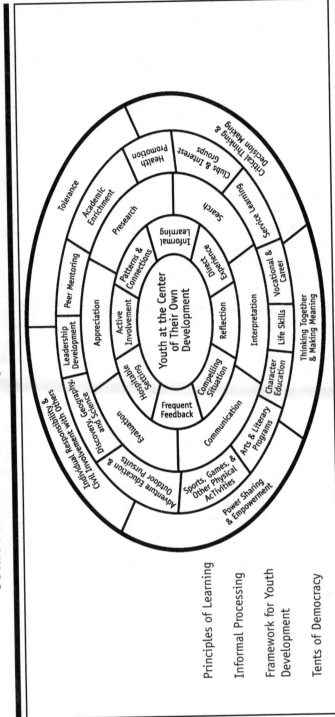

Principles of Learning

Informal Processing

Framework for Youth
Development

Tents of Democracy

Source: Adapted from Switzer, T. J., Callahan, W. P. & Quinn, L. (1999, March) *Technology as facilitator of quality education. An unfinished model.*
Paper presented at Society of Information Techology and Teacher Education, San Antonio, TX.

sonal value of the information), presearch (discovering what resources are available to learn more about a particular subject), search (using the "best" of the resources to do in-depth study of a particular topic), interpretation (internalizing and synthesizing the information so that youth fully understand), communication (sharing information with others), and evaluation (assuring yourself that you have adequately communicated the information).

The next circle in the Intime Learning Model identifies different program areas that can be employed in youth development programs. A program area can be thought of as the content of the activity, and the formal education refers to content standards. The program areas included in this model as related to youth are: peer mentoring; academic enrichment; leadership development; health promotion; clubs and interest groups; service learning; vocational and career; life skills; character education; the arts, crafts, and literary; sports, games, and other physical activity; adventure education and outdoor pursuits; as well as discovery, geography, and science. These are discussed in greater depth in Chapter 6. In the future, it will be advantageous for youth workers to develop observable behaviors tied to each of these program areas. This will provide a basis for assuring that there are consistencies when interpreting these program areas.

The outer circle of the model identifies the elements of democratic learning. These include tolerance, critical thinking and decision mak-

ing, thinking together and making meaning, power sharing and empowerment, and individual responsibility and civil involvement with others. These tenants are consistently associated with democratic principles and contributing to a democratic society. As one can see, this model has great potential for organizing a construct for viewing the complex, challenging, and demanding process of youth development. The Intime Learning Model can be accessed at www.intime.uni.edu.

CHARACTER EDUCATION

We can think of one's character as the distinctive traits, qualities, and attributes of a person. In other words, they are the individual's distinguishing characteristics. When we think about a person's character, we think about his or her patterns of behavior, reputation, and those qualities that best define him or her as an individual. Youth workers often work to help youth identify and strengthen those characteristics that form the foundation for positive adult behaviors in a democratic society. For the individual youth, the formulation of one's character is central to the process of one's passage through adolescence.

Character education is not a new concept. As Ranum, Baumgartner, and Grover (1998) have written, character education ". . .is not a new idea." In fact, Jane Addams wrote in the early 1900s that ". . .all education should be geared toward the building of character, toward what is called in *German bildung,* the shaping and forming of self over time" (Elshtain, 2002, p. 376). Not only has character education been a fundamental part of our formal educational system, it has also been a major focus for youth organizations involved in informal education. From a historical perspective, youth service organizations have engaged in a variety of strategies aimed at building of youth. In years past, these strategies were known as moral education, character building, values clarification, and values development. Today it is called character education.

Character education can be viewed from many different perspectives. Linkona (1993) has identified two historical goals of education. The first is to help youth to gain knowledge, and the second is to help them develop their character in a positive fashion. He suggests that character has three components: moral knowledge, moral feeling, and moral action. Moral knowledge refers to the ability of an individual to develop an awareness of various moral dimensions in life situations, to understand moral values, to have perspective, to engage in moral reasoning, to be able to make wise decisions, and to have knowledge of oneself including the ability for self-criticism. Moral feeling refers to a person's conscience, self-esteem, empathy, self-control, humility, and the desire to pursue what is good. Moral action refers to an individual's confidence, will, and habits in making moral decisions. As Linkona (1993) notes, good character consists of "knowing the good, desiring the good, and doing the good—habits of the mind, habits of the heart, and habits of action."

In 1992, at what is known as the Aspen Conference, a group of twenty-nine youth leaders and educators purposed a list of moral values that our society should seek as a whole. These values can serve as "a common denominator" for not only individuals, but also for youth organizations and youth workers seeking to promote character education. The core moral values are as follows:

- Trustworthiness.
- Respect.
- Responsibility.
- Justice and fairness.
- Caring.
- Civic virtue and citizenship.

(Josephson Institute, 1992, p. 80)

Youth workers and youth organizations can build character education programs around these values. First, youth workers can model these moral values by establishing trust with the youth with which they work; showing respect, caring, and operating in a fair manner. They can help youth understand how these moral values are important in their lives through community oriented service learning programs, engaging in conversation and praxis, promoting cooperative learning opportunities, and providing instruction.

The 4-H has created a character education program known as *BOOMERANG!* This program focuses on the moral values of belonging, mastery, independence, and generosity. More specifically, the curriculum is targeted on helping youth to focus on concern for others, communication, problem solving, sportsmanship, self-responsibility, community service/volunteering, character, accepting differences, cooperation, decision making, and self-discipline. The learning model involves having participants experience activities, share their experience with others, process the experience, generalize the experience to form principles, and finally to apply what they have learned to another situation.

YOUTH WORK AS A SOCIAL INSTRUMENT

Youth are in a constant state of becoming. They are constantly evolving and serve as a source of new ideas, concepts, and perspectives. Youth cultures represent a force for change and are influenced by and as have a significant impact on modern society (Braungart & Braungart, 1994). Not all youth movements are perceived in a positive way. In fact, from an historical perspective, there have been periods of time when great social upheaval and unrest have occurred with youth directly confronting existing institutions, values, customs, and norms. Since the early nineteenth century, there have been several periods of great unrest. For example, the 1960s generation reflected a global youth movement wherein youth acted out in a rebellious fashion against adult society.

During the periods of time when youth challenged the existing status quo, adult populations often looked to youth workers and youth programs as a process for curbing and controlling this unrest, as well as for maintaining traditional values. For example, when the character and nature of work changed, as well as the conditions within which youth were employed, youth programs were established to fill their "idle hours" with positive leisure activities that were wholesome in nature. In more recent times, it was thought that if youth were only happy, they would be less disruptive. Youth workers were employed to create what was discussed earlier as the "fun morality." These were experiences for youth that attempted to make them happy with little thought to the developmental possibilities of such activities.

As one can see, not all youth development programs have at their core, integrating or empowering youth. There is a fundamental, philosophical difference between viewing youth as an asset to society and viewing youth as out-of control, disruptive to society, and therefore in need of being controlled. Youth are often disenfranchised, alienated, isolated, lonely, viewed negatively, have limited mobility, and are held at bay from participating fully within society. The efforts of many community leaders to develop programs and services for youth are well intended, but are often done to help diminish delinquent behaviors, fill time, or even placate youth. Thus youth programs become an instrument of social control; often the attempt of adult society to regulate, order, or promote conformity to an existing value structure. All youth workers and youth organizations impart values to youth. Some organizations work to incorporate youth as valued members of society. Others work to control youth, to encourage conformity to existing standards. Youth can and do discriminate; they are able to distinguish the philosophical patterns that give rise to an organization's *raison détre*, learning strategies, and programs and services.

SUMMARY

The exploration of ideas, concepts, and approaches to youth work can be helpful in developing a philosophy to guide one's professional actions. In this chapter, we have presented and discussed a number of models, concepts, and approaches to youth work that we believe must be considered in crafting a foundation for practicing youth work. There are a number of approaches that can be employed by youth workers. We have identified three basic strategies: the remedial approach, the prosocial approach, and the integrative approach. Further, we have provided information regarding the goals, strategies, and purposes of a variety of youth work orientations.

At the center of the work of youth workers is democratic learning. Democratic learning provides a philosophical foundation upon which youth workers can structure experiences and learning environments for youth. It is predicated on the assumption that all individuals should be treated with dignity and respect. Youth workers should assist youth in developing the skills necessary to function effectively in a democratic society. These skills often include reflective thinking,

communication, creativity, problem solving, conflict resolution, and tolerance.

It is our belief that youth work is a form of education and learning, and the type of learning that takes place in the settings where youth workers practice can be thought of as informal learning. It is not mandated nor is it organized solely by a syllabus, lesson plan, or curriculum. Youth workers often are at their best when engaging youth in conversation, helping them to gain a perspective on the challenges of adolescence. They often employ a praxis to assist them in helping youth learn from reflecting on their actions. We have also pointed out that youth learn in different ways, and youth workers should work to accommodate the varying types of learning strategies that can be employed in any given youth program or service.

REFERENCES

Addams, J. (1909). *The Spirit of Youth and the City Streets*. New York, NY: Macmillan.

Bandura A., (1996). *Social foundations of thought and action: A social cognitive theory*. Englewood Cliffs, NJ: Prentice Hall Inc.

Benson, P. (1997). *All kids are our kids: What communities must do to raise caring and responsible children and adolescents*. San Francisco, CA: Jossey-Bass.

Benson, P., Leffert, N., Scales, P. C., & Blyth, D. A. (1998). Beyond the "village" rhetoric: Creating healthy communities for children and adolescents, *Applied Developmental Science, 2*,(3), 138-159.

Braungart, R. G., & Braungart, M. M. (Eds.). Youth Culture (1994). In Outhwaite, W. & Bottomore, T. (Eds.). *The Blackwell Dictionary of Twentieth-Century Thought.* Oxford: Blackwell Publishers.

Brightbill, C. K. (1960). *The challenge of leisure.* Englewood Cliffs, NJ: Prentice-Hall, Inc.

Brightbill, C. K. (1961). *Man and leisure: A philosophy of recreation.* Englewood Cliffs, NJ: Prentice-Hall, Inc.

Bronfenbrenner, U. (1979). *The ecology of human development: Experiments by nature and design.* Cambridge, MA: Harvard University Press.

Brooks, J. G., & Brooks, M. G. (1993). *In search of understanding: The case for constructivist classrooms.* Alexandria, VA: Association for Supervision and Curriculum Development.

Bruner, J. (1996). *The culture of education.* Cambridge, MA: Harvard University Press.

Callahan, W. P., & Switzer, T. J. (2001). Technology as facilitator of quality education: A model [On-line]. Available: http://www.intime.uni.edu/model/modelarticle.html

Curtis, H. S. (1914). *Play and recreation in the open country.* Boston, MA: Ginn and Company.

Curtis, H. S. (1915). *The Practical Conduct of Play.* New York, NY: Macmillan.

Curtis, H. S. (1917). *The Play Movement and its Significance.* New York, NY: Macmillan.

de Oliveira, W., & Edginton, C. R. (1999). Youth and human services. In H. D. Harris & D. D. Maloney, (Eds.), *Human Services: Contemporary issues and trends.* (pp 255-268). Boston, MA: Allyn and Bacon.

Dewey, J. (1938). *Democracy in education.* New York, NY: Macmillan.

Duckworth, E. (1964). "Piaget Rediscovered." In *Piaget Rediscovered* edited by R. E. Ripple and V. N. Rockeastle, pp. 1-5. A report of the Jean Piaget conference at Cornell University

Elshtain, J. B. (2002). *The Jane Addams reader.* New York, NY: Basic Books.

Euwell, P. T. (1997). Organizing earning: A point of entry [On-line]. httpwww.intime.uni.edu/model/learning/learn_summary.html

Freire P., (1968). *Pedagogy of the oppressed.* New York, NY: Continuum.

Glanz F. M., Lewis F. M., & Pimer, B. K. (1997). *Health behavior and health education.* San Francisco, CA: Jossey-Bass Publishers.

Goodman, N. (1978). *Ways of worldmaking.* Indianapolis, IN: Hackett.

Hill, P. (1933). *The kindergarten child in the New Deal.* American Childhood, *19,* 5-6.

Hughes, J. L. (1896). *Fröebels educational laws for all leaders.* New York, NY: D. Appleton & Co.

Jeffs, T., & Smith, M. K. (1999). *Informal education.* Ticknall, Derbyshire: Education Now Publishing.

The Josephson Institute of Ethics. (1992). *Ethics: Easier said than done.*

Kohlberg, L., & Meyer, R. (1972, November). Development as the aim of education. *Harvard Educational Review, 42*(4), 449-496.

Lee, J. (1917). *Play and education.* New York, NY: Macmillan.

Lee, J. (1925). *The normal course in play.* New York, NY: A. S. Barnes & Company.

Linkona, T. (1993). *Educating for character.* Des Plaines, IL: Bantam.

Locke, J. (1689). Two treatises of government. In P. Laslett (Ed.), *Two treatises of government.* Cambridge, England: Cambridge University Press.

Mursell, J. (1955). *Principles of democratic education.* New York, NY: Norton.

Nash, J. B. (1938). *The organization and administration of playgrounds and recreation.* New York, NY: A. S. Barnes & Company.

Nash, J. B. (1953). *Philosophy of recreation and leisure.* St. Louis, MO: The C. V. Mosby Company.

Pappas, M. L., & Tepe, A. E. (1997). *Pathways to knowledge: Follett's information skills model* (3rd ed.). McHenry, IL: Follett Software.

Ranum, B., Baumgartner, C., & Grover, V. (1998). *Boomerang! Character education program.* Ames, IA: Iowa State University.

Rothblatt, S. (1993) The limbs of osiris: Liberal education in the English-speaking world. In S. Rothblatt & B. Wittrock, (Eds.), *The European and American university since 1800: Historical and sociological essays.* Cambridge, MA: University of Cambridge Press.

Rousseau, J. C. (1762, 1960). Social contract. In Sir Ernest Barker (Ed.), *Social contract: Essays by Locke, Hume, and Rousseau.* London, England: Oxford University Press.

Smith, M. K. (1988). *Developing youth work: Informal education mutual aid and popular practice.* Milton Keynes: Open University Press.

Wiles, J., & Bondi, J. (1979). *Curriculum development: A guide to practice.* Columbus, OH: Charles E. Merrill Publishing.

CHAPTER SIX

Programming with Youth

INTRODUCTION

The planning of programs for youth is a challenging yet rewarding endeavor for youth workers (Edginton & Edginton, 1994, p.111). Crafting youth programs involves the creation of opportunities for youth to enhance their cognitive, social, physical, emotional, and moral development. Youth programs enable youth workers to effectively reach youth. Programs enable youth workers to engage youth in meaningful, relevant ways that contribute to their development. Therefore in this context, programming is the central task of youth work. Youth workers, in collaboration with youth, seek to establish opportunities which support the development of youth.

Youth programming does not have a beginning or ending. It is like the flow of a river, a continuous process of engagement with one experience leading to another. One engagement with a youth provides a foundation for additional encounters. One program builds on another, providing support to the overall strategy of youth development that helps prepare youth in their journey through adolescence to adulthood. In this chapter, we will discuss the nature of youth programming, present guidelines and a model for youth-centered program planning. In addition, we will include a short discussion of the process of building ownership. Last, various program areas and formats that can be incorporated into the work of a youth service organization will be presented.

WHAT IS YOUTH PROGRAMMING?

Programs serve as vehicles that enable youth to experience desired ends or benefits. Any given program exists on a continuum from what is highly structured to those with little or no structure. Any activity along this continuum is considered a youth program. For example, instructional classes with highly identifiable learning goals are examples of structured programs. They may have a syllabus with identified learning objectives, specified course content, and very precise evaluation criteria. On the other hand, a conversation in a hospitable environment where youth congregate with a youth worker is less structured. These kinds of conversations may even occur randomly without a great deal of preplanning other than the fact of being at a given location at a particular time. Both are youth programs.

There is a great deal of support for the establishment of such programs. The Carnegie Corporation of New York's landmark report *A Matter of Time: Risk and Opportunity in the Nonschool Hours* (1992, p.38) suggests that many studies and program evaluations have indicate that youth programs have a great deal of impact on healthy youth development. In synthesizing the research literature, they report the following:

- Young people, their parents, and other adults want such programs.
- Young people value and want more opportunities to help them build personal and social skills.
- Young people and adult alumni value their own participation in nonschool youth programs.
- Participation in community-based youth development programs is especially appreciated by minority youth and young people growing up in single-parent families.
- Participation in community-based youth development programs can promote positive behavior and reduce high-risk behavior. (Carnegie Corporation of New York, 1992, p.38)

As one can see from viewing the above, there is a great deal of support for youth programs by youth, parents, adults, and community members.

Youth Programming Building Blocks

What are the building blocks of quality youth programs? A report published by the National Academy of Sciences has suggested that there are several elements that are important in building successful and effective youth programs. They are as follows:

- Physical and psychological.
- Structure that is developmentally appropriate.
- Emotional moral support.
- Opportunities for adolescents

to experience supportive adult relationships.

- Opportunities to learn how to form close, durable human relationships.
- Opportunities to feel a sense of belonging and valued.
- Opportunities for skill building and mastery.
- Opportunities to develop confidence in one's abilities to master one's environment (a sense of personal efficacy).
- Opportunities to make a contribution to one's community and to develop a sense of mattering.
- Strong links between families, schools, and broader community resources in decision making; opportunities for leadership, and involvement in community. (Gambone & Arbreton, 1997, p. 6).

Program Intentionality

In recent years a great deal of discussion has occurred regarding the importance of creating programs promoting "intentionality." This concept, when tied to programming, suggests that programs need to move beyond a casual approach, wherein the focus is one of building the attitudes, skills, values, and knowledge of youth. Intentionality implies that youth programs have a plan, aim, end, or purpose. In other words, they are crafted purposely for some deliberately intended purpose. Witt (2002) suggests that program intentionality finds the youth worker asking the question "What do we want to have happen and how are we going to make it happen?"

The emergence of program intentionality as a concept moves beyond what we have referred to as the "fun morality." There was a period of time when it was thought if the focus of youth should be exclusively on insuring their happiness; if we could make youth happy, they would be content, probably less rebellious, and in-step with societal expectations. In this sense, youth programming is more instrumental in nature. That is, a youth program should serve as a means to an end. The means are pathways that provide youth with opportunities to have their needs addressed, to grow and develop as they explore and discover their capabilities and potentials as individuals. The ends are multiple but are focused primarily on assisting youth in becoming self-reliant individuals capable of functioning effectively as adults in a democratic society.

GUIDELINES FOR YOUTH PROGRAMMING

Youth programming must be linked to the basic needs of youth. If we view programming in this context, it helps establish a focus for the efforts of youth workers. First, understand the needs of youth and then build programs around these needs. What are the basic needs of youth as it relates to programming? Building on the work of Pittman (1991) and Scales (1991), Edginton and Edginton, (1994, pp.88-89) have suggested that youth programs should be designed around the following:

- **A need for positive social interaction.** Youth want to belong and need opportunities to form positive social relationships with adults and peers.
- **A need for safety, structure, and clear limits.** Expectations, structure, and boundaries are important for youth, so that they feel secure and also have a clear picture of the areas that they can/cannot explore.
- **A need for belonging and meaningful involvement in family, school, and community.** Youth have a desire to be a part of and to participate in activities related to their families, their schools, and their communities.
- **A need for creative expression.** Youth need opportunities to express to others who they are and how they feel. Music, writing, sports, cooking, and other activities help to achieve this goal.
- **A need for feeling self-worth/ giving to others.** Involvement in meaningful and worthwhile effort related to larger goals is extremely important to youth.
- **A need for physical activity.** Youth have tremendous energy and require a great deal of physical activity and time for fun.
- **A need to feel a sense of independence, autonomy, and control.** Youth have a desire to mature, to become more independent, and to exert some control and influence over their lives.

- **A need for closeness in relationships.** Youth need opportunities to form close relationships with peers and adults. They also have a need for relationships with caring adult role models.
- **A need to feel a sense of competence and achievement.** It is important for youth to have opportunities to achieve success and to receive recognition.
- **A need for a sense of individualism, identity, and self-definition.** Youth need to have opportunities to become individuals and to define their sense of identity and self-concept, based on positive input from others.

These types of guidelines provide a way of linking programs and other services directly to the needs of youth. In establishing experiences for youth, the aforementioned items can be seen as benefits or the expectation of benefits upon which programs can be developed. Obviously, it is important that as programs are developed, youth are provided the opportunity for input crafting organization and implementation of said programs. Youth need to build a sense of ownership as a part of the process of program development.

Delgado (2002) has suggested that there are a number of principles for programming. These are found in Exhibit 6.1. Discussing core elements of youth development programs, the University of Washington School of Social Work (Catalano, Berlund, Ryan, Lonczak, & Hawkins, 1999) has identified 15 items that can be used in describing what youth development programs contribute. They suggest that youth development programs should contribute to the following: 1) promoting bonding; 2) fostering resilience; 3) promoting social competence; 4) promoting emotional competence; 5) promoting cognitive competence; 6) promoting behavioral competence; 7) promoting moral competence; 8) fostering self-determination; 9) fostering spirituality; 10) fostering self-efficacy; 11) fostering clear and positive identity; 12) fostering belief in the future; 13) providing recognition for positive behaviors; 14) providing opportunities for prosocial involvement; and 15) fostering prosocial norms.

Linear Programming vs. Developmental Programming

One way of framing the programming process is to view it in the "context of time." Context of time refers to how one views the process of participation within a program as related to its goals and objectives. On one hand, we can view the time spent by youth within a program in a linear fashion. In other words, there are specific program goals and objectives to be accomplished within an explicit timeframe or period. In this context, a systems approach to programming, the youth worker presents a very definitive program plan designed to reach a set of goals and objectives that can be measured and obtained within a specified time period. For example, in teaching swimming there are specific behaviors to be demonstrated by a youth

that are thought to be obtainable and whose successful achievement can be measured within a designated period of time. Such an approach does not necessarily take into consideration the fact that the development of youth varies, depending upon the individual.

The proposition that the development of youth varies, leads to another proposition for programming. That is, that youth programming should reflect the developmental needs of individuals and not be tied to a specific time period. Such a process of programming is more open, reflective of individual developmental needs, and not necessarily tied to a specific timeframe or even a set of short-term benchmarks. Again, using the example of swimming, progress is often measured in the linear approach of programming by the ability of the individual to demonstrate selective behaviors within a specific timeframe. Contrary to this would be the developmental approach to programming, which would focus on each person's developmental needs and not how much time there is to achieve specific behaviors. The measure of success would be whether or not a person learns to swim in the long haul, rather than meeting a prescribed set of goals and objectives.

In the creation of youth programs, both linear and developmental approaches are employed. There are many variables that influence the utilization of either one or both of these program strategies. A youth service organization's vision or mission statement may stipulate one or multiple approaches to pro-

Exhibit 6.1
Principles of Youth Development Programming

- Seek to deepen creativity, provide critical tools for negotiating developmental stages, and provide multiple avenues for the processing of cognitive information.
- Emphasize innovative, dynamic, and comprehensive approaches to serving youth.
- Provide youths with opportunities to succeed and contribute to their community.
- Build on youth assets and what youths value.
- Have multiple clear, high, and realistic expectations for participants.
- Provide youths with a sanctuary wherein they can generalize their learning—and in a fun manner.
- Be voluntary and provide youth with decision-making powers in shaping programming.
- Be built on quality staff and programming and a willingness to invest resources in support of staff.
- Emphasize positive intergenerational mentoring relationships.
- Actively seek to involve parents and other people significant in the lives of participants.
- Require long-term institutional commitment and seek to be comprehensive.
- Serve as vehicles for delivering conventional services to youth, if necessary, in unconventional settings and at unconventional times.
- Systematically involve other organizations (formal and informal).
- Prepare youth to live in a multicultural world by stressing the importance of interethnic/interracial relations among participants.

Source: Delgado, M. (2002). *New frontier for youth development in the twenty-first century*. New York: NY: Columbia University Press, 164.

gramming. An organization's funding sources may dictate a set of expectations regarding how programs are to be implemented. Accrediting bodies often establish standards or guidelines for programming, to which agencies respond in the development of their programs. Some programs focus their efforts on providing quantity as opposed to quality services. Still others are focused on providing the greatest good for the greatest number versus attempting to individualize their services. Certainly, the personal bias of a youth worker may also influence his or her emphasis on one programming approach over another and/or how the two are mixed.

YOUTH-CENTERED PROGRAMMING

The process of program planning must be youth centered. It must provide opportunities for youth to be involved in every step in the process in order to make programs and services meaningful, relevant, and effective for youth. High-yield youth programs are programs that make a difference in the lives of youth in terms of assisting youth in building their competence, and resilience to manage their journey through adolescence. Effective programs ". . .provide opportunities for values to be developed, beliefs to be considered, and behaviors to be shaped." (Edginton and Edginton, 1994, p.111) As these authors have noted, and we will repeat several times in this book and especially in this chapter, ". . .the program planning process works best when youth are empowered to participate in the process" (1994, p.111).

Youth-centered programming implies that the focus of youth workers in establishing programs and services is and should be the youth themselves. The program planning process should always have at its core the needs of youth and ways to involve them in all aspects of program development. Figure 6.1 provides a step-by-step process for planning, organizing, implementing, and evaluating programs and services for youth. The six steps are: 1) preprogram design elements, 2) program planning phase, 3) goals and objectives, 4) program design elements, 5) program implementation elements, and 6) program evaluation.

The following discussion provides brief background information for each of these elements.

PreProgram Design Elements

In preparation of actually beginning the process of program planning, there are a number of steps that need to be taken. These are known as preprogram design elements (Edginton, Hanson, Edginton, & Hudson, 1998). Some of the activities that the youth worker might be involved in are: 1) identifying the actual planning process to be employed; 2) locating, recruiting, selecting, and/or assigning individuals who may be a part of planning teams, including youth, community volunteers, and other professional staff; 3) assigning responsibilities, in other words, who is to carry out various tasks or assignments that are necessary in the planning process; and 4) reviewing past programs and other historical records that can be useful in understanding previous challenges, issues, methods, and strategies used in planning, implementing, and evaluating programs. In other words, a youth worker should step back, think about what needs to be done, what has been accomplished in the past, and who might be involved in the current effort.

Program Planning Phase

The program planning phase involves six critical elements (Edginton, Hanson, Edginton, & Hudson, 1998). They are: 1) needs assessment, 2) agency requirements, 3) community/agency resources, 4) benefits structure, 5) review of youth

Figure 6.1
Youth Centered Program Planning

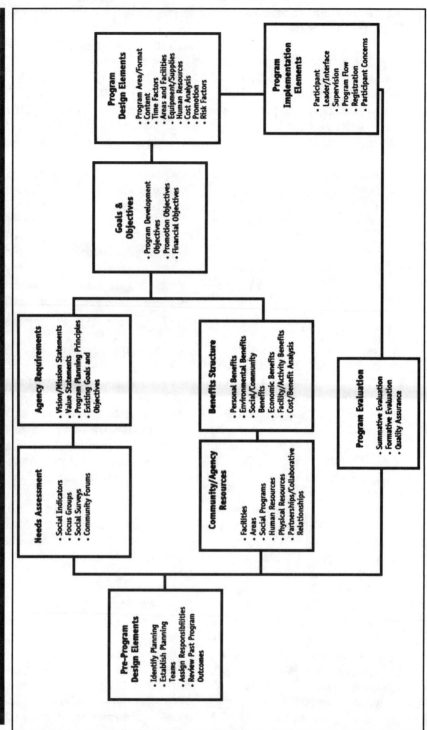

Source: Adapted from Edginton, S., & Edginton, C., (1994) Youth Programs: Promoting Quality Services. Champaign, IL: Sagamore Publishing p. 113.

development factors; and 6) soliciting youth involvement. Obviously, this is the heart of the program planning process. Needs assessment may involve many different tasks. Some of the ways of identifying needs are to use normative standards, review basic youth needs, review social indicators, utilize focus groups, conduct social surveys, and promote community forums for the purpose of soliciting information. There isn't one single way of assessing needs, and the youth worker may enlist various strategies. One should never overlook the direct approach of simply asking youth what they would like to do. Next the youth worker will want to look at agency requirements. What is the mission of the organization? What does it value? What program planning principles have been established, and what are the existing goals and objectives? A review of the resources available in the community is useful. Some programs are facility dependent. Others require unique human resources to implement. Still others require collaboration and building of partnerships with other community agencies. Next is to understand and establish the benefits desired by youth. There are many different ways of classifying benefits. All should be reviewed as a part of the program planning process. Youth development strategy should also be reviewed. What competencies are to be promoted? What values to be sought? What youth development strategies are best suited to aid in promoting selective competencies and values? Last the youth worker must solicit youth involvement. This may be done through an advisory group, program planning groups, and actually finding ways to ensure that youth have prominent leadership roles in the process.

Goals and Objectives

Goals can be thought of as the ends sought by the youth worker. Usually they are broad in nature. On the other hand, objectives tend to be more specific and action oriented. There are different types of program development objectives, promotional objectives, and financial objectives. Program development objectives are usually written in performance or behavioral forms that can be observed in some fashion. Promotional objectives refer to the ways in which the intent or benefits of programs are communicated with youth. Financial objectives refer to the management of fiscal resources. Most youth service organizations are nonprofit in nature, however, they must have financial support to run their activities. Further, many nonprofit organizations subsidize selected programs and require others to break even or even generate a profit. Some thought needs to be given by the youth worker to what strategies are to be employed in financing programs and what financial ends are to be sought.

Program Design Elements

There are many variables that go into designing youth programs. Consideration of the content of a program, also known as program areas, as well as its format are essential issues to be considered. Time factors and the location of the program are

Exhibit 6.2
To Program or Not to Program?

Let Kids Do Nothing—It Can't Hurt

Summer is coming soon. I can feel it in the softening of the air, but I can see it, too, in the textbooks on my children's desks. The number of uncut pages at the back grows smaller. The loose-leaf is ragged at the edges, the binder plastic ripped at the corners.

An old remembered glee rises inside me. Summer is coming. Uniform skirts in mothballs. Pencils with their points left broken. Open windows. Day trips to the beach. Pickup games. Hanging out.

How boring. Of course, it was the making of me, as a human and writer. Downtime is where we become ourselves, looking into the middle distance, kicking at the curb, lying on the grass staring at the tedious blue of the summer sky. I don't believe you can write poetry, compose music or become an actor without downtime, a hiatus that passes for boredom but is the quiet moving of the wheels inside that fuel creativity.

And that is one of the saddest things about the lives of American children. Soccer, acting classes, tutors—the calendar of the average middle-class kid is so over the top that soon Palm handhelds will be sold in Toys R Us. Children are as overscheduled as we are, and that is saying something.

This has become so bad that parents have arranged to schedule times for unscheduled time. Earlier this year the privileged suburb of Ridgewood, New Jersey announced a Family Night, when there would be no homework, no athletic practices and no after-school events. This was exciting until I realized that this was not one night a week, but just one single night. There is even a free-time movement, and Web site: familylife1st.org.

How about letting the kids do nothing? It's pathetic to consider the lives of children who don't have a moment between piano and dance and homework to talk about their day or just search for split ends, an enormously satisfying leisure activity of my youth. There is ample psychological research suggesting that what we might call "doing nothing" is when human beings actually do their best thinking, and when creativity comes to call. Perhaps we are creating an entire generation of people whose ability to think outside the box is being systematically stunted by scheduling.

A study by the University of Michigan quantified the downtime deficit: In the last twenty years, American kids have lost about four unstructured hours a week. Their has even arisen a global Right to Play movement. In the Third World, it is often about child labor, but in the United States it is about the sheer labor of being a perpetually busy child. In Omaha, Nebraska, a group of parents lobbied for additional recess. Hooray, and yikes.

(continued)

Exhibit 6.2 (continued)

How did this happen? Adults did it. There is a culture of adult distrust suggesting that a kid who is not playing softball or attending science programs—or both—is huffing or boosting cars. If kids are left alone, they will not stare into the middle distance and consider the meaning of life and how come your nose in pictures never looks the way you think it should, but instead will get into trouble.

There is also the culture of cut-throat and unquestioning competition that leads even the parents of preschoolers to gab about prestigious colleges without a trace of irony. This suggests that any class in which you do not enroll your first-grader will put him at a disadvantage in, say, law school.

Finally, there is a culture of workplace presence (as opposed to productivity). Try as we might to suggest that all these enrichment activities are for the good of the kid, there is ample evidence that they are really for the convenience of parents with way too little leisure time of their own.

Summer used to be a time apart for kids, a respite from the clock and the copybook, the organized day. Every once in a while, either guilty or overwhelmed or tired of listening to me keen about my monumental boredom, my mother would send me to some rinky-dink park program that consisted almost entirely of three-legged races and making things out of Popsicle sticks.

Now, instead, there are music camps, sports camps, fat camps, probably thin camps.

I mourn hanging out in the back yard. I mourn playing Wiffle ball in the street without a sponsor and matching shirts. I mourn drawing in the dirt with a stick.

Do most adults really want to stand in line for Space Mountain or sit in traffic to get to a shore house that doesn't have enough saucepans? Might it be even more enriching for their children to stay at home and do nothing?

For those who say they will only watch TV or play on the computer, a piece of technical advice: The cable box can be unhooked, the modem removed. Perhaps it is not too late for American kids to be given the gift of enforced boredom for at least a week or two, staring into space, bored out of their gourds, exploring the inside of their own heads.

"To contemplate is to toil, to think is to do, "said Victor Hugo.

"Go outside and play," said Prudence Quindlen.

Both were right.

Source: Quindlen, A. (2002, May 13). Let kids do nothing It can't hurt. *The Des Moines Register*, P. 7A.

also important. Areas, facilities, supplies, and leadership are all often elements that must be reviewed. It's important to think about how the program is to be promoted and what risk elements may be involved in the implementation of the program. Youth today often seek risky opportunities; therefore, youth workers must give careful consideration in establishing risk management plans to ensure the safety of participants. It's also important to analyze the costs of a program in terms of personnel, supplies/equipment, facilities, promotion, and other administrative costs. The establishment of fees and charges may be directly linked to the financial objectives established by the organization.

Program Implementation Elements

Program implementation is the actual realization or execution of the program. Of critical importance is the interaction of the youth worker with youth. This is known as the leader/participant interface. There is nothing more important than this relationship in establishing quality youth programs. Consideration must also be given to the program flow or animation of the program. Often programs are planned so that they unfold in a linear fashion; youth experiencing one event and then moving on to the next. However, room must be given so that youth have some control over how programs actually happen or occur. The youth worker can visualize in his or her mind a sequence of events, but must be open to empowering youth with the ability to change that sequence. A part of the implementation process is the way in which we provide recognition to participants. This can be done in a highly formal or informal manner. Of course, strategies for supervising programs in an ongoing way must also be well thought out, as well as the ways in which we handle instantaneous feedback from youth.

Program Evaluation

The last step in the process is program evaluation. There are two basic types of evaluation: formative and summative evaluation. Formative evaluation takes place during the life cycle of the program, and summative evaluation occurs at the end of the program. Formative evaluation helps bring about corrective measures or reinforce existing strategies as the program proceeds in an ongoing fashion. Summative evaluation is an opportunity to look back and think about ways to change or improve a program offering. Youth workers are increasingly involved with the concept of quality assurance. Quality assurance is a way of improving programs incrementally, by establishing benchmarks and monitoring the implementation of these benchmarks with an eye toward continuous improvement.

Although each of the steps is self-contained and each requires the focused attention of the youth worker, they must be viewed as a holistic process. Although each of the elements stands independent from one another, youth-centered program planning must be viewed in its broadest context in order to assure success.

BUILDING OWNERSHIP AND PROMOTING DEMOCRATIC LEARNING

As indicated, it is essential if youth programs are to succeed that youth workers assist youth in building a sense of ownership for the programs and services in which they participate. In a sense, building ownership is linked to promoting democratic learning. Youth workers seek to assist youth in shared decision making, problem solving, and learning tolerance for the views of others. To promote youth ownership, we must empower them. To empower suggests that one has been authorized or given authority to direct or influence those affairs that impact on their lives. Empowering others suggests that you are permitting them to engage in or do something on their own behalf. Successful youth workers work to enable youth to do what they are competent at performing, or they work to build competence within youth that will move them toward the goal of having control and greater personal responsibilities.

Youth workers in this sense function as guides rather than serving in a directive fashion or autocratic fashion. Promoting ownership and empowering youth, finds youth workers giving advice or assistance to youth, rather than telling them exactly what to do. This may involve providing instruction, helping to point out the various advantages or disadvantages to a course of action, and/or helping to shape the course of action that an individual may take. It involves taking a risk on the part of the youth leader. They must provide youth with opportunities to assume responsibilities so that they may gain real-life experiences that assist their development. Providing this sort of guidance to youth often involves giving positive feedback to enable youth to modify their behaviors to achieve their ends. Discouraging comments and discounting individuals can be detrimental in this process. The youth worker empowers youth by affirming and supporting them as individuals and by assisting them in their decision making.

A FRAMEWORK FOR YOUTH PROGRAMMING

There is no universal framework or model available outlining all of the areas in which programming for youth may occur. There are virtually no limits to the possibilities for programming for youth. One is only limited by one's imagination, creativity, and ability to think innovatively. Of course, youth themselves may be the very best resource available to the youth worker when it comes to generating program ideas.

There are a few models that have been developed to help create a framework for programming for youth. The National Collaboration for Youth (2001) has suggested that programming should focus on the broader developmental needs of youth rather than deficit based approaches that are only concerned with addressing problems. This concept is consistent with the idea of positive or prosocial youth development; that is, youth are an asset and youth workers should work to strengthen individuals through their programming efforts rather than seeing youth as a problem.

In developing youth programs, it is useful to think of two interacting components. The first is known as youth program areas. This refers to the actual content of programs. The second is the way in which the program is organized or the program format.

Program Areas

The National Collaboration for Youth (2001) suggests that there are a wide array of programs that could be provided by youth service organizations including: leadership development, character enrichment activities, mentoring activities, community youth centers and clubs, after-school programs, weekend programs and summer programs, sports and recreation, health promotion, academic enrichment, camping and environmental enrichment, workforce preparation, community service, civic participation, special interests groups, and youth-led programs. Edginton and de Oliveira (1995) have offered a program framework for youth development that includes the following areas: academic enrichment, leisure activities, health promotion programs, peer mentoring, life skill building, vocational/career, leadership development, service learning (community/civic), outreach services, and clubs/special interest groups.

We have combined these frameworks and added additional items to create a new program framework for youth. Figure 6.2 presents these areas. Following is a discussion of each of these youth program dimensions.

Peer Mentoring. A popular approach to youth programming is known as peer mentoring. Essentially it involves youth meeting youth. One's peer is one of equal rank, ability, or value. A peer mentor is usually an individual trusted by another who provides wise counsel, assistance, instruction, guidance, or other useful information. Edginton and de Oliveira (1995, p.26) have written that ". . .the concept of mentoring can be thought of as a process where the individual provides wise and trusted advice to another. A mentor is often seen as an individual with special levels of knowledge, skill, and/or experience." They suggest that the key element in mentorship is the development of a relationship of trust between individuals. We would also add that peer mentorship also involves building respect between individuals.

Academic Enrichment. Youth development programs are often directed at assisting youth towards advancing their knowledge, skills, or ability in some fashion. This is done through the provision of some form of scholastic, educational, or learning activity. Such learning activities can be organized in either a formal or informal fashion. Academic enrichment programs are focused on assisting individuals gain greater proficiency or improve their skills, knowledge, and abilities in some

Figure 6.2
Youth Development Program Areas

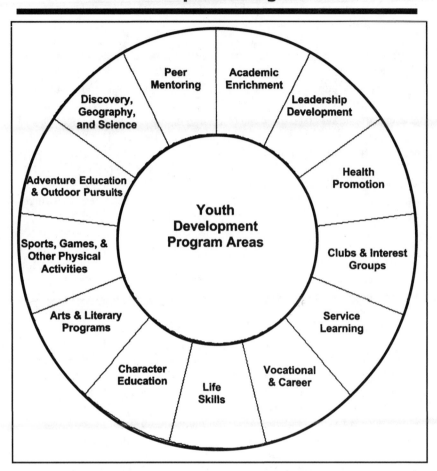

Adapted from Edginton, C. R., & de Oliveira, W. (1995). Youth development: A program framework. *PERS Review Hong Kong, 1*(2), 22-27.

fashion. Edginton and de Oliveira (1995, p. 22) have noted that such learning environments contribute to growth and knowledge, critical thinking, and cognitive abilities. They write ". . .such programs may assist youth by proficiency, improvement, and by adding to enriching their knowledge or skill programs." Such programs are often provided in a parallel and collaborative fashion with other learning environments. When connected in such a fashion with either the school or the home environment, these types of programs can be very powerful learning experiences for youth. Another approach would be to provide remedial programs that help uplift the level of youth in selected areas. Youth learn at different rates and as a result may not reached predetermined standards. Remedial programs help students gain proficiency, meet minimum standards, and perhaps advance their knowledge and skills in selected areas.

Leadership Development. One youth service organization has as one of its important values the statement that "today's youth are tomorrow's leaders." We believe this to be the case and feel that it is essential to invest in the development of the leadership potential of youth. Many youth programs are focused on this theme—that of building leadership competencies and abilities and finding the potential within youth to practice leadership and become leaders. "Leadership development is a program area that is dedicated to promoting opportunities for youth that place them in leadership roles and also assists

youth in identifying, discovering, and developing the knowledge, skills, and competencies necessary in exercising leadership" (1995). As Edginton and de Oliveira (1995, p. 23.), citing such noted contemporary management authors as Warren Bennis, Bert Nanus, and Tom Peters, have written "leaders ought to help shape and elevate the motives of others. They create images, metaphors, and models that focus attention; in effect, their efforts create meaning for others." They further note that leadership involves passion, flexibility, and excitement as well as the wisdom to reconcile followers' needs and wants in such a way as to promote a common vision or end. These authors support the idea that leadership development is an important program function for youth workers noting that "helping youth develop or discover their potential for leadership and build capacity for leadership within youth is a prime goal of many youth service organizations" (Edginton & de Oliveria, 1995).

Health Promotion. Health promotion is an overarching concept that is directed at the encouragement of positive health behaviors and lifestyle. Health promotion is difficult to define as it is conceptually viewed differently by individuals, as well as across disciplines and professional areas of study. From one perspective, health promotion can be thought of as "a process that helps individuals enjoy their lives more fully" (Edginton, Hanson, Edginton, & Hudson, 1998, p.232). On the other hand, Schlaadt (1983) suggests that health promotion promotes a lifestyle that is dedicated to encouraging desirable health practices and an optimal lifestyle. Still further, health promotion programs are often viewed as programs of intervention. The U.S. Department of Health and Human Services (2004) has defined health promotion as any combination of health, education, and related organizational, economic or political interventions designed to facilitate environmental changes conducive to health. Finally, we may think of health promotion programs as ones which support the search for optimal health and vitality, encompassing physical, emotional, intellectual, spiritual, interpersonal and social, and environmental wellbeing. Youth workers often are engaged in the provision of programs that provide opportunities for individuals to gain information regarding such issues as drug and substance abuse, alcohol consumption, sexual behavior, family dynamics, interpersonal relationships, fitness, stress management, dietary nutrition, and lifestyle changes. An example of a health promotion program is one known as TEEN (Total Education and Enrichment Network). This program serves youth ages 18 to 21 and addresses the perils of substance abuse, teenage pregnancy, early fatherhood, gangs, and dropping out of school. It is operated by the City of Phoenix (Arizona) Parks, Recreation and Library Department.

Clubs and Interest Groups. Youth often "hang together" in groups. They are motivated by their desire to be with each other and to pursue common interests. From a youth program perspective, the creation of clubs and interest groups can facilitate the need for youth to be with one another and engage in common activities. In a sense, a gang is as much an interest group as is a Boy Scout or Girl Scout troop. Both provide opportunities for youth to be with one another. For example, the Boy Scouts of America organize individuals into patrols; patrols in turn are formed into a troop. These units are usually neighborhood based, providing individuals with an opportunity to enhance their skills, develop physically and mentally, promote teamwork, build self-confidence, personal reliance, and build a sense of pride. As Fine and Mechling (1993), have proposed, the formation of groups by youth provide a sense of place and importance, a sense of belonging, loyalty, selfless rendering of service and even sacrifice for others, peer-sponsored morality, significant amounts of enjoyment, as well as goal-directed activity. Edginton, Hanson, Edginton, and Hudson (1998, pp. 172-173) suggest definitions for both clubs and interest groups. They suggest that a club is "a group of persons organized for some particular purpose. . .formed on the basis of age group, activity interest, or for some exchange of information and ideas." In a similar fashion, they suggest that ". . .an interest group is a collection of individuals that has formed around an activity, issue, or program area."

Service Learning. Service learning programs provide opportunities for youth to support community needs in a meaningful and worthwhile way. This type of program allows youth to give of themselves altruistically and learn at the same time from meaningful opportunities and life experiences. Although there is no universally ac-

cepted definition of service learning, many definitions have emerged. The National Center for Early Adolescence (2001) defines service learning as a form of community service that involves youth combining meaningful volunteer service with

Exhibit 6.3
National Youth Service Day

Youth Service America sponsors an annual National Youth Service Day, celebrating the contributions that youth make to their communities through year-round service. This organization is dedicated to strengthening the effectiveness, sustainability, and scale of the youth service and learning fields. Youth Service America has as its vision "making service and service-learning the common expectation and experience of all young people in America."

Youth Service America envisions a powerful network of organizations committed to increasing the quality and quantity of volunteer opportunities for all youth in America to serve locally, nationally, and globally. They are committed to building a strong youth service field to create healthy communities and to foster citizenship, knowledge, and the personal development of young people.

The goals of National Youth Service Day are as follows:

• To MOBILIZE youth to identify and address the needs of their communities through service;
• To RECRUIT the next generation of volunteers; and
• To EDUCATE the public about the role of youth as community leaders.

National Youth Service Day is a program operated in collaboration with the National Youth Leadership Council. Over 60 national partners promote the event. Youth Service America works with 50 lead agencies that coordinate city-wide and state-wide celebrations of National Youth Service Day.

Source: Youth Service America. (2003). National Youth Service Day [On-line]. Available: www.YSA.org/NYSD

ongoing reflection. Likewise, Lau (2002) has suggested that service learning provides opportunities for youth to engage in meaningful community services that address human and community needs together with structured opportunities intentionally designed to promote learning and development. Another view of service learning suggests that it is

. . .a carefully monitored experience in which a student has intentional learning goals and reflects actively on what he or she is learning throughout the experience. Service learning programs emphasize the accomplishment of tasks which address community issues and include features which foster participants' learning about larger social issues and an understanding of reciprocal learning and service which can occur between students and community members," (University of Northern Iowa, 1995).

Most forms of service learning require action followed by reflection. This is known as a praxis and will be discussed more fully in chapter seven.

The benefits of service learning are numerous. Edginton and de Oliveira (1995, p. 24) have noted that

. . .service learning programs engage youth in prosocial behaviors, helping them to develop healthy interpersonal skills, foster emotional

growth, encourage care and responsibility, gain an understanding of community service, increase the ability to work with others, assist in the development of career objectives, expand willingness to learn and assist in the development of a sense of self.

Schine (1990, p. 8) proposes that "the central need or task in adolescence is what scholars call identify formation—trying to find the answer to the question: Who am I?" Service learning programs assist in this discovery process. Still further, Edginton and Edginton (1995, p. 6) have noted that "service learning may be instrumental in helping youth learn to work with others, gain an understanding of community service, develop life skills, demonstrate caring and commitment, and other benefits."

Vocational and Career. The idea of vocation can be thought of as an individual's "calling." There are two ways of viewing the concept of vocation. First is from a philosophical perspective. When questioning his or her life's calling or quest in life, an individual youth is seeking to discover his or her life's purpose. From a theological perspective, one may be called to serve others, to act compassionately, to give of oneself in an altruistic fashion, and to be a caring and concerned individual, as well as in a myriad of other ways. One's life calling provides a foundation for one's self-concept and has a dramatic impact on the way in which one lives one's life. The search for a calling is ongoing, similar to the process of "becoming." It is often a quest that one pursues with critical self-examination and inquiry throughout one's life.

A second perspective on dealing with the concept of vocation and career is to think of it as finding one's self in the marketplace. We all use our jobs to define our self-concept. When a person is asked who they are, it is often asked in the context of what do you do for a living? One's job becomes a major way of defining one's self-concept. Certainly youth workers assist youth in preparing themselves for the job market; in finding a career, an occupation, a job. Youth need direction, counsel, information, and support as they search for a career. They often require assistance to enhance their skills in preparing a resume, interviewing, and successfully engaging others in the workplace. Youth workers can help youth in developing a variety of knowledge, skills, and competencies required for a successful entry level insertion into the job market.

Life Skills. One of the important program areas addressed by youth workers is that of assisting youth in development life skills that help youth meet daily challenges, as well as aiding them in their journey through adolescence to adulthood. Pittman and Wright (1991, p. 3) have written:

> Life skills training is the formal teaching of requisite skills for surviving, living with others, and succeeding in a complex society. Because of pro-

found changes in our society over the past few decades, it can no longer be assumed that these skills are automatically learned.

Adolescents need help in acquiring a range of social competencies to cope with academics, to meet fundamental challenges of forming stable human relationships, to maintain hope about their future, to understand and adopt health promoting behaviors, to make wise decisions about life options and to optimize use of social networks.

Adolescents need general problem solving skills, planning and decision-making skills, cognitive strategies for resisting peer or media influences, skills for increasing self-monitoring and self-regulation, and coping strategies to deal with everyday stresses.

As one can discern from viewing the above statements, life skill development is an important program component for youth service organizations. According to Edginton and de Oliveira (1995, p. 25), "...life skills include the ability to handle conflict, ability to make decisions and solve problems, ability to make positive and healthy choices, ability to value others, ability to achieve success in school/employment and other practical skills and knowledge."

Character Education. Character education, character building, moral education, and values development have all been important program features of youth service organizations over the past century. It is not a new concept. In Chapter 5 we discuss this, indicating that character education is pursued by youth workers as a way of helping identify and strengthen those characteristics that form the foundation for positive adult behaviors in an adult democratic society. The Boys and Girls Clubs of America operate several character enhancing programs as a part of their core program. For example, they have established a recognition that promotes and celebrates a club member's service to the Club, community and family, academic performance, spiritual values, life goals, and poise and public speaking ability." The City of Phoenix (Arizona) Parks, Recreation and Library Department focuses on character-building strategies in their programs. They note that they ". . .will build character with programs that challenge the mind, body, and spirit."

The Arts and Literary Programs. Arts, crafts, and literary programs are very popular among youth. We define arts as including the performing arts (music, dance, drama), the visual arts (decorative arts and crafts), and the new arts (photography, computer graphics, radio, and television). Literary programs include activities in categories such as writing, communications,

reading, foreign studies, and discussion groups. (Edginton, Hanson, Edginton, & Hudson, 1998, p. 212). The Arts is another core program area of the Boys & Girls Clubs of America. They note that ". . . programs in this area enable youth to develop their creativity and cultural awareness through knowledge and appreciation of the visual arts, crafts, performing arts, and creative writing." Likewise, the City of Phoenix (Arizona) Parks, Recreation and Library Department sponsors a variety of art programs where youth are exposed to performing and visual arts. Summer programs emphasize a full slate of "drawing, dance, drama, music, and other special interest classes." In addition, they operate numerous literacy-based programs, including a summer reading program and a library outreach program.

Sports, Games, and Other Physical Activity. Sports, games, and fitness activities are popular among youth. We can think of sport as an activity that demands a combination ". . .of physical skill, endurance, purpose, and enthusiasm." (Edginton, Hanson, Edginton, & Hudson 1998, p.214). Sports have more precise rules and regulations. There are different types of sports including individual, dual, and team and games that require varying degrees of skill and ability. Some games are very complex; others are simple, requiring less organization and skill. There are three basic kinds of games: low-organized, table/board, and mental. In recent years there has been a greater emphasis on the importance of youth fitness. The U.S. Surgeon General's report (Satcher,

Exhibit 6.4
Youth Centers

There is a wide array of youth centers throughout the United States. These types of facilities often provide youth with an opportunity to "drop in or hang out" with others. Resources in such facilities may be well developed, including gymnasiums, computer rooms, arts and crafts areas, venues for table games such as billiards, and meeting and lounging areas. Youth centers also feature opportunities to hold dances, set up coffee shops, provide counseling and other information. On the other hand, facilities may be rather spartan, providing the opportunity to furnish, decorate, and in a sense, take ownership of the resource through initiative.

For example, the San Carlos (CA) Youth Center is supported by funding from the City of San Carlos and the San Carlos Youth Center Foundation. Programs of the San Carlos Youth Center include after school drop-in, dances, an annual teen conference, camps, personal development workshops, sports programs and classes, as well as numerous special events. Working in collaboration with other community agencies, the San Carlos Youth Center is especially connected with the San Carlos school district, providing such programs as a homework center, science fair, and physical education programs.

Source: San Carlos Youth Center. (2002). *Annual report to the community*. San Carlos, CA: Youth Center Foundation.

2001) suggests that America's youth are unfit and increasingly obese. Interestingly, youth enjoy fitness activities and participate when the social conditions are supportive. Many youth have difficulty participating in traditional school-based physical education programs. Yet youth will participate in wellness and fitness centers, bowling centers, and in extra curricular activities where the environment encourages skill development, personal achievement, and even social ends, as contrasted with mandatory programs or competitive athletic programs.

Adventure Education and Outdoor Pursuits. Youth often seek risk. Outdoor education and outdoor pursuits programs provide opportunities for youth to be exposed to risk but also the exhilaration that comes from being in the out-of-doors and interacting with nature. There are many different terms that are associated with this program area, including outdoor recreation, adventure tourism, conservation education, eco-tourism, environmental education, environmental interpretation, natural history, nature education, and outdoor education. The scope of activities for youth is virtually limitless. Table 6.1 provides a list of some of the possibilities that may be available for youth. Outdoor activities provide a great medium for helping individuals gain an awareness of self (especially where they are challenged), improve their social living skills, learn about the environment, and, as mentioned, be exposed to some element of risk.

Discovery, Geography, and Science. These three terms have been lumped together and refer in general to program opportunities that enable youth to discover the physical environment. The study of science includes opportunities for discovery and enhancement of one's cognitive abilities in the areas of biology, chemistry, geology, mathematics/computer science, and physics.

The study of geography is broader, encompassing the study of Earth, its division into continents and countries, and the climate, plants, animals, natural resources, inhabitants, and industries that form these divisions. The word discovery implies that youth are provided with the opportunity to find out about and to explore the existence of some phenomena. In the aforementioned areas, the process of discovery creates opportunities for new insights and perspectives. Such luminating learning experiences often heighten an individual's appreciation, awareness, and value of the world in which they live.

Program Formats

As mentioned, a format is the way in which activities are organized or structured. Edginton, Hanson, Edginton, and Hudson (1998, p. 256) have defined a program format as ". . .the configuration or way in which experiences are sequenced and linked to one another to increase the likelihood that . . . [youth] will achieve desired benefits." Farrell and Lundegren (1991, p. 101), Russell (1982), Kraus (1985, p. 186), and Rossman (1995, p. 53) have all proposed a variety of different program formats that can be used in youth programming. Some of these include: self-improvement, competition, social, participant/spectator, self-directed, clubs, trips and outings, special events, classes, open facilities, voluntary services, workshops, instruction, free play, performances, exhibitions, leadership training, special interest groups, drop-in, and skill development. In reviewing this list, one can see that some authors identify selected program areas as program formats. This may very well be the case as some programs imbed properties of both what could be defined as a program area and a program format.

We have chosen to simplify this discussion and include the following as program formats: competitive, drop-in/open, instructional classes, club, special events, and outreach programs.

Competitive. This program format emphasizes competition. There are basically three types of leagues, tournaments, or contests—self-per-

Table 6.1
A Partial List of Adventure Education
and Outdoor Pursuits

Adventure education	Ice skating	Safety and survival courses
Air surfing	Interpretative activities	Sailing
Alpine skiing	Jet skiing	Sailboarding
Archery	Jogging	Sand sculpturing
Aquatic safety	Kayaking	Scuba diving
Backpacking	Kites	Sightseeing
Ballooning	Kite fighting	Skeet and trap shooting
Beach activities	Luge	Ski camping
Beach volleyball	Motor boating	Ski orienteering
Bicycling	Mountain biking	Ski touring
Bicycle touring	Mountain climbing	Skiing
Bird-watching	Mountaineering	Skin diving
Board sailing	Nature art	Skydiving
Boating	Nature education	Sledding
Bow hunting	Nature interpretation	Snorkeling
Bungee jumping	Nature photography	Snowboarding
Bushwhacking	Nature study	Snowmobiling
Camping	Navigation	Snow play
Canoeing	Nordic skiing	Snow sculpturing
Caving	Ocean kayaking	Snowshoeing
Climbing	Off-road motorcycles	Spearfishing
Collecting berries	Off-road vehicles	Speed skating
Collecting firewood	Organized camping	Spelunking
Cooperative tripping	Orienteering	Sunbathing
Conservation education	Ornithology	Surfing
Cross-country skiing	Outdoor pursuits	Survival skills
Curling	Outdoor survival skills	Target shooting
Cycling	Outdoor swimming	Tent camping
Day hiking	Paddling	Tobogganing
Diving	Parachuting	Touring
Downhill skiing	Parasailing	Trail hiking
Ecological activities	Photography	Tubing
Environmental education	Picnicking	Upskiing
Environmental interpretation	Pleasure boating	Visiting historic sites
Family gatherings	Pleasure driving	Visiting prehistoric sites
Fishing	Primitive camping	Visiting museums
Fitness walking	Rafting	Volksmarching
Flower gathering	Rapelling	Walking
Gardening	Recreational vehicles (RV camping)	Waterskiing
Glacier climbing	Resident outdoor school	White-water rafting
Golfing	Rifling	Wildlife observation
Hang gliding	River camping	Wildlife photography
Heli-skiing	River running	Wilderness trekking
High ropes adventure	River safety	Windsurfing
Hiking	Rock art hunting	Winter camping
Horseback riding	Rock climbing	Winter skiing
Hot air ballooning	Rockhounding	Wreck diving
Hunting	Ropes courses	Yachting
Ice boating	Rowing	
Ice fishing	Running	

Source: Adapted from Edginton, C., Hudson, S. D., Dieser, R. B., & Edginton, S. R. *Leisure Programming, A Service-Centered and Benefits Approach* (2004) 4th ed. p. 237

petuation, round robin, and elimi-nation. (Edginton, Jordan, DeGraaf, & Edginton, 2002, p. 361).

Drop-in/Open. Using a drop-in format for programs gives youth a sense of freedom. Activities in this format are organized so that they can be ongoing, self-directed, or spontaneous. Youth drop-in when they want to, and become involved in activities at will (Edginton & Edginton, 1994,p. 161).

Instructional Classes. Classes help people acquire specific leisure competencies, skills, or knowledge. There are two approaches to instruc-tion. . .the humanistic and the systems approach. The humanistic approach focuses on growth and de-velopment of each individual, whereas the systems approach mea-sure minimal standards of competence (Edginton et al., 2002, p. 361).

Club. A club is a format de-signed for a group with a special interest. Clubs are a big hit with youth, because they can choose things they are interested in, and they have a sense of perceived free-dom (Edginton & Edginton, 1994, p. 161).

Special Events. Special events—programs organized in a unique manner deviating from the routine—often take months of plan-ning, but can be implemented in a matter of hours or even minutes (Edginton et al., 2002, p. 361).

Outreach Programs. These programs are taken to participants in their own locale. This type of pro-gram format may involve mobile recreation equipment and roving leaders and often occurs in densely populated urban areas where entire programs can be organized and implemented on site (Edginton et al., 2002, p. 361). Edginton and Edginton (1995) have suggested that outreach programs can be viewed from several different orientations, including: 1) an activity/program strategy, 2) therapy/intervention, 3) state of mind/attitude, 4) free in-terface/presence, 5) as defined by time and/or location, and 6) holis-tically.

PROCESSES FOR ORGANIZING YOUTH PROGRAMS IN THE COMMUNITY

Youth programs are in and of the community. The ways in which communities choose to allocate re-sources or make decisions about the types of youth programs it will offer depends on what a given locale val-ues. Conceptually, there are several strategies that can be employed within a community to provide ser-vices. One is the market system and another the political governmental system. However, the great majority of youth programs in any given com-munity come about as the result of the work of nongovernmental, non-profit organizations. Each of these types of approaches to allocating resources requires a different set of assumptions.

There are a number of ap-proaches that can be used in the process of organizing a community's resources in order to provide youth programs. There are four basic ap-proaches that can be employed by youth workers to influence the allo-

Exhibit 6.5
Information Shops

Information Shops have emerged primarily in the United Kingdom with the idea of providing an area of information, counseling, and advising to youth. The aims of information shops are the following :

- To make information available and attractive to young people and give them the support and power to act on this information.
- To promote the development of information through high-quality, high-street Information Shops, and involvement of other youth information projects in a nationally coordinated initiative.
- To make it easy for young people to seek the help they need about issues affecting their lives. The information or counseling might be needed because of a crisis, such as a bereavement or homelessness, or it might be about opportunities for work, education, travel, or leisure activities.

In the U.K. these facilities provide information regarding eating disorders, sexual abuse, physical abuse, rape, self-harm/suicide attempts, bereavement, pregnancy, sexual identity, education, employment, environment, family, housing, justice, finances, and sports (National Youth Agency, 1994). These types of facilities promote a consolidation of information to enable "one-stop shopping" for youth. Counseling is an important component of these services and confidential meeting space with staff is provided. Further, health workers are available to youth to support their concerns.

Source: National Youth Agency (1994). *Directory of Information for Young People.* Leicester, UK: National Youth Agency.

cation of community resources on behalf of youth. They are: social planning, community development, social action, and social marketing.

Social Planning. Social planning is a task-oriented approach directed toward a rational and logical way of distributing community resources. It can be thought of as a way of creating a focus toward the achievement of community goals. Basically, social planning employs a process of using the knowledge and expertise of professionals to plan, organize, and deliver youth programs. Youth workers work to diagnose the needs of youth by fact gathering and then try to create programs based on the identification of these needs. Youth workers in this role are seen as program planners, analysts, and program implementers. The youth worker sees him or herself as the expert, and youth are the customers who receive the services that are provided. Social planning can employ a good deal of involve-

Exhibit 6.6
A Place to Hang: Children Feel Right at Home in Rec Center Especially for Them

It's 4:45 p.m. Thursday, a school day. Several middle-schoolers are venting pent-up energy in the recently opened Good Samaritan Game Room in a basement at Sixth Avenue and Hickman Road. The sound of laughter mixes with the noisy chiding typical of kids, the plock of pool balls being hit and the musical melodies of a Nintendo game. About 15 children, mostly two year-olds come and go during the afternoon. They rotate from the computers to the ping-pong table, foosball table, dartboard and pool table.

Mark Nelson, 38, Director of Youth Ministries for Good Samaritan Urban Ministries and the adult on duty, shoots pool with three preteen boys who rival his own sixfoot height. "We see this as an opportunity to reach kids, as an alternative to being on the streets and as an alternative to drugs and to capture their attention early enough so we have a opportunity to disciple them," Nelson said.

Paris Smith, 12, a seventh grader at Harding Middle School, is using the foosball table as a barrier for his game of tag with another seventh grader. "If I wasn't here, I'd be watching TV at home," he said. Veola "Peaches" Hicks, 13, an eighth-grader at Harding, recently moved to Des Moines from Virginia and doesn't have many friends yet. She sits at a computer playing a game of solitaire. I try to come every time "it's open," she said. This game room, which opened this summer for eleven to fifteen year-olds, was Nelson's idea.

It became reality with the help of adults in the 2001 Greater Des Moines Leadership Institute and a handful of kids who live in the complex where the game room is located, and with contributions of money and services from local individuals and businesses.

Good Samaritan helps mostly single moms and their children by providing affordable housing and other services to assist them in improving their lives. The organization maintains about 120 housing units, several located in the seven brick buildings that comprise the complex at Sixth and Hickman.

The game room is the second in the complex. Another game room set up a few years ago in another basement was so popular with younger children that high school kids felt out of place there, Nelson said. It became apparent something was needed for kids older than ten. When Nelson was approached in January by members of the 2001 Greater Des Moines Leadership Institute looking for a project, he eagerly told them about his idea for the game room for older kids. "We could all connect to their need," said Kevin Currie, who is in business development for Septagon Construction Co. and one of the fifty-four members of the 2001 class of the Leadership Institute. The mission is to develop leadership skills and involvement among community members.

"We considered several different projects, but this one was doable in the time frame we had before our June 1 graduation," Currie said. They visited the existing game room, then toured the basement that would become the site of the new center. "It was just a wreck down there. It was filled with asbestos and it was dark and dank," said Joy Schiller, Wellness Director at Des Moines University Osteopathic Medical Center and a member of the 2001 Leadership Institute class. The class solicited money and in-kind services and materials to convert the basement into a recreational area. Schiller said the goal was to collect about $6,000. When they were done, they had collected about $17,000 in donations.

Professionals cleared the asbestos and rewired the basement. Other workers leveled the floor, reworked the utilities, drywalled the ceiling, tore down and built walls, and cleaned, painted and carpeted. The leadership class left an autograph. On a purple-painted wall near the pool table, fifty-four white stars represent each of the members who worked on the project. When everyone was finished with the physical labor, the result was an open recreation room with game areas and places for computers, Nintendo games, TVs and PlayStations, tables and chairs. "This project had a lot of appeal to us because we were trying to get the kids actively involved so they would have pride of ownership," Schiller

(continued)

Exhibit 6.6 (continued)

said. About a half dozen children living in the Good Samaritan housing helped regularly with the project, working alongside the adults on Saturdays and evenings.

Tara Williams, 12, was one of them. "It was fun. We got to paint," she said. Tara and the other children who helped regularly were rewarded with a trip to Toys "R" Us to select games and game tables. The young people pick up in the game room after each use and clean it every other week or so. "I think they've already caught on to that ownership thing," Nelson said. Picking up is one of the six house rules posted on a sign beginning "Da House Rulz." The number one rule: "Love your neighbor as yourself, Mark 12:31." Other rules remind kids to wear shirts and shoes and to respect others. Food, foul language and fighting are prohibited. Everything must be put away after use. "We have pretty strict consequences if they don't behave," Nelson said. One discipline he imposed is to bar kids from the room until they write an apology to the appropriate person. Unfortunately, not everything has been smooth. Someone broke into the game room and stole the PlayStation games. "We think we know who did it and what happened," Nelson said, who hopes to recover the stolen equipment. Although the game room was finished in June, it wasn't open much this summer. Children from Good Samaritan housing attended camp the week after it opened. The epoxy paint applied to the floor wouldn't dry and had to be cleaned and repainted. Nelson, who runs the mentoring and tutoring programs for Good Samaritan

DETAILS
What: Good Samaritan Game Room

Where: Basement in southwest building in Sixth and Hickman housing complex.

Who: For 11-15 year olds who live in Good Samaritan housing and for teens in the neighborhood around Sixth Avenue and Hickman Road.

Hours: About 4-5:45 p.m. Mondays and Thursdays.

Equipment: Pool table; ping-pong table: Seta Dreamcast, Nintendo and PlayStation games; electronic dartboard; air hockey; foosball table; computer with games and other software; stereo and CDs; bicycle repair tools.

Creation of the game room: Came together through the efforts of Mark Nelson, youth ministries director for Good Samaritan Urban Ministries; children living in Good Samaritan housing; members of 2001 class of the Greater Des Moines Leadership Institute; and corporate, business and individual donors who contributed money, services and materials.

Needed: Adult volunteers so the game room can be open more often

Urban Ministries and is also a chief financial officer for the organization, is too busy with other duties to keep the room open as much as he'd like. His goal is to have it open every weekday. For now it is open Mondays and Thursdays from about 4 to 5:45 p.m. He is in the process of trying to hire more staff and is looking for volunteers. The Good Samaritan game room is open for children in the neighborhood as well as those who live in the organization's housing. About 15 minutes before the room closes Nelson has a short

(continued)

Exhibit 6.6 (continued)

discussion and Bible study for anyone who wants to stay. Talk lately has been about concerns in the wake of recent terrorism and the importance of prayer. Nelson, who left the corporate world after fourteen years to work for Urban Ministries, looks at his work with the youth as part of his ministry. The game room helps him get to know the kids and do what he calls "discipline them." "In order to speak truth in a child's life, you have to develop their trust," he said.

Source: Boeckman, J. (2001, October 10). A place to hang: Children feel right at home in rec center especially for them. *The Des Moines Register*. pp. 1E and 6E.

ment on the part of youth as a part of the process of information gathering in the assessment of needs. This approach is also sometimes referred to as direct service delivery.

Community Development. Community development is built on a different set of assumptions than social planning. It is built on the idea that youth workers can build a partnership with youth. Youth workers work collaboratively with youth to help them identify their needs and plan programs that are of value to them. In this approach, the role of the youth worker is to help youth gain knowledge and information regarding the processes that they can use to develop service programs to meet their needs. In this sense, youth workers serve as enablers, catalysts, coordinators, coaches, teachers, and, most importantly, facilitators. Youth workers promote self-help, the teaching of process skills, and values related to democratic learning and community service. Basically, youth workers assist individuals by stimulating them to think about and participate in the

community while meeting their needs. Youth workers as community developers help individuals to develop their leadership capabilities and assist in the process of clarifying values, issues, and concerns. Community development can be thought of as indirect service delivery.

Social Action. Youth are often marginalized in many communities across the United States. Their needs and ideas are often diminished. The social action strategy presumes that youth are in fact disadvantaged. Youth workers work on behalf of youth to address this concern, attempting to force the system, institutions, and organizations to change and to be responsive to the needs of youth. Basically, youth workers attempt to shift the allocation of resources and power so that youth needs are met. Youth workers in this approach to dispersing community resources act as agitators, brokers, negotiators, organizers, and, most importantly, advocates and activists. Youth workers using social action as a strategy understand that they must acquire power to achieve social justice and equity.

Social Marketing. Marketing has captured the interest of youth service organizations, especially those operating in the market sector in the nongovernmental, nonprofit area. The basic underlying assumption in social marketing is that an organization should have as its basic strategy meeting the needs of those that it serves. Adding the word social to marketing further emphasizes the importance of the fact that the marketing process has to do with human beings and the need to find a way to promote the common welfare of individuals within the community or society as a whole. Individuals using social marketing focus their efforts on initially analyzing needs and then initiating what is known as the "market mix" to meet these needs. The market mix addresses such items as the services to be delivered, the location/scheduling, the cost or price of a program, and the way it is promoted. Further, social marketing is concerned with identifying discreet target markets (there really is no such thing, but there are people with needs, especially youth) and then determine the most effective way of satisfying the needs of these groupings. Youth workers using social marketing act as analysts, planners, implementers, and promoters.

SUMMARY

The crafting of youth programs is challenging. Programs are vehicles that are used to connect with youth in a meaningful and relevant fashion. They assist in promoting the cognitive and social, emotional, and moral development of youth. Program experiences provided to youth exist along a continuum. At one end of the continuum are the random, yet highly productive, encounters that youth workers often have with youth as they work to connect with them through conversation. At the other end are programs that are highly organized and structured, often with detailed curriculum guides, lesson plans, and course objectives. There is no question that society as a whole supports the establishment of youth programs, and in fact, it has become an important focus of many, many communities across the United States.

In this chapter, we have proposed a model for program planning called "youth-centered programming." This model suggests that the youth must be at the center of the process of program planning. The implication of this is that youth will assume responsibility for their own development with the assistance of youth workers and other community members. The model has six components including: 1) preprogram design elements, 2) program planning phase, 3) goals and objectives, 4) program design elements, 5) program implementation elements, and 6) program evaluation. An essential component of the process of youth program development is building a sense of ownership by youth for programs and services. Ownership is established when youth are empowered to share in decision-making and problem-solving, as well as program planning, organizing, and implementing strategies.

A framework for offering youth programs was provided. The framework included program areas and program formats. Program areas refer to the content of the activity and include: peer mentoring; academic enrichment; leadership development; health promotion; clubs and interest groups; service learning; vocational and career; life skills; youth centers and information shops; character education; the arts, crafts, and literary programs; sports, games and other physical activity; adventure education and outdoor pursuits; and discovery, geography, and science. Program formats refer to the way in which a program is structured or organized. Program formats discussed include: competitive, drop-in/open, instructional classes, club; special events, and outreach programs.

REFERENCES

Bennis, W. & Nanus, B. (1985). *Leaders*. New York, NY: Harper & Row.

Carnegie Council on Adolescent Development. (1992). *A matter of time: Risk and opportunity in the nonschool hours*. Report of the task force on Youth Development and Community Programs. New York, NY: Carnegie Corporation.

Delgado, M. (2002). *New frontiers for youth development in the twenty-first century*. New York, NY: Columbia University Press.

Edginton, C. R., Hanson, C .J., Edginton, S. R. & Hudson, S. D. (1998). *Leisure programming: A service-centered and benefits approach*. (3rd ed.). Boston, MA: WCB McGraw-Hill.

Edginton, S. R., & Edginton, C. R. (1994). *Youth programs: Promoting quality services*. Champaign, IL: Sagamore. Publishing

Edginton, S. R., & Edginton, C. R. (1995). *Youth outreach and service excellence*. U.S. Army Child and Youth Services.

Edginton, C. R., & de Oliveira, W. (1995). Youth development: A program framework. *PERS Review Hong Kong, 1*(2), 22-27. Refereed.

Farrell, P., & Lundegren, H. M. (1991). *The process of recreation programming*. State College, PA: Venture Publishing.

Fine, G. A., & Mechling, J. (1993). Child saving and children's cultures at century's end. In S. B. Health & M. E. McLaughlin (Eds.), *Identity and inner-city youth* (pp. 120-146) New York, NY: Teachers College.

Gambone, M. A., & Arbreton, A. J. A. (1997). Safe havens: The contributions of youth organizations to healthy adolescent development [On-line]. Philadelphia, PA: Public/Private Ventures. Available: www.aspe.hhs.gov/hsp/positiveyouthdev99.

National Center for Chronic Disease Prevention and Health Promotion (2004, October 7) *Healthy Schools, Healthy Youth*. Retrieved from www.cdcgov/healthyyouth/index.htm

National Collaboration for Youth (2001). National Youth Development agenda [On-line]. Available: http://www.nydic.org/nydic/statements/html.

National Youth Agency. (1994). The information shop for young people: statistical report. http://www.info4yp.demon.co.uk/shop.htm

Peters, T. (1987). *Thriving on chaos.* New York, NY: Knopf.

Pittman, K. J. (1991). *Promoting youth development: Strengthening the role of youth serving and community organizations.* New York, NY: Center for Youth Development and Policy Research.

Pittman, K. J., & Wright, M. (1991). *A rationale for enhancing the role of the non-school voluntary sector in youth development.* Washington, DC: Center for Youth Development & Research, Academy for Educational Development.

Pittman, K. J., Irby, M., & Ferber, T. (2000). *Unfinished business: Further reflections on a decade of promoting youth development.* Takoma Park, MD: The Forum for Youth Investment.

Rossman, J. R. (1995). *Recreation programming: Designing leisure experiences.* Champaign, IL: Sagamore Publishing.

Russell, R. V. (1982). *Planning programs in recreation.* St. Louis, MO: Mosby.

Scales, P. (1991). *A portrait of youth adolescents in the 1990s.* Carrboro, NC: Center for Early Adolescence.

Schine, J.A. (1990). A rationale for youth community service. *Social Policy, 20*(4), 5-11.

Schlaadt, R. G. (1983, Winter). Wellness or lifestyle management. *The ACHPER National Journal.*

Witt, P. A. (2002, October). *Youth Development: The Importance of Intentionality.* Paper presented at the meeting of the National Recreation and Park Association, Tampa Bay, FL.

CHAPTER SEVEN

Leadership and Working with Youth

INTRODUCTION

Leadership is a key ingredient in the success of any youth service organization. Youth work is stimulating, rewarding, and fulfilling. Yet at the same time, youth work can be challenging, demanding, and intense. Youth workers require a high order of ability in order to effectively perform. Youth leaders need to be visionary, inspirational, motivating, empathetic, and cheerful, as well as consistent, fair, firm, and dependable in their interactions with youth. No youth worker can act in a professionally responsible fashion without careful examination of his or her leadership capabilities and capacity.

What does it take to be a great youth worker? What leadership skills are required for success in working with youth? This is a difficult and complex question to answer. Clearly, there is no recipe that can be universally applied to every youth work situation; however, there are some general guidelines that can be applied to youth work. Such guidelines are broad in nature and provide only a starting point in the discussion of leadership strategies for working with youth. Clearly, great youth workers have the ability to motivate others. They have ability to inspire and bring out the best in those with whom they work. Further, great youth workers are individuals who demonstrate empathy for others. They have the capacity to understand the viewpoints of others, to walk in their shoes, to listen, and to give social-emotional support. Great youth workers also operate with integrity; a wholeness or consistency in their actions. They are principled individuals whose actions reflect their values and beliefs. Last, we often find that great youth workers have the ability to use their intuitive abilities or emotional intelligence to help them connect effectively with others. These are just some of the elements that contribute to a youth worker's effectiveness.

In this chapter, leadership and leadership strategies in working with youth will be discussed. We will attempt to define leadership and discuss the ways it is manifested in youth work. Further, the art of conversation as a primary leadership responsibility of youth workers will be presented. Use of the concept of praxis as an important leadership strategy—a way to assist youth reflect on their life experiences—will be included in the discussion. Next, this chapter will present an engaging concept known as leader presence and suggest how the efforts of youth workers can be enhanced through their knowledge of this concept. Last, we will discuss several leadership functions which we believe capture the many important activities in which youth workers are engaged.

What is Leadership?

The concept of leadership means different things to different people. As Rost (1993, pp. 97-98) has indicated ". . .the word leadership has many different meanings and in fact has come to mean all things to all people." He has further written that leadership can be equated with

what one person does to a group of people (1993, pp. 97-98). More succinctly, Rost suggests that leadership can be defined as ". . . an influence relationship among leaders and followers who intend real changes that reflect their mutual purposes (1993, p. 102). A leader must be able to influence others, thus leadership can be viewed as a process of influence. Further, leadership is about building relationships. Leaders and followers are involved in relationships which may be unequal because the patterns of influence among individuals are divergent. For a leader to aid another individual or group he or she must seek real changes. The changes must be substantial and transforming in nature. Last, our definition suggests that individuals join together in a relationship that is mutually beneficial. They join together for some common purpose or value.

As Edginton, Hudson, and Ford (1999, p. 11) have written, "leadership can be best be viewed as a process whereby a leader uses his or her influence to enable mutually desired change to occur." They further note that leadership "is the process employed by the leader to assist individuals and group in identifying and achieving their goals. Leadership may involve listening, persuading, suggesting, doing, and otherwise exerting influence on others." Leadership when applied in an effective fashion can be thought of as an art that is directed at influencing individuals, building relationships, and achieving some mutually desired end. In support of this approach to leadership,

Russell (2001, p.12) has written that leadership can be "defined as interpersonal influence exercised by a person or persons, through the process of communication, for the attainment of goals."

Leadership and Empowerment

Leadership and empowerment are often discussed in the same context today. Empowering others involves giving up one's power and authority. Certainly, youth workers promote the idea of empowering youth. Their goal is to give youth influence; to provide them with a voice to express their present concerns and hope for the future. This at times is also referred to as assisting youth in developing ownership. Ownership can only occur when youth have been empowered to have influence over their own lives and those elements that impact on their being or becoming.

There are numerous ways to empower youth. It is thought that the ultimate expression of leadership is giving away responsibility and authority to others that respond in an accountable fashion. When youth perceive that they are free and have the ability to make decisions, solve problems, and direct resources, they are often more highly motivated and will in fact, be more dedicated and committed to an endeavor. Youth need to have the opportunity to risk, to generate their own ways of accomplishing tasks, and build other relationships that assist them in achieving their objectives. The freedom to express one's views is not only central to living in a democratic society, but it also assists youth in developing a greater sense of self-confidence and self-worth.

Levels of Leadership

Leadership in youth service organizations manifests itself in many different contexts. There are youth workers who interact with youth on a face-to-face basis. These are often referred to as direct service leaders. Their job is one of interacting directly, often on a one-to-one basis, with youth. They are often engaged in direct conversation with youth, as well as other direct service activities such as teaching, coaching, or counseling. Still another level of leadership occurs at the supervisory level. Individuals involved in supervisory roles working with youth often have the responsibility of planning, organization, and implementing a program area such as sports, teen center activities, or overseeing a number of direct service youth workers. Last, individuals involved in administrative positions also must demonstrate leadership skills. Their leadership is more conceptual in nature, often involved in providing a vision to the entire organization and/or coaching other workers by providing guidance in the form of instruction, motivation, or problem solving.

THE ART OF CONVERSATION

Creating opportunities to listen, converse, interact, or dialogue with youth is a key component of youth work. However, conversation with youth as an end in itself is often dismissed as being a byproduct of the involvement with youth in structured programs and services. As Jeffs and Smith (1999, p. 21) have suggested, "conversation is central to our work as informal educators, yet we undervalue it. Some of us may be uncomfortable just sitting around and talking." Conversation with youth may very well be the most important leadership function practiced by youth workers. In conversing with youth, we create the opportunity to more effectively understand their needs, aspirations, challenges, and concerns. Conversation provides us with an opportunity to learn about youth—discovering their innermost thoughts and feelings. Such knowledge is absolutely essential in assisting youth in meeting the challenges of adolescence.

Conversation is a two-way process. It requires that youth workers be good listeners, as well as framers of an inquiry to assist youth in clarifying their values and life choices. Learning to listen with empathy, sincerity, and genuine interest in others is a prime responsibility of the youth worker. One must often shed one's preconceived, often judgmental, expectations of others. To truly listen with empathy, one must have an open mind and an open heart. As Jeffs and Smiths (1999, p. 23) suggest, in order for two or more people to communicate, they must

• cooperate
• think about others' feelings and experiences, and
• give each other room to talk.

As these authors note, conversation is a reciprocal process. They go on to also note that "to fully engage in conversation, we have to be in a certain frame of mind. We have to be with that person, rather than seeking to act upon them." (Jeffs & Smith, 1999, p. 25). In other words, having a conversation with someone requires that an individual be open to another's viewpoint. It requires that the youth worker give social-emotional support to the ideas, feelings, and expressions of the youth with whom they are interacting. Such conversation requires an affirmation of others. The youth worker must be careful not to talk over, put down or project their own ideas in an obtrusive, haughty, or overbearing manner, or even try to intellectualize the thought of another. Rather, the youth worker should attempt to listen with empathy, assist youth in clarifying their concerns, and provide social-emotional support to them throughout their conversation.

Youth today want more than ever to have a positive and productive conversation with an adult. The youth worker provides an important outlet for youth by enabling them to share with him or her their inner concerns in a fashion that is nonjudgmental, safe, and nonthreatening. Youth want to dialogue with others. Conversation with others for youth is important as it provides an outlet for an expression of their concerns, as well as their creative thoughts. Just talking with youth may in fact be the most important activity of a youth worker's day.

LEADERSHIP AS A PRAXIS

Youth workers deal with youth in such a way as to help shape their perceptions of life. The challenge to youth workers is to provide experiences where youth can gain from their participation. The knowledge that comes from one's life experiences is invaluable. We may think of knowledge as existing in two domains. One is conceptual knowledge; the other is the knowledge that comes from the experience of living one's life.

A key factor in assisting youth gain knowledge from life experiences is to aid them in reflecting on these experiences. This type of reflection is known as a praxis. A praxis simply refers to practice as distinguishable from theory. The power of a praxis is in the opportunity that it provides for individuals to act and then reflect on their experiences. A praxis can be a very significant learning strategy for youth. Action followed by reflection provides the opportunity to learn and then in turn change, modify, strengthen, or improve one's future actions. The praxis becomes a way of framing one's life experiences as a learning opportunity. We can also think of this process as what is known as "phenomenological pedagogy" or the learning or teaching that comes from life experiences.

What is the role of the youth worker in facilitating a praxis? First, youth must be immersed in an experience or action; there must be a base of life experience that provides a significant opportunity for reflection. The youth worker must converse with youth in such a way as to unobtrusively allow the individual to think about the meaning and implications of their life experience. In other words, the youth worker must frame their dialogue with youth in such a way as to enable them to think for themselves, rather than imposing a value structure or ideas on their experience. Rather than using didactic learning methods, the youth worker's efforts are framed in a heuristic fashion. That is, their work is focused on helping youth to discover or learn by crafting questions to assist youth in framing meaning from their life experiences.

Assisting youth by promoting praxis is an important form of youth work leadership. Carefully crafted dialogues aimed at assisting youth gain meaning from their life experiences is an important function of youth workers. Praxis, in this sense, is a leadership opportunity for youth workers. Conversation with youth, as indicated above, is central to youth work. The successful crafting of opportunities for reflection by youth, leading to greater meaning and learning, is often present in all encounters with youth. Therefore, the use of praxis should be viewed as a fundamental leadership strategy of youth workers.

LEADER PRESENCE

There are intangible qualities to one's interactions with others. At times just being in the presence of another individual can be very commanding. No words need to be exchanged, no dialogue, merely the presence of another individual may impact one's being. Such is the case with the work of youth leaders. One's simple presence may have a important influence on the development of the youth with whom they come in contact.

We can think of one's presence as one's bearing, personality, and even appearance. One's presence is often characterized by dignity, poise, and confidence. Even the way one carries oneself is a part of the presence he or she conveys to others. We all have been influenced by other individuals whom we admire, respect, and even model our own lives after. We have been transformed by people who are kind, gentle, charismatic, visionary, compassionate, empathetic, forgiving, caring, energetic, enthusiastic, and who express a zest for life. We have all encountered individuals in our lives that have had a great deal of impact on us because of these qualities and others. Obviously, the mere presence of another individual in our sphere can be a very powerful and moving influence.

De Oliveira, Edginton, and Edginton have discussed the idea of presence in youth work. They have coined the term "leader presence." These authors have indicated that one's presence "conveys a greater, spiritual essence through an individual and his or her works." (1996, p. 38). They go on to suggest that ". . .leaders use their presence to influence values, attitudes, and behaviors" (1996, p.38). Clearly, a youth leader's energy, warmth, sincerity and genuine love of others have the power to transform youth

(De Oliveria, Edginton & Edginton, 1996, p.38). "Simply by living one's life in contact with others where such characteristics are present conveys meaning. Expanding on the idea of role modeling, the concept of leader presence promotes more encompassing relationships" (De Oliveria, Edginton & Edginton, 1996, p.38). As de Oliveira, Edginton and Edginton (1996, p. 39) have written, "youth leaders get to know youth and let the youth get to know them. One of the products of this mutual learning is a caring and loving relationship." These authors suggest that influence occurs, sometimes unintentionally and unobtrusively, from a mingling of the life essences of individuals. In this sense, leadership occurs as each individual is influenced by the other.

Much of the influence of youth workers can be seen in the context of leader presence. We have, as indicated, viewed the process of leadership as one of influence. Youth workers are in a position to influence the lives of youth simply because of their presence. Youth look to youth leaders as role models. They often scrutinize the actions of youth leaders and draw from them meaning that influences their lives. The actions of the youth worker as observed by youth have a great deal of power and influence on the behavior of youth. We can all think of individuals who have influenced us in our lives simply because of the quality of their presence. A coach, a teacher, a counselor, a religious leader, a grandparent, a parent, a sibling, and still many others, are all identified as individuals who have influenced the lives of youth. The influence of such individuals has often been by virtue of the quality of their presence.

The idea of presence emerges from the concept known as the "pedagogy of presence" (Gomes da Costa, 1991). This concept implies that one may come to understand the leadership potential of one's presence as a method of learning and influence. The idea of presence is drawn from Christian theology, which suggests that believers invite the presence of Jesus Christ to dwell within them as a transformational experience (and we might add a great process of influence). We have all met individuals who demonstrate Christ-like behaviors, suggesting to us that their actions are an outward manifestation of the internal qualities of Jesus Christ within them. The Hebrew word, *shekhina,* suggests an ". . .all-embracing presence that is perceptible in all forms of human experience and encounters" (Kiely, 1996). Thus, one's presence, from a theological perspective, becomes a powerful condition that has great potential to influence all exchanges between individuals.

LEADERSHIP FUNCTIONS

In the last hundred years, a great deal has been written on the topic of leadership. Still further, many assumptions about effective ways of leading or working with others have been proposed. Rather than repeat the voluminous literature related to leadership, we have identified those functions or ele-

ments that we believe are important in youth work. We have chosen to focus on these primary functions of youth workers: relationship building; inspiring and transforming individuals; assisting, clarifying and building values; and developing collaborative relationships. These functions are all accomplished in the framework of providing service to youth and others.

Youth workers are involved essentially in connecting with youth. They do so by building relationships with youth and others. Youth workers are involved in inspiring and transforming youth, assisting them in their journey through the often chaotic, yet critical period of identity formulation associated with adolescence. As a part of the galaxy of human service professionals, youth workers operate in service to others, often in an altruistic fashion. Still further, youth workers assist youth in clarifying and building values to guide life's decisions. In addition, youth workers promote democratic learning as a fundamental focus for their efforts. Last, youth workers are involved in building collaborative relationships with individuals, other organizations, and the community as a whole.

Leadership as Relationship Building

A key element in working with youth is building a relationship of trust, confidence, and mutual respect. Without establishing a relationship built on respect for one another, it would be difficult for any leader to be successful in working with youth. Therefore, the building of relationships, or the act of being connected in meaningful and relevant ways to youth, is central in the work of youth leaders.

The youth leader must connect with individuals, groups, and even the community at large in order to engage youth. Relationship building often involves joining, linking, and building an affinity for youth. It requires the establishment of an understanding of their needs, wants, desires, and interests. Relationship building involves constructing an awareness of others. To do so, the youth leader must operate with a great deal of compassion, sensitivity, and genuine interest, and concern for the well-being youth.

The importance of building relationships is a central theme found within the literature on the topic of leadership. Stogdill and Coons (1957) identified consideration, or one's relationship orientation with others, as a key element in the leadership style of an individual. Likewise, Blake and Mouton (1978) have written that successful leaders are those concerned with both people and production. They use the term "human relations orientation" and suggest that much can be accomplished by individuals committed to a common goal that leads to a relationship of trust and respect. Fiedler (1967) suggests that one's leadership style must be situationally determined. He notes that when there is a high degree of favorableness toward the leader it often exists because of several factors, one being the relationship that exists between the leader and others. Still further, Hershey and Blanchard (1977) note

that one's human relationship orientation is a part of his or her leadership style; and they suggest that one's task-relevant knowledge can impact on the style used in working with others.

All the aforementioned studies point out the importance of building relationships with others as part of the leadership mix. Youth workers who relate well to others—attempting to understand each individual's needs, desires, and interests—and take time in building relationships of trust and confidence, will often be able to connect effectively with youth. How does one build relationships with others, especially youth? First, it takes time. One has to exhibit patience, tolerance, and a genuine interest in others. Connecting with youth often requires a genuine effort to understand the language and perspective of the world from the youth's view. Youth workers must operate in a nonjudgmental, supportive fashion with youth. They must embrace others, opening themselves to divergent views, values, and ways of learning, knowing, and understanding.

Leadership and Inspiring a Transformation of the Spirit

Leadership, at its best, is aimed at inspiring others. Youth workers work to instill the best in youth. They work to instill a sense of hope—hope in the present, hope for the future, hope in oneself, hope for others, and hope for the community. Youth often possess feelings of alienation, isolation, and loneliness. The outside world, as well as one's inner self, can often be chaotic, harried, and sometimes frightening. Youth have great needs in finding their way in life, of becoming what they envision for themselves in the future.

One of the main purposes of youth work is to provide a sense of hope. Transforming and uplifting the human spirit inspires youth to fulfill his or her future expectations. This may involve helping youth craft future callings or life scenarios that are desirable and then helping youth by lighting the path to achievement. Youth look to youth leaders as role models. They are some of the most important heroes. Their every action is often scrutinized in detail by youth. A youth leader's every action possesses the power to transform the lives of the youth with whom they work. As mentioned above, the presence of the youth worker is a powerful tool in and of itself.

Burns (1978) has helped us learn of the power of transformational leaders. He suggests that there are two types of leaders: transactional and transformational. Transactional leaders exchange one reward or other units of value with an individual in exchange for desired behaviors. On the other hand, transformational leaders work to lift individual to focus on higher needs. They work to help individuals transcend their own self-interest, seeking more altruistic, common ends. They work to instill a sense of commitment towards worthwhile ends, and encourage individuals. Transformational leaders often touch the soul of others, raising their level of consciousness, assisting them to

make a difference in their own lives and those of others.

Leadership and Building Values

From a historical perspective, youth workers have focused on promoting, encouraging, reflecting, clarifying, and mirroring values. In the past, youth workers have been engaged in what was known as moral education, values development, and character building. Today it is more prominently referred to as character education. Values are the social principles, goals or standards that are held by individuals or by a community or society collectively. Values provide guidelines for living one's life. Leadership focused on building values is a direct responsibility of youth workers, yet is played out at times in a subtle, often unobtrusive fashion.

The values of a youth worker are transmitted to youth through many mechanisms. As mentioned above, the presence of the youth worker alone can serve to promote selected values. In the youth work field, values such as humility, love, compassion, tolerance, consistency, coherence, hope, courage, integrity, commitment, understanding, and respect for others are communicated to youth through the efforts of youth workers. As is also mentioned above, it is important for youth workers to remember that youth view them and their behaviors, searching for the symbolic meaning of that behavior. Youth look to youth workers for understanding, guidance, and clarification regarding how values may be applied in their lives.

The leadership literature has approached the study of values in several ways. First, much attention in the leadership literature has been to identify those traits that contribute to a person's effective leadership style. Such traits as a person's ability to relate well to others, operate with integrity, be fair-minded, dependable, and caring are often viewed by individuals as a reflection of an individual's basic value structure. Kouzes and Posner (1995) have identified some of the traits (reflecting individual values) that people admire in leaders. These are honesty, vision, inspiration, competence, fair-mindedness, support, broad-mindedness, straightforwardness, dependability, courageousness, cooperativeness, imagination, caring, determination, ambition, loyalty, self-control, and independence (Kouzes & Posner, 1995). Covey (1989, p. 18) has made a strong case for the importance of being value-driven, principled, and ethical in one's activities as a leader. He notes that "the foundation of success—things like integrity, fidelity, temperance, courage, justice, patience, industry, simplicity, modesty, and the golden rule—were pillars upon which individuals built leadership styles. "In more recent times, he suggests that a new ethic emerged focused on the function of individuals' personalities and focused on building a positive mental attitude and finding ways to "lubricate the process of human interaction." Covey goes on to note that the use of "human influence strategies" instead of focusing on an individual's fundamental character and values "is fundamentally flawed, marked by duplicity and insincerity . . .and in the end will fail" (1989, p. 21).

Leadership and Promoting Democracy

As we have suggested, a central integrating theme in youth work is democratic learning. As such, it seems reasonable to suggest that youth workers should evidence democratic principles as a part of their leadership style in working with youth. What does this mean? Basically, the way in which the youth worker interacts with youth can be seen as *laissez faire*, autocratic, or democratic. These leadership styles represent various strategies for interacting with others. An individual employing a *laissez faire* strategy would allow youth to act without interference or direction. An authoritarian leader would demand or enforce unquestionable obedience to authority. The democratic leader would promote greater individual freedom and action with a bias toward treating individuals in an equitable fashion. Thus, democratic leadership promotes the principle of equality of rights, opportunities, and treatments in relating to and interacting with youth.

How can democratic principles be incorporated into one's leadership style? Shared problem solving, shared decision making, consensus building, and the promotion of equity among individuals are the major strategies for incorporating democratic principles into one's leadership style. Democratic leaders value the input of youth and attempt to build commitment through participation.

When working with youth, democratic youth workers attempt to help youth develop a sense of ownership for their life experiences as well as programs and service which may be organized in support of the needs of youth. This shared sense of ownership promotes a greater commitment, even a greater sense of belonging, to the programs and activities provided by a youth organization. A democratic leadership style requires an individual to be open to the perspectives, wishes, and desires of others. Youth workers employing a democratic leadership style work actively to incorporate the needs, interests, and wants of individuals into a collective whole.

From an historical perspective, the modern study of leadership focused on an analysis of *laissez faire*, authoritarian, and democratic leadership styles. The pioneering research of Lewin, Lippitt, and White (1939) at The University of Iowa, investigating the effects of various leadership styles on the behavior of youth, established the basis for research in this area. These authors observed the impact of various leadership styles on the behavior of youth involved in activities such as mask-making and model airplane construction. They found that youth were more hostile and aggressive when responding to authoritarian leaders than when compared to individuals using a democratic leadership style. They found similar responses when comparing laissez faire leaders with democratic leaders. Overall, they were able to determine that youth participating in the study liked democratic and *laissez faire* leaders more than the authoritarian ones. Thus, as one can see in reviewing these early studies involving leadership, these investigators established the appropriateness and usefulness of the democratic style of leadership in working with youth.

Leadership and Promoting Collaboration

Whether working with individuals in a micro sense or working with a community at large in a macro sense, youth workers are involved in building and promoting collaborative relationships and partnerships. To collaborate means to work together. Edginton, Hudson, and Ford (1999, p. 56) wrote:

> Building collaborative relationships between individuals is a key element in contemporary concepts regarding leadership. Collaboration means to work together or to cooperate with others. The hallmark of collaborative effort is found in the process of "teaming" with other individuals. Those who collaborate do not work independently but rather, work to produce synergistic opportunities between individuals or group members. The idea of synergistic, collaborative behavior is that the work of the team will out-perform the combined outputs of individuals working alone.

Youth Work: Emerging Perspectives in Youth Development

Certainly, youth workers focus on working together with youth. Their goal is to engage youth by promoting dialogue, engaging them in programs and services, and in a general sense, to work with youth to advance and reflect their ideas, concepts, and sense of the future. As Kouzes and Posner (1995, p. 11) have written, "...leadership is a dialogue not a monologue." Youth workers using a collaborative leadership style are focused on building relationships of trust, listening attentively, and establishing ways of collective decision making. Also, youth workers work to build a infrastructure in the community by building collaborative partnerships and relationships. Networking is an important part of the function of the youth worker. By extending oneself into the community and interacting with other individuals, groups, and community organizations, the youth worker is helping assist youth in broadening their base of support and extending the resources that are available in meeting their needs.

The literature regarding collaborative leadership has evolved considerably in the last several decades. Mabey (1994) has proposed a Collective/Collaborative Leadership Model. She suggests that leadership should be seen as a shared, collaborative process where the effort between leaders and collaborators results in action that reflects their mutual interest. A key factor in the establishment of the Collective/Collaborative Leadership Model is the need for leaders to find ways to empower collaborators. Mabey notes there are a number of different types of collaborative leadership including: personal leadership (self-management with internal dialogue), team leadership (small groups, the family), organizational leadership (strategic planning, convening meetings of individuals/teams), citizen leadership (participation in community life), and community leadership (collective action leading to community change). Eisler (1995) has promoted a gender-based leadership paradigm comparing the masculinity-dominated model with the femininity partnership-driven model. This model suggests that males and females bring different values to leadership situations. Feminine traits such as creating nurturing environments, empathy, nonviolence, caring, compassion, conflict resolution, and an egalitarian approach to working with others are a part of this model. Youth workers employing this model would work to connect with youth in a nonabusive manner, valuing their individual differences and the inherent worth of each person. Belasco and Stayer (1993) have also promoted the idea of collaborative leadership. They use the analogy of the flight of geese in the V formation, noting that leadership roles change frequently as individual geese tire. Hallmarks of the Belasco and Stayer model of collaborative leadership involve open communication, trust, shared responsibility, and commitment by all to the goals of the group.

DEVELOPING A NEW MODEL OF LEADERSHIP IN YOUTH WORK

What the field of youth work lacks is a model of leadership that informs youth agencies and program providers about what ought to be done in youth programs and how it ought to be done. Without such a model, youth workers are left to their own devices when making decisions about issues central to program leadership, vision, and ethics. One model of leadership that might prove useful for informing the practice of youth work is the relational leadership model.

The relational model of leadership views relationships to be the key to leader effectiveness (Komives, Lucas & McMahon, 1996) and is congruent with our understanding of what "good" youth program leaders do. Effective youth workers or youth program leaders are able to build positive relationships with young people, interact with them in developmentally positive ways, and empower them to become active participants in the communities of which they are a part, as well as promote in young people a moral and ethical sense of right and wrong in such a way that they are able to govern their own behavior.

Some in the field of leadership may view the term "relational leadership" as redundant because all leadership involves relationships, but the term does have strength, as Komives and colleagues have stated, "in affirmation of repetition" (Komives et al., 1996, p.22). Regardless of the term itself, the elements that make up relational leadership (see Table 7.1) provide a useful framework through which youth program providers can make decisions about what should be expected of program leaders, as well as participants.

Defining Relational Leadership

Relational leadership, of course, focuses on the role relationships play in establishing the context within which members of an organization or community of individuals interact. It is believed that "leadership is always dependent on the context, but the context is established by the *relationships* we value" (Wheatley, 1992, p.144). This way of thinking is consistent with that of traditional youth work practice, where our focus is on the ways in which youth workers and young people interact, the ways of relating that the patterns of interaction form, and the developmental significance of those relationships and patterns of interaction (Magnuson & Randall, unpublished manuscript).

In order to promote positive relationship development, this model of leadership suggests that leaders and participants should be, and should expect others to be as follows:

• Inclusive—of people and diverse points of view.

• Empowering—of others who are involved.

• Purposeful—there is individual commitment to a goal or activity.

Table 7.1
Relational Leadership Model

Leadership Component	Knowing (Knowledge/ Understanding of)	Being (Believing that)	Doing (Skills in)
Inclusive— of people and diverse points of view.	Self and others citizenship, frames and multiple realities, world views, organizational, cultures.	Differences in people are valuable, and fairness and equality are important in the treatment of all people. Everyone can make a difference.	Developing talent Listening, building coalitions. Framing/ reframing, engaging in civic discourse.
Empowering— of others who are involved.	Power, empowerment, impact of power on policies and procedures, self esteem.	Everyone has something to offer. Concern for the growth and development of others is necessary and important. Contributions of others are to be solicited and valued. Power, information, and decision making are to be shared willingly.	Gate-keeping sharing information, learning at individual and team levels, encouraging or affirming others, building capacity of others, promoting self-leadership, practicing renewal.
Purposeful— having an individual commitment to a goal or activity, also having the individual ability to establish a common purpose, a vision for a group.	Change process and models, roles of mission/ vision.	An attitude that is hopeful, positive, and optimistic helps everyone. Individuals, groups, and organizations can make a difference.	Identifying goals, Envisioning, making meaning, thinking creatively, involving others in vision-building process.

Source: Komives, S. R., Woodward, D. B. Jr., & Associates (1996). *Student services: A handbook for the Profession* (3rd. ed.). San Francisco, CA: Jossey-Bass.

When present, "these aspects of relational leadership. . .become foundational to working smarter" and together—both program leaders and participants (Komives et al., 1996, p. 22). They help leaders and participants to relate and work together in supportive and meaningful ways.

Being Inclusive in Youth Programs

The usual perspective that guides activity within youth programs is that of the adults who are leading these programs. Group tasks and rules are commonly established without consideration of the perspectives, ideas, and feelings of young people. Youth, if they want to participate in these programs, are expected to follow and respect the decisions that the program leaders have made, without challenging the program leader's authority.

As one can imagine, this type of program structure sets up a combative situation between youth, who are developmentally dealing with the task of establishing who they are as individuals, and adult leaders when there is a disagreement between the two over a particular aspect of program life (e.g., rules, proposed activity). In order to establish and maintain the kinds of relationships that are developmentally supportive for young people, youth program leaders must strive to be inclusive; they must make efforts to understand, value, and engage the diverse views that exist amongst themselves and program participants.

"Being inclusive means understanding, valuing, and actively engaging diversity in views, approaches, styles, and aspects of individuality, such as sex or culture, that add multiple perspectives to a group's activity" (Komives et al., 1996, p. 73). It is important for program leaders to recognize the importance of each individual within the program. The goal should not be to achieve unity by having everyone conform to the same standard of imposed rules; rather, the goal should be to bring the differing and varying perspectives of all group members together to form a shared vision of group life within youth programs.

Being inclusive also means making an effort to develop the strengths and talents of every group member so that everyone can contribute to the group's goals. Program leaders can enhance the learning of young people by helping them discover and develop their strengths and talents. This, however, requires that leaders strive to bring out the interests of the youth with whom they are interacting. Individuals cannot develop their strengths without being given the chance to participate in those activities that they are most interested in. By beginning with the interests of each individual youth, respecting those interests, and helping youth engage those interests, program leaders can promote a sense of inclusiveness and support the individual development of each young person.

One last comment about being inclusive in youth programs: It is essentially that youth program leaders gain a good understanding of themselves and others. This means gaining an understanding of both how you, as a leader, view and interact with the world around you (e.g., the beliefs you hold, the prejudices you have), as well as how different people might interact with and view that same world differently. This also means maintaining and promoting an atmosphere of respect for the differences of people, in general, within youth programs. All members of a youth program, leaders as well as youth, must ensure that everyone communicates their ideas and beliefs without fear of criticism and disagrees with each other with civility.

Being Empowering in Youth Programs

While inclusiveness is a crucial aspect of relational leadership, so is empowering the members of a group. In youth programs, this means fostering an atmosphere that encourages individual, as well as group, participation in all aspects of the program. Within the framework of relational leadership, two dimensions of empowerment are crucial: 1) the sense of self that claims ownership, claims a place in the process, and expects to be involved and 2) a set of environmental conditions (in the group or organization) that promote the full involvement of participants by reducing barriers that block the development of individual talent and involvement (Komives et al., 1996).

In other words, empowerment is claimed ("I have a legitimate right to be here and say what I feel and think") as well as shared with others ("You should be involved in this;

you have a right to be here too; tell us what you think and feel"). For young people, expressing their feelings and ideas, when they differ from others, can be challenging because they are working so hard to find their place in the world in relation to everyone else. They have a need to be different, but they also desperately want to fit in. What is crucial is that leaders of youth programs demonstrate that everyone in the program is a valued member. The leader should strive to develop a sense of membership or belonging among all group members, but also encourage everyone to express him or herself and participate so that the group can learn and grow from the ideas held by each individual.

Central to the issue of empowerment is the idea of power. Program leaders must be willing to share power with young people, and young people must be willing to assume responsibility for group outcomes within the program. The traditional approach to youth work is that the adult leader is in charge, but this approach fails to develop leadership skills in young people who desperately need a place where they can assume a leadership role. Program leaders must strive to collaborate with young people in order to empower all group members to become active program participants.

Being Purposeful in Youth Programs

A third aspect of relational leadership is being purposeful. Youth leaders, more often than not, choose activities in their programs based on the need to keep young people busy.

Rarely do youth workers (mostly because of time and resources) choose the activities in a purposeful manner. In others words, it is rare that program leaders consider what benefit youth might gain, or even what negative outcomes might be generated, while participating in certain activities. It is generally believed that anything that a youth worker chooses to do will be inherently better than what a young person may do on his or her own.

This attitude is unacceptable. Youth workers must make a commitment to being purposeful in their actions within youth programs. Group activity should be chosen intentionally for the purpose of benefiting the young people who will be participating in the activity. This should be done by seeking to understand the interests of the youth, finding a common direction for the group as a whole, and building a sense of common vision in relation to group activity.

It is not what program leaders choose to do in youth programs that should be of initial concern, but rather how it is being done. This requires program leaders to have an understanding of how certain activities or experiences will benefit young people, and then to purposely choose those activities that they see as being most useful.

Ideal and Unrealistic or Real and Possible?

A common response by youth workers to those who suggest a certain way of being in youth programs, as has been proposed in this article, is "what you're suggesting is ideal."

There is a belief that when working with young people there simply must be established rules to which youth must conform, whether they like the rules or not, for their own good; that youth cannot, and should not, be trusted with making decisions in programs or sharing in the leadership responsibilities. It is almost as though the worst is expected of young people, and that they simply require the guidance of an adult in order to choose the "right" thing to do.

This perception of young people is precisely why youth leaders need to strive to be different. In order to be effective program leaders, they must strive to create respectful and meaningful relationships with the young people in their programs. In schools, adults can get away with, although it is not developmentally beneficial, an autocratic brand of leadership or instruction; however, in youth programs, where participation is voluntary, relationships are much more central to the effectiveness of adults. Adults simply cannot ignore the significance of their relationships with young people and expect them to follow them just because they're in a leadership position. For this reason, it is crucial that youth workers strive to make the principles suggested by the relational leadership framework a reality.

Leadership and Serving Others

Youth leaders work in service to others. In the leadership literature, the idea of servant leadership emerged based on the writings of Robert Greenleaf (1977). Greenleaf

promoted the idea that servant leadership involves the creation of caring
environments which emphasize
teamwork, shared problem solving,
and community building. The idea
of servant leadership is drawn from
a Christian theological perspective.
At the Last Supper of Jesus with his
disciples, he washed their feet as a
symbolic gesture of friendship and
equanimity. In doing so, Jesus promoted a sense of community in
which all shared, rather than the
hierarchical relationship that we find
in many groupings. Thus the idea of
servant leadership was established
from a Judeo-Christian perspective.

Youth workers as servant leaders work to assist the development
of youth. Their role is one of creating a nurturing, supportive
relationship, in contrast to a more
controlling leadership style. The
youth leader as a servant worker sees
his or her role as one of giving support, providing encouragement, and,
in general, affirming youth. In the
process of affirming youth, the
youth worker as a servant leader
seeks to find value in all individuals. They promote a sense of empathy
for others as well as a sense of par-
ity and equanimity. From this
perspective, the youth worker attempts to free his or her personal
bias in such a way as to compassionately embrace others.

DeGraaf, Jordan, and DeGraaf
(1999) have suggested that servant
leadership is an affective strategy for
the human services. They write that
servant leadership ". . .emphasizes
increased service to others and a
sense of community." They further
note that such services focus the

work of professionals on a desire to
help people. In Greenleaf's model of
servant leadership, he emphasizes
characteristics such as listening,
empathy, healing, awareness,
persuasion, conceptualization, fore-
sight, stewardship, commitment to
the growth of others, and community building. As indicated, youth
workers employing servant leadership work to create ethical, caring
environments based on teamwork,
affirming impartially the essence of
others, and building a sense of fellowship between and among youth
workers and youth.

SUMMARY

Leadership is a central and
important component of youth work.
Leadership can be thought of as process of influencing others. It involves
building relationships, inspiring others, building values, promoting
democracy, encouraging collaboration, and serving others. Creating the
opportunity for youth to engage in
conversation with youth workers is
an important process and product of
youth work. Today, more than ever,
youth need the opportunity to engage in a dialogue with an adult, to
express their feelings, concerns, and
hopes for the future. Within the process of conversation, youth workers
seek to assist youth to reflect on
their actions. This is known as praxis
and is a very powerful way of shaping youth's perceptions of how they
live their lives. Leaders also influence youth simply with their
presence. Youth leaders have intangible qualities that influence their
interactions with youth. They live

out their values and beliefs through their actions, and these in turn can have an impact on the lives of youth.

REFERENCES

Belasco, J. A., & Stayer, R. C. (1993). *Flight of the buffalo*. New York, NY: Warner.

Blake, R. R., & Mouton, J. S. (1978). *The new managerial grid*. Houston, TX: Gulf.

Burns, J. M. (1978). *Leadership*. New York, NY: Harper & Row.

Covey, S. R. (1989). *The seven habits of highly effective people*. New York, NY: Simon & Schuster.

DeGraaf, D. G., Jordan, D. J., & DeGraaf, K. H. (1999). *Programming for parks, recreation, and leisure services: A servant leadership approach*. State College, PA: Venture Publishing.

de Oliveira, W., Edginton, S. R., & Edginton, C. R. (1996, January). Leader presence. *Journal of Physical Education, Recreation and Dance, 67*(1), 38-40.

Edginton, C. R., Hudson, S. D., & Ford, P. M. (1999). *Leadership in recreation and leisure service organizations*. Champaign, IL: Sagamore Publishing.

Eisler, R. (1995). *Sacred pleasure*. New York, NY: Harper

Greenleaf, R. (1977). *Servant leadership: A journey into the nature of legitimate power and greatness*. New York, NY: Paulist Press.

Hersey, P., & Blanchard, K. (1977). *Management of organizational behavior: Utilizing human resources* (3rd ed.). Englewood Cliffs, NJ: Prentice-Hall.

Jeffs, T., & Smith, M. K. (1999). *Informal education: Conversation, democracy and learning*. Ticknall, Derbyshire: Education Now Publishing Cooperative Limited.

Kiely, R. (Ed.) (1996). *The Good Heart: A Buddhist Perspective on the Teachings of Jesus*. Boston, MA: Wisdom Publications.

Komives, S. R., Woodward, D. B. Jr., & Associates (1996). *Student services: A handbook for the Profession* (3rd ed.). San Francisco, CA: Jossey-Bass.

Kouzes, B., & Posner, K. (1995). *The leadership challenge: How to keep getting extraordinary things done in organizations* (2nd ed.). San Francisco, CA: Jossey-Bass.

Lewin, K., Lippitt, R., & White, R. K. (1939, May). Patterns of aggressive behavior in experimentally created social climates. *Journal of Social Psychology, 10*, 271-299.

Mabey, C. (1994). Youth leadership: Commitment for what? In S. L. York & D. J. Jordan (Eds.), *Bold ideas: Creative approaches to the challenge of youth programming*. Cedar Falls, IA: Institute of Youth Leaders, University of Northern Iowa.

Magnuson, D., & Randall, S. (2002). *ECHOES after school learning programs: A first report*. Cedar Falls, IA: Institute of Youth Leaders, University of Northern Iowa.

Maslow, A. (1978). *Motivation and personality* (3rd ed.). New York, NY: Addison-Wesley.

Rost, J. C. (1993). *Leadership for the twenty-first century*. Westport, CT: Praeger.

Russell, R. V. (2001). *Leadership in recreation.* Boston, MA: McGraw-Hill.

Stogdill, R. M., & Coons, A. E. (1957). *Leader behavior's description and measurement.* Columbus, OH: Bureau of Business Research, Ohio State University.

Wheatley, M. J. (1992) *Leadership and the new science.* San Francisco, CA: Berrett-Koehler.

Mentoring Youth

INTRODUCTION

Effective youth development programs often offer young people opportunities to develop positive relationships that connect them to peers and adults in their communities (Villarruel, Perkins, Borden, & Keith, 2003). These peers and adults may exhibit qualities that are important for youth to grasp and understand in their development. One example of an effective program arrangement highlighting this concept is mentoring.

This chapter is focused on mentoring as an important element of youth development and youth work. Specifically the chapter will discuss the origins, common concepts and processes, programmatic models, and conceptual difficulties associated with mentoring as an approach to youth work. Each of these topics are critically important to understanding mentoring as an effective approach to working with young people.

WHAT IS MENTORING?

Mentoring is a unique program arrangement involving the care of youth as the primary purpose of design (Rauner, 2000). A mentoring relationship can occur between a coach and a player, a teacher and a student, and a youth worker and a youth. "Mentoring relationships comprise a special category of caring relationships, distinguished by their intensity, their developmental focus, and their impact on a young person's development into adulthood" (Rauner, 2000, p. 83). A mentor may come from the same demographic, socioeconomic, or ethnic background as the youth. A mentor is a friend, overseer and confidante; this person, at times, is the "conduit" for the youth's introduction into young adulthood.

Walker (2001) describes this conduit as a need for a caring adult, someone who will guide and challenge a young person as he or she journeys the path toward maturity. A mentor serves as a partner to a young person along the path of life, aiding in his or her understanding of right and wrong and the consequences that result from his or her actions. A mentor is as involved with the youth's joy of successful accomplishments and the pain of setbacks as if those decisions and results were his or her own.

A properly mentored youth, or "mentee," receives important knowledge, guidance, and care on succeeding in life from the mentor. This success can include proper communication skills, behavior management techniques, and conflict resolution methods. A mentee receives knowledge and also is a receptor for past personal interactions and thoughts of the mentor. A mentor may use past actions or decisions to illustrate an important point to the mentee.

However, the process of mentoring should not be thought of as the simple transmission of knowledge from a mature adult to a young person, but rather as a process of sharing life experiences and mutual understanding. Mentoring adults are not simply a vehicle through which the young are shaped and molded to fit some social ideal. Mentoring is about the development of self, something that can only occur between two individuals sharing beliefs, goals, struggles, and other life situations. The mentor helps a young person make sense of the elements of his or her life, and at times, a young person does the same for his or her mentor.

Mentoring experiences are not only beneficial for the youth, but also for the mentor. Delgado (2002) stresses the rewards that mentors receive in their relationship with the mentee. One of these rewards is the concentration on bettering the future. Mentors are often adults who want to continue improving the quality of life for successive generations. A mentoring opportunity is one way to directly affect the well-being of a youth.

Erikson (1963) illustrated this direct focus for well being when discussing generativity in adults. Generativity is described as being productive in society. Generative adults want to help youth become active members of society; methods include guidance, modeling, and collaboration with youth (Kleiber, 1999). Mentoring is a way for adults to be productive and leave their "mark" on society by positively affecting youth (Logan, 1986). Adults who mentor youth understand that they are a part of a common goal with other youth workers to establish positive patterns of interacting with young people.

MENTORING PROGRAMS IN THE UNITED STATES

Today mentoring is gradually becoming known as one of the most effective approaches for working with young people in youth work settings. The idea of establishing and maintaining positive relationships with young people in order to meet their greatest needs (i.e., sense of belonging, care, guidance, friendship) has its roots in the process of mentoring that can occur between a young person and a caring adult. However, this idea is not new. In fact, the belief in the power of relationships to positively influence young people is a well-established understanding in the field of youth work in the United States.

The Origins of Youth Mentoring in the United States

The oldest and best known mentoring effort in the United States is the Big Brothers Big Sisters of America (BBBSA) youth development program. BBBSA traces its roots to the work of Ernest K. Coulter who helped organize the first Children's Court in New York City (Greif, 1997, p. 5). Coulter, in 1904, working as a clerk in that Children's Court, sifted through the court records and noticed that the majority of youth passing through New York City's criminal system were not only repeat offenders, but also came from fatherless homes. Coulter believed that the most powerful way to reach these young people would be to organize adults who would establish positive interpersonal relationships with them on a regular basis (Greif, 1997).

As Greif (1997) has outlined, Coulter took his concern to New York City's most influential business, professional, and community leaders. Coulter shared the stories of the young boys he had seen sentenced to reformatory institutions because of their criminal tendencies and pleaded with the church members:

> There is only one way to save a youngster and that is to have some earnest, true man volunteer to be his Big Brother, to look after him, help him do right, make the little chap feel that there is one human being in the great city who takes a personal interest in him, who cares whether he lives or dies. I call for a volunteer. (Cited in Greif, 1997, p. 5).

Forty men responded to Coulter's plea, promising to initiate a relationship with a boy from the Children's Court caseload. These mentoring activities spread throughout the city, and in 1909, several men, including Ernest, came together to form the first mentoring agency in the United States—Big Brothers of New York City, Inc. These efforts mark the first of their kind in the United States to reach young people through the process of mentoring (Greif, 1997).

Mentoring Today

The Big Brothers philosophy quickly spread throughout the United States, and today the agency serves more than 100,000 children each year. Since those first efforts in New York City, more than one million mentoring relationships have been initiated (Jekielek, Moore, & Hair, 2002). Today, nearly 4,500 mentoring programs exist throughout the United States, and mentoring has become the most scientifically validated approach to meeting the unique needs of young people-especially those young people identified as being "at risk" and with little hope of reaching adulthood successfully (Rhodes, 2002; Miller, 2001).

However, the approach of mentoring young people is not limited to youth serving agencies. Mentoring takes place in a wide variety of settings, including churches, schools, and athletic fields, as well as on street corners. Rather than being simply a style of programmatic structuring, mentoring today is more a philosophy, guiding those interested in being actively involved in the lives of youth—one emphasizing the importance and power of positive relationships.

This trend toward an increased interest in mentoring as a viable approach for working with young people has been fueled in a variety of ways. First, practitioners and researchers in the field of youth work are increasingly moving from a prevention orientation toward a relational orientation of youth work. Second, youth workers, recognizing the reality of the lives of many youth (e.g., divorced parents, impersonal school experiences, low-income home), have come to understand that meeting the relational needs of young people can positively influence youth academically and socially, as well as emotionally. Finally, a variety of recent evaluations of mentoring programs have suggested that such programs provide a safe and trusting environment in which young people and adults can initiate and maintain positive relationships (Rhodes, 2002).

THE CONCEPT OF MENTORING

The concept of mentoring includes promoting relationships between an experienced, healthy adult and a young person. Within these one-on-one relationships, adults are thought to foster the development of character and competence in young people (Rhodes, 2002). Emphasis is placed on the development of a close personal relationship over time, in which an adult actively seeks to get to know the young person's hopes, dreams, and beliefs, as well as his or her struggles and challenges, in order to assist the young person's individual development (Hamilton & Hamilton, 2004).

As Greif explains, mentoring involves, "a one-on-one relationship, the youth is given undivided attention. The focus is on the child and his or her thoughts, feelings, and dreams. This develops the child's sense of importance, self-esteem, and competence." (1997, p. 9). In this way, mentoring is conceptualized not as a one-time intervention, but rather as a series of relational experiences, established over time, that work to form a close, positive relationship between a young person and a positive adult role model that influences the developmental outcomes of a young person so that he or she is able to form successful adult tendencies.

This process is similar to the educational process described by psychologist Lev Vygotsky in his conception of the Zone of Proximal Development (Vygotsky, 1978).

Vygotsky maintained that the child follows the adult's example and gradually develops the ability to do certain tasks without help or assistance. The Zone of Proximal Development represents the difference between what the child can do with adult help and what he or she can do without guidance. The adult serves as a role model, presenting the child with possibilities and solutions to problems that he or she would not consider alone, challenging his or her current understandings.

Mentors are believed to help fill the gap between what young people are able to achieve on their own and what they might achieve with some guidance. Through the consistency of their giving and guiding, mentors are believed to, over the course of their relationships with young people, assist youth to places where they would not have been able to arrive alone. The justification for mentoring as a viable educational approach is that positive adult role models are able to help young people succeed as individuals and become the kinds of people they might not otherwise be (Hamilton & Hamilton, 2004).

EFFECTIVE MENTORING PROCESSES

A variety of processes have been found to be associated with the development of positive youth-mentor relationships. Achieving the positive results through the process of mentoring depends on promoting certain helping behaviors and quali-

ties in mentors. The helping behaviors and qualities most identified in the literature include: 1) consistency of time together; 2) commitment to relationship, 3) openness and honesty; 4) genuine concern and caring; and 5) participation (Hamilton & Hamilton, 2004; Beam, Chen, & Greenberger, 2002; Rhodes, 2002; Mahoney & Schweder, 2002; Miller, 2002; Jackson, 2001; Tierney, Grossman, & Resch, 1995). Each of these processes are described below.

- *Consistency of Time Together.* Effective mentors have been found to spend three to four hours a week with their protégés (Tierney et al., 1995). Consistency of time spent together, researchers argue, is the one of the most critical components of successful mentoring (Rhodes, 2002; Miller, 2002; Jackson, 2001; Tierney, Grossman et al, 1995). Without such consistency, mentors and mentees are unlikely to establish the closeness and trust necessary to advance their relationships to a state where the adult's guidance can contribute to the youth's life in a meaningful way (Hamilton & Hamilton, 2004).

- *Commitment to Relationship.* In addition to committing to consistently spending time with young people, effective mentors also have been found to commit to at least one year in the duration of their relationship with a youth. The commitment to establishing a long-term relationship with a youth is critically important. This has been found to be true because many of the youth participating in mentoring activities have a great deal of inconsistency in their lives, as well as because committing oneself to a youth demonstrates to a young person that he or she is important to someone, which translates into increased levels of perceived self-worth (Tierney, Grossman, & et al., 1995).

- **Openness and Honesty.** Successful mentoring relationships are believed to be characteristically open and honest (Beam, Chen, & Greenberger, 2002). Being open and honest means letting a young person see his or her mentor for the person he or she is, and vice versa (Greif, 1997). "It means being able to talk about and translate personal life experiences, good and bad. By being open and honest, a (mentor) encourages his (mentee) to do the same" (Greif, 1997, p. 28).

- **Genuine Concern and Caring.** Researchers stress the importance of mentors expressing their genuine concern for the well-being of the young people with whom they interact (Tierney, Grossman, et al., 1995; Greif, 1997). Typically, care in youth mentoring relationships is demonstrated through regular contact and open dialogue between mentors and youth (Grief, 1997). Spending time together, sharing life experiences, translating life experiences, and offering guidance in troubling situations, represent ways in which effective mentors have been found to communicate concern and care for the youth in their company (Mahoney & Schweder, 2002).

- **Participation.** Successful mentors have been described as taking an active role in their relationships with young people (Rhodes, 2002). This quality, more than any other, applies to how a match between a mentor and youth will go (Greif, 1997). Youth "often mirror back the involvement and interest their (mentors) put into the relationship. The more energy and enthusiasm a (mentor) displays, the more likely he is to get that same energy and enthusiasm back" (Greif, 1997, p. 29).

Each of the behaviors and qualities outlined above have been found to be attributes of successful youth-mentor relationships. Inversely, youth-mentor matches lacking these qualities often not only fail to establish perceived relational closeness, they often prove to create a many iatrogenic (untended negative) effects. Such negative outcomes of ineffective mentoring relationships have been found to include: 1) manipulation, 2) humiliation, 3) the abuse of power, (4) youth social withdrawal, and 5) youth anti-social behavior (i.e., fighting, rebellion) (Eby & McManus, 2002; Eby, McManus, Simon, & Russell, 2000). Establishing consistency of time spent together, relational commitment, openness and honesty, genuine concern and caring, and active participation has been found to be critically important for predicting the success of youth-mentor relationships (Hamilton & Hamilton, 2004; Beam, Chen, & Greenberger, 2002; Rhodes, 2002; Mahoney & Schweder, 2002; Miller, 2002; Jackson, 2001; Tierney, et al., 1995).

MODELS OF YOUTH MENTORING AND ADOLESCENT CHANGE

Competing perspectives on youth work have spawned a variety of models for developing and implementing youth mentoring programs. Specifically, the deficit and developmental models of youth work have been most influential in shaping efforts to mentor youth. A third model is unique to mentoring alone—naturally occurring mentoring. Each of these models offers a different perspective on the process of mentoring, as well as the role of adults in the lives of youth.

The Deficit Model of Mentoring and Adolescent Change.
The deficit model of mentoring and adolescent change has at its roots the influential work of psychologist G. Stanley Hall (1904). As noted in Chapter 2, Hall generalized the life experiences of young people as representing a period of challeng-

ing transitions. He theorized that young people "are on an emotional seesaw: giddy one moment and depressed the next, apathetic today and impassioned tomorrow" (Rice & Dolgin, 2002).

From this perspective, young people are characterized as "problems to be managed" (Roth, Brooks-Gunn, Murray, & Foster, 1998). Because the transition from childhood to adulthood is considered a turbulent one, the deficit model holds that "problems of mental and behavioral functioning (are) inevitable unless preventive action (is) instituted at developmentally propitious times" (Lerner, Brentano, Dowling, & Anderson, 2002). Adult intervention is believed to be necessary when youth deviate from the path of normal development in order to protect young people from experiencing ongoing developmental crises.

Mentoring from this perspective typically takes the form of structured mentoring programs, where youth who are considered to be "at risk" are matched with an adult who is to serve as a role model. Within this framework, mentors concentrate on helping youth develop the skills they currently lack. Mentors may model appropriate social behaviors, interpersonal skills, or other skills associated with maturity. The goal is to assist a young person back onto the path toward positive or normal development.

A central obstacle to providing such intervention efforts for youth, argues deficit model supporters, is the preoccupation of young people with establishing autonomy from their caregivers (Lerner et al., 2002). Because of young people's desire for separateness, their relations to those adults closest to them are characterized as conflicted and detached (Hall, 1904); and thus adult-youth relations, at least from the perspective of young people, lack trust and mutual respect (Rhodes, 2002).

The Developmental Model of Mentoring and Adolescent Change

The developmental model of mentoring and adolescent change holds the view that young people are "resources to be developed" (Lerner et al, 2002, p.15). Youth, like all human beings, are believed to be actively engaged in an ongoing process of personal development that occurs throughout one's life span. Adolescents are considered to be on the path to an "idealized personhood"—an adult status marked by making culturally valued contributions to self, others, and institutions" (Csikszentmihalyi & Rathunde, 1998, p.15).

Developmental researchers are focused on the "search for characteristics of individuals and their ecologies that, together, can be arrayed to promote positive developmental change" (Lerner et al, 2002, p.15). For example, the Search Institute offers a list of forty developmental assets argued to be important factors in the process of positive developmental transitioning (Benson & Pittman, 2001). The more "assets" present in the lives of young people, holds the developmentalist,

the better the chance of a young person maturing in a positive manner.

Mentoring from this perspective is focused on increasing positive developmental experiences in the lives of young people. Such experiences may include helping youth build a positive relationship with an adult, encouraging youth to interact with peers and family members in positive ways, and challenging young people to use their time in a productive manner. By increasing positive developmental experiences, argue developmentalists, young people are more likely to become the sorts of individuals society wishes them to be.

At the center of this point of view are physical groupings of people (e.g., social networks, groups, society, communities, culture), with a concentration on the relations that exist between the social contexts influencing the lives of young people. Developmentalists argue these social networks should be organized in such a way as to support and promote adolescent growth (e.g., offering opportunities for meaningful participation, skill development, positive personal relationships), for it is within these networks that young people are thought to learn the skills required in order to successfully transition into the adult world (Philip & Hendry, 2000).

Naturally Occurring Mentoring Relationships

Although the modern conception of mentoring is typically focused on structured mentoring practices (i.e., those relationships formed in structured organizations), naturally occurring mentoring has recently become of interest to researchers from various fields of study (e.g., communication studies, education, child and youth care) (Darling, Hamilton, Toyokawa, & Matsuda, 2002). This model of mentoring is focused on the supportive relationships young people develop with the significant adults in their lives within a variety of settings outside formal youth mentoring programs. From this perspective, mentoring is believed to occur naturally as young people establish close personal relationships with neighbors, superiors within work settings, ministers, teachers, or even family members (Darling et al., 2002).

Naturally occurring mentoring relationships are defined more broadly than are those taking place in structured settings (i.e., formal mentoring/youth programs). Naturally occurring mentoring relationships are defined as "powerful, supportive, emotional ties between older and younger persons in which the older member is trusted, loving, and experienced in the guidance of others" (Klaw & Rhodes, 1995, p. 553). On the surface, this definition of a mentoring relationship appears to be closely tied to those descriptions of structured mentoring relations; however there is a key distinction.

The naturally occurring model of mentoring relationships separates the image of a mentor from the act of mentoring (Klaw & Rhodes, 1995). In doing so, the model broadens the contexts in which a young person is thought to benefit from the guidance of a mentor. Mentors are not thought to influence a young person's development exclusively within a structured mentoring program, rather they are believed to exist in any setting where adults and youth are allowed to interact in a meaningful way (Rhodes, 2002).

THE STAGES AND DEVELOPMENT OF MENTORING RELATIONSHIPS

Youth mentoring relationships have been characterized as developing in a series of four stages (Ensher & Murphy, 1997). Each stage represents a quantitative change in the nature of the youth-mentor relationship; characteristically having more or less established relational openness and closeness (Rhodes, 2002; Ensher & Murphy, 1997). These stages are briefly described below.

- *Introductions.* Participants look for similarities and make judgments. A young person and his or her mentor actively seek to find common understandings, experiences, and interests. They are seeking to connect, at least on a superficial level, so that relational growth is possible.

- *Relationship Building.* Youth and mentor engage in positive activities that give them things to talk about and remember and opportunities to spend time together. Commitment to the mentoring relationship is crucial. The young person at this relational stage is trying to determine whether or not his or her mentor can be trusted and counted on, and whether or not he or she is truly interested in him or her as an individual.

- *Growth.* Through relatively open communication and role modeling, the mentor provides emotional and instrumental support to the young person. As shared experiences occur and mutual understanding is gained, the young person and his or her mentor are able to establish a positive mentoring relationship.

- *Maturation.* The pair focus on the youth's goals, and the mentor begins to derive benefits as well. Because care has been demonstrated and trust has been established, the adult mentor has more influence on the young person's life. It may be that the mentor has become an important confidant for the young person, someone that the youth trusts with thoughts and feelings that he or she may not be willing to share with anyone else in his or her social circle.

- *Transition.* The relationship declines or is redefined. Because of the circumstances of life, the mentoring relationship is forced to change. Possibly the young person has moved on to college or has become in-

volved in a variety of activities that make finding regular time to meet with his or her mentor more difficult. Regardless of the circumstances, all mentoring relationships reach a point in which the relationship changes from what it initially was.

This process of relational growth and development should not be thought of as a linear process. In fact, a mentor and youth may experience several of these stages at the same time. Rather, "These stages . . .serve as a compass for (mentors) to gauge their level of involvement, predict periods of instability, and assess progress" (Rhodes, 2002, p. 97). Each stage is thought to be an indication of the effectiveness of a youth-mentor relationship, and the knowledge one possesses of each stage can be used to understand a young person's relational behavior (Rhodes, 2002; Ensher & Murphy, 1997;).

For example, a relationship at the introduction stage is predictably not emotionally close or stable, and thus is most likely not as successful as mentoring relationships at other succeeding relationship levels. With such an understanding of a relationship, a mentor or mentoring program coordinator, is thought to be able to draw conclusions about the causes of a young person's behavior (e.g., a young person may be withdrawn during the introduction stage due to relational uncertainty).

BENEFITS OF MENTORING RELATIONSHIPS

Research investigating the benefits of mentoring relationships suggests that benefits are reciprocal (Rhodes, 2002). In other words, both youth and their adult mentors have been found to benefit from the relationships that they establish together. Adult mentors and youth may not experience the same types of benefits, but they have both been found to be positively influenced by the experiences that they share. Specific benefits to each, both youth and mentors, will be discussed below.

Mentoring Benefits for Youth

In a major evaluation of the influences of mentoring relationships on youth development, Tierney, Grossman, and Resch (1995) outlined the following ways in which youth benefit from their participation in mentoring relationships with adults: 1) educational achievement, 2) health and safety, and 3) social and emotional development.

First, youth are believed to benefit academically by improved school attendance, improved chances of going on to higher education; promotion of better attitudes toward others, including their parents; and, though minimally found in evaluation studies, an improvement in grades achieved (Tierney et al., 1995). Second, youth-mentor relationships have been found to benefit the health and safety of young people by preventing substance abuse and reducing negative youth behaviors, including fewer misdemeanors and felonies (Tierney et al., 1995). Third, mentoring relationships have been found to benefit the social and emotional development of youth by promoting positive social attitudes and relationships and improving perceptions of young people's self-worth (Tierney et al., 1995).

Mentoring Benefits for Adult Mentors

Evidence outlining the benefits of mentoring for adult mentors is less scientific, but it is no less prevalent in the literature. As an example, long-time Big Brother Irv F. Westheimer, founder of the second Big Brother agency in the nation, located in Cincinnati, Ohio, reflected on what his mentoring experiences meant to him: "Looking back over the years. . .feel that they (youth) have given me more than I have given them. They have given me added faith in myself. They have given me the greatest experience of my life" (Cited in Grief, 1997, p. 7).

Mentors have been found to describe the following benefits of their relationships with youth that lead to the development of perceptions such as those described above: 1) increased understanding of the experiences of young people today, and 2) increased understanding of their own childhood experiences. Each of these benefits have been described as contributing to adult mentors' perceived benefits of their relationships with their mentees; as young people and adult mentors share their lives with each other, mentors gain more clear understanding of the experiences of youth, thus promoting self-reflection on their own childhood experiences (Tierney et al., 1995).

SUMMARY

Mentoring has emerged as a viable way for a youth worker to become an influential member of a young person's social support group. Because of the relational disconnect that many young people experience in their daily lives, mentors are able to fulfill the vital need young people have to feel connected to a positive adult role model. By establishing positive relationships with youth, mentors are able to develop the trust and insight required in order to meet the unique needs of each individual young person. Youth programs, in a general sense, can never be programmed in such a way as to meet the needs of every young person. However, because of the close personal relationships they are able to establish, individual mentors can fill this void. They are able to enter the lives of young people in influential ways, often becoming the confidants young people need as they experience the struggles associated with growing up in today's complex society.

As the transition from a prevention orientation toward a more relationally based orientation continues to transform the field of youth work, it is likely that mentoring will continue to gain interest among youth work researchers and practitioners alike. The central focus on promoting positive youth-mentor relationships will continue to make mentoring an effective approach to youth work. However, the effectiveness of such efforts will be influenced by the philosophies and perspectives (e.g., deficit model, developmental model) adopted by program providers.

REFERENCES

Beam, M. R., Chen, C., & Greenberger, E. (2002). The nature of adolescents' relationships with their "very important" nonparental adults. *American Journal of Community Psychology, 30*(2), 305-325.

Benson, P. L., & Pittman, K. J. (Eds.), (2001). *Trends in youth development: Visions, realities, and challenges*. Boston, MA: Kluwer Academic Publishers.

Csikszentmihalyi, M., & Rathunde, K. (1998). The development of person: An experiential perspective on the ontogenesis of psychological complexity. In R. M. Lerner (Ed.), *The handbook of child psychology: Theoretical models of human development*, (5th ed., 635-684). New York, NY : John Wiley & Sons, Inc.

Darling, N., Hamilton, S. F., Toyokawa, T., & Matsuda, S. (2002). Naturally occurring mentoring in Japan and the United States: Social roles and correlates. *American Journal of Community Psychology, 30*, 245-270.

Delgado, M. (2002). *New frontiers for youth development in the twenty-first century: Revitalizing and broadening youth development*. New York, NY: Columbia University Press.

Eby, L. T., & McManus, S. E. (in press). Negative mentoring experiences from the mentor's perspective. *Journal of Vocational Behavior.*

Eby, L., McManus, S., Simon, S., & Russell, J. (2000). The protégé's perspective regarding negative mentoring experiences: The development of a taxonomy. *Journal of Vocational Behavior, 57,* 1-21.

Ensher, E. A., & Murphy, S. E. (1997). Effects of race, gender, perceived similarity, and contact on mentor relationships. *Journal of Vocational Behavior, 50,* 460-481.

Erikson, E. (1963). *Childhood and society* (2nd ed.). New York, NY: Norton.

Greif, R. S. (1997). *Big impact: Big brothers making a difference.* Boston, MA: New Hat Publishing.

Hall, G. S. (1904). *Adolescence: Its psychology and its relation to physiology, anthropology, sociology, sex, crime, religion and education.* New York, NY: Appleton and Company.

Hamilton, S. F., & Hamilton, M. A. (Eds.). (2004). *The youth development handbook: Coming of age in American communities.* Thousand Oaks, CA: Sage.

Jekielek, S. M., Moore, K. A., Hair, E. C., & Scarupa, H. J. (2002). *Mentoring: A promising strategy for youth development.* Washington, DC: Child Trends.

Klaw E. L., & Rhodes J. E. (1995). Mentor relationships and the career development of pregnant and parenting African-American teenagers. *Psychology of Women Quarterly, 19*(4), 551-562.

Kleiber, D. A. (1999). *Leisure experience and human development: A dialectical interpretation.* New York, NY: Basic Books.

Lerner, R. M., Brentano, C., Dowling, E. M., & Anderson, P. M. (2002). Positive youth development: Thriving as the basis for personhood and civil society. In R. M. Lerner, C. S. Taylor, & A. von Eye (Eds.), *New directions for youth development: Theory, practice and research: Pathways to positive development among diverse youth* (Vol.95). San Francisco, CA: Jossey-Bass.

Logan, R. D. (1986). A reconceptualization of Erikson's theory: The repetition of existential and instrumental themes. *Human Development, 29,* 125-136.

Mahoney, J. L., & Schweder, A. E. (2002). Structured after-school activities as a moderator of depressed mood for adolescents with detached relations to their parents. *Journal of Community Psychology, 30,* 69-86.

Miller, A. W. (2002). *Mentoring students and young people: A handbook of effective practice.* Sterling, VA: Stylus Publishing.

Philip, K., & Hendry, L. B. (1996). Young people and mentoring: Towards a typology? *Journal of Adolescence, 19,* 189-201.

Rauner, D. M. (2000). *They still pick me up when I fall: The role of caring in youth development and community life.* New York, NY: Columbia University Press.

CHAPTER NINE

Multiculturalism

INTRODUCTION

Multiculturalism in youth work is analogous to gazing at a paint palette and the canvas for which the colors will be applied. Each color has distinct characteristics, and when applied to the canvas begins to create a large piece of art. As the artist progresses through the work, there are multitudes of color combinations that can occur to reach the end product. The artist works and reworks the paints, looking for the best combination to create the masterpiece. There may be a large amount of one color and a dab of another, but together they form the final product.

Multiculturalism is the celebration of the different "colors" on the palette and how inclusion of the different colors can drastically improve the "canvas" of a youth's life. The artist is the youth worker—the inclusion of unique qualities from various cultures starts with him or her. The different colors themselves are the unique characteristics that each youth brings to the field of youth work. The application of the colors is how youth workers plan to incorporate these characteristics and qualities into their practice of multiculturalism. The piece of art is a program or service that involves the youth and youth workers, together with the plan of maintaining a multicultural perspective. The one difference is that with an artist, the final piece is completed with few alterations. The beauty of youth work is that there is no final piece of art; the different colors can always be reworked to benefit the youth population being served.

What is diversity? How can encapsulation affect the development of youth? What are some educational steps in helping youth develop an attitude of tolerance and acceptance of various cultures? These and other points are discussed in the following chapter on multiculturalism. To have a strong framework of understanding, we will analyze various concepts related to multiculturalism and see a few examples of youth work agencies that have created and implemented programs related to multiculturalism.

In this chapter, the meaning of diversity and the different characteristics that make up an individual are discussed. These characteristics are the foundation for the issues that are related to diversity that youth and workers may deal with on a daily basis. The discussion continues with a closer look at various detrimental actions related to multiculturalism—stereotyping, encapsulation, prejudice, discrimination, and ethnocentrism—and how these actions can adversely affect the growth of youth. In addition, the different points associated with culture are presented, as well as the idea of culture shock and how it can affect workers and youth. The chapter concludes by outlining what multicultural education is, the proper language and communication methods between workers and youth, and the pitfalls associated with not educating youth properly about the benefits associated with multiculturalism.

WHAT IS DIVERSITY? WHY IS IT IMPORTANT TO YOUTH WORK?

Youth workers often work with diverse populations, providing services to individual youth with varying characteristics, qualities, skills, abilities, and needs. It is essential that youth workers have

knowledge of the topic and concept of diversity. There are many issues related to the concept of diversity that impact youth and youth work. As youth work has evolved in the United States over the past one hundred years, the social, cultural, economic, and political melieu has evolved providing for the emergence of various issues relating to diversity. Such concerns provide a new and continually evolving context that influences the practice of youth work. As society continues to evolve, such issues shall continue to emerge, providing new and demanding challenges to the field of youth work. Knowledge of issues relating to diversity and the ways in which they influence youth work, is essential for effective professional practice. Various challenges have arisen in the quest to develop youth that can be viable members of a diverse community. Youth workers may have to address one or more of these issues when guiding youth in and out of the workplace.

In this chapter of the book, we will introduce a number of concepts and issues related to diversity. More specifically, we will discuss the concept of diversity and discuss primary and secondary characteristics that are related to diversity. In addition, topics related to diversity issues that youth workers must address when working with youth will be included. Some of the issues to be discussed include changing demographics, family structure, role and sexual orientation, racism, encapsulation, stereotyping, discrimination, prejudice, self-fulfilling prophecy, ethnocentrism, ethnorelativism, and the spread phenomenon.

Defining Diversity

Diversity is a celebration of differences among people that seek to encourage the appreciation of those differences in the pursuit of equality and fairness. (Hernandez, 1989 as cited in Jordan, 2001). Each youth possesses unique characteristics, or qualities, that define who he or she is; some of those are by choice and others are by nature. These characteristics provide youth workers with a glimpse of each youth's heritage, value system, or interests in life. Such characteristics are called primary and secondary characteristics of diversity.

An exploration of the primary and secondary characteristics related to diversity can be useful in impressions of individual youth (Loden & Rosener, 1991). We can think of a youth's primary characteristics as the individual qualities that others see, and which are usually beyond a person's control. Examples of primary characteristics are race, ethnicity, physical and mental abilities, and age. Primary characteristics are an integral part of how youth are socialized within the context of their environment. The way in which individuals act positively or negatively toward others is often based upon the primary characteristics of that person.

Secondary characteristics are equally important to understanding youth. We can think of secondary characteristics as the qualities of an individual that are within that person's control and are not visible to the eye. Once interaction is established between the youth worker and those he or she is engaging, sec-ondary characteristics often emerge and impact one's perception of the individual. Examples of secondary characteristics related to youth include such factors as one's economic status, geographic place of birth, and religion. Secondary characteristics are equally important in the process of understanding youth as individuals and influence our impressions of them.

An example of a program promoting diversity is the Diversity Initiative sponsored by the Boys and Girls Clubs of America. This program, offered in collaboration with the Anti-Defamation League (ADL) is organized as an initiative to teach youth and youth workers how to promote and celebrate diversity and combat and prevent prejudice, bigotry, and discrimination. The program has three elements. The first component is directed toward assisting youth workers to examinate their own biases and learn how to facilitate discussions about prejudice and discrimination. Designed as a staff development tool, this component also is aimed at helping individuals gain an awareness of and respect for others. The Boys and Girls Clubs of America, as its second component, has developed a guidebook that provides lessons and activities to foster a greater understanding and appreciation of diversity for youth. Last, a component focused on peer mentoring and a training program that assists youth to teach others in the community about dealing with diversity and discrimination, is included in the program (Boys & Girls Clubs of America, 1999).

Changing Demographics

As indicated in chapter one, we live in a more youthful society. When compared with 50 years ago, the number of adolescents in the United States has nearly doubled. This means that there are more youth, and that according to future estimates, that number will continue to increase. It is evident that their needs will have to be addressed, and not only programs and services are required, but also social policy enacted to support their needs. As this portion of the populations grows in relationship to others, their voice will be stronger, their economic power greater, and their social influence larger.

Not only is the percentage of youth as a part of the total population growing, but also America is becoming a more heterogeneous society. The size of the various ethnicities and races as a percentage of the total population is steadily increasing. McLoyd (1994) notes that as the population in the United States continues to grow, the influx of various ethnicities will continue to rise. As we enter the twenty-first century, the numbers of what are considered traditional minority groups will expand, with a majority of overall youth populations comprised of minority groups (McLoyd, 1994). As the composition of youth populations continues to diversify, youth development organizations may need to strongly consider hiring volunteers and workers who reflect the demographics of the youth involved with their programs and services. The following descrip-

tion of a program created by the Phoenix Parks, Recreation and Library Department illustrates factors relevant to youth today.

The City of Phoenix Parks, Recreation and Library Department has developed a number of unique educational and awareness programs aimed at instilling cultural pride. One of their services known as the Rights of Passage Program is focused primarily on helping youth make the transition from adolescence to adulthood. According to City of Phoenix Recreation Supervisor Rene Bera, "we give young people a chance to see the world is bigger than their neighborhoods, and that opportunities are available to them if they believe in themselves" (Vision 2000, p. 8). This sixteen-week instructional program promotes pride in self, family, and culture. At the conclusion of the program, youth are engaged in an inspiring ceremony celebrating their passage into adulthood. This organization's vision regarding diversity is one of creating a "mosaic in motion." Their goal is to foster and promote tolerance and understanding among youth. This organization believes that it is important to provide bold, creative, and innovative services that "...continually evolve to meet the societal and personal challenges that confront twenty-first- century youth" (City of Phoenix Parks, Recreation and Library Department, 2000).

Structure of the Family Unit

The construction of the family unit is an important factor related to diversity. The traditional two-parent nuclear family is not as prevalent today as in past generations. Today there are nearly ten million single parent households (U.S. Census, 2000). The present family structure is unique and varied, with examples including single parent, intergenerational parents, and foster care as a few examples. Youth workers should maintain an understanding that all youth are not raised with the same family framework as themselves, and that each individual framework carries with it meanings that the youth incorporates into their existence.

Changing Role and Sexual Orientation

Several school systems foster norms, values, and beliefs of intolerance and rejection for youth who are gay, lesbian, or bisexual (Nichols, 1999). This climate inhibits youth from developing a sense of acceptance and belonging, of feeling comfortable with who they are. This is also the time in a youth's life when they are forming their own identity and navigating through the different choices they can make in life. A welcoming climate, regardless of a youth's sexual orientation, encourages interaction with peers and breaks down barriers that may be constructed due to misinformation, stereotyping, prejudice, and discrimination.

Youth workers can facilitate an environment of acceptance by developing areas within a facility that are appropriate places to discuss and share about issues related to sexual orientation. If a youth is discriminated against due to their sexual orientation, a "diversity area" affords the opportunity to disclose feelings, thoughts and emotions related to the discriminatory acts (Nichols, 1999). A youth worker can spearhead the construction of a "diversity area" and the discussions that may occur within it. Facilitating discussions of this nature may require specific training, and it would be appropriate to research the data related to this topic.

Racism

America has a long history of racism. Although we have granted civil and other legal rights to promote equity and fairness for various groups in American society, we still are plagued with racism. Hazekamp and Popple (1997) define racism as the domination of one group over another based upon perceived racial differences. These racial differences may originate from beliefs involving the primary and secondary characteristics of an individual. Pedersen (1994) suggests that racism is a pattern of systematic behaviors resulting in the denial of opportunities or privileges to one group by another. He states there are two forms of racism: overt and covert. Overt racism is the intentional judgment of one group as inferior to another. Covert racism is unintentional, rooted in misinformation and wrong assumptions. It can interfere with youth work through actions of:

- Color-blindness—the youth worker's belief that all youth are treated equal.
- Color consciousness—the youth worker's belief that all the youth's problems are due

to his or her cultural background.

- Transference—the youth may transfer previous experiences with a specific culture to a worker representative of that culture.
- Countertransference—the youth worker may transfer previous experience with a specific culture to a youth that is part of that culture.

An examination of beliefs by the youth worker will help outline the steps needed to successfully interact with youth. Multicultural education, which will be discussed later in the chapter, is a move forward in shaping the proper procedures when working with youth.

Encapsulation and Associated Downfalls

Often youth and youth workers are insulated inside their own cultural context, deriving meaning from the symbols, rituals, customs, and norms of their given culture. As a result, this perspective often shapes their understanding of the world. This concept can potentially limit a youth worker's—as well as a given youth's—understanding of others from a different cultural context. This concept is known as cultural encapsulation.

Cultural encapsulation is referred to as ignoring certain cultures (Wrenn, 1962). Pedersen (1994) identifies five characteristics of cultural encapsulation: 1) reality is defined according to one set of cultural assumptions and stereotypes;

2) a person becomes insensitive to other cultures and assumes his or her view is the only correct way; 3) the individual's assumptions and stereotypes have no proof of validity; 4) technique-oriented jobs contribute to cultural encapsulation; and 5) when there is no evaluation of cultural variations, there is no responsibility to others except from the person's viewpoint. Cultural encapsulation is a lack of understanding other cultures due to the close-mindedness of the individual only seeing the world through his or her culture's "lenses."

Through encapsulation, individuals run the risk of excluding various cultures. Cultural groups may be excluded for a variety of reasons. For example, an individual may not have enough knowledge of a cultural group and perceive them as a risk. Lack of exposure, misguided information, and unreliable sources may lead to the misinterpretation of a cultural group. In addition, if an individual is not able to understand what someone from a different cultural group verbally communicates, the conclusion may be that the individual is not capable of being understood and should be avoided. This is unfortunate because the most important communication is nonverbal and the emphasis should be made to communicate in ways other than verbally. Last, it may take time to understand another culture, and in some cases people don't want to devote their time in that manner. For example, to build methods of communication can include agreement on actions, words, terms, and symbols. This can take several encounters with someone before basic patterns of communication are established, using time this way might be perceived as wasteful or unnecessary. The attitude can be one-way learning (that person should adjust to me) instead of two-way (we can find a medium for mutual understanding). Exclusion of cultures robs individuals of the opportunities to learn and experience traditions, customs, and practices and inhibits others from illustrating how significant their culture is to the societal framework. The following example illustrates the importance of discussing diversity early in youth's lives to avoid the dilemma of encapsulation.

The Multicultural Association of Fredericton, New Brunswick, Canada, offers a summer camp for youth ages six to eleven that focuses on social cohesion and developing harmonious relationships between youth of various backgrounds (MCAF, 2001). The philosophical foundation behind the Rainbow of Cultures Summer Camp is to create and execute an educational, cross-cultural experience for youth through fun summer activities. Campers have the opportunity to get to know others of differing ethno-cultural backgrounds in a fun and natural setting, creating friendships that often last longer than the duration of camp. The vision of the Multicultural Association of Fredericton is to sustain a supportive and proactive climate in which people of all backgrounds can come together for social interaction, economic self-sufficiency, and cultural enrichment, to make a creative contribution to the community and to take a stand on issues of common concern (MCAF, 2001). This vision is incorporated in the Rainbow of Cultures Summer Camp through meaningful exchanges and active participation of all the youth that attend the camp.

Stereotyping, Discrimination, and Prejudice

Youth are often engaged in conscious and unconscious stereotyping of their peers and others. Stereotyping is the habit of making rigid assumptions about others based upon the primary and secondary characteristics associated with diversity (Jordan, 2001; Sue & Sue, 1990). Stereotypes can be negative or positive, and are by no means always accurate (Pelled, Eisenhardt, & Xin, 1999). Such stereotyping may affect human behavior, thus affecting interactions between individuals from different cultures. Stereotypes are encouraged by denying their existence and subsequent effects on people's lives, ignoring or accepting when they occur, and supporting them through actions (King, Chipman, & Cruz-Janzen, 1994 as cited in Jordan, 2001). A downfall of stereotyping, that is detrimental to interaction, is the inability to recognize the unique differences of people, plus the limitless potential of growth experienced by the people interacting.

Youth workers can help youth overcome stereotyping by helping them become aware of their assumptions. For example, a youth worker may engage in active conversation with youth, guiding them in discovering the pitfalls associated with their assumptions about others. Still further, a youth worker can model the types of behaviors that embrace others regardless of their characteristics. Also, youth workers need to guard themselves, making sure that they do not engage in such stereotyping. It is often easy for a youth worker to slip unconsciously into behaviors wherein individual youth are viewed with some bias or favoritism.

Prejudice and discrimination are interrelated concepts within the discussion of multiculturalism that may play a significant part during the developmental stages of youth. Prejudice is the belief or preference of one person or culture over another. Prejudice can take the form of fear, anger, or hatred by one person towards another (Hirsch, Kett, & Trefil, 1993). Discrimination is the act of making a distinction about a person based solely upon prejudice, then upholding that distinction through actions toward that person, such as labeling or stigmatizing (Dattilo & Williams, 1999). Stigmatized individuals are confronted with preserving their self-esteem in the face of unmitigated claims of inferiority (Wallace & Wolf, 1991). While prejudice and discrimination may be witnessed in the actions of youth and youth workers, the introduction of multicultural education tactics and terminology may help alleviate prejudice and subsequent discrimination in youth and youth workers.

Self-fulfilling Prophecy

A youth worker may think that a certain youth in the program is incapable of participating in an activity. This perception may influence a youth's behavior in such a way as to limit or inhibit his or her opportunities. For example, a youth worker serving individuals with disabilities may perceive that these youth are limited in some fashion and incapable of higher levels of achievement, mastery of skills, or even advanced cognitive reasoning. These perceptions become a self-fulfilling prophecy wherein the youth worker's actions and language limit the participation and possible success of a youth.

According to Rosenthal and Jacobson (1968), a self-fulfilling prophecy occurs when one person's expectations become an accurate prediction of another person's behavior. The interaction between the youth worker and a youth may include verbal and nonverbal communication (e.g., little positive feedback, facial expressions, body language) that influences the youth's participation in the activity. As a result, the youth does not participate in the activity, which reinforces the worker's belief.

Youth workers need to guard against participation in self-fulfilling prophecy when working with youth. Youth workers need to see and encourage possibilities for youth, and not be enveloped by perceived limitations. Ways to support youth and avoid self-fulfilling prophecy include active verbal and nonverbal support, continuous unconditional encouragement, and finding ways to empower youth to fulfill their potential. Youth workers should engage youth in such a way as to expand their horizons by broadening their exposure to the world around them.

Spread Phenomenon

Closely related to the idea of the self-fulfilling prophecy is that of the "spread phenomenon." Picture yourself working with a youth that you perceive to be in trouble, imperfect, and at risk. How does this perspective influence your association and interaction with the youth? The metaphors that we create in our minds to help us visualize the needs of youth have great impact upon our work with youth. If we see them in a certain light—for example, rebellious and needing to be controlled, versus being at the forefront of cultural change by providing fresh new perspectives—this will influence our response to the youth. If the initial position is adopted, then one's efforts as a youth worker will be focused on attempting to control the behavior of youth to conform and comply with society's existing norms, customs, rituals, and rules. On the other hand, if we view youth culture as contributing in a positive way to the progressive movement of culture, then youth and their perspectives and ideas will be embraced, encouraged, and welcomed.

The spread phenomenon helps us understand that there may be a link or connection between one's perception of a given characteristic and how we think that this factor may spread to other behaviors. Further, the spread phenomenon suggests that one's perception is usually negative, in that the association that is often made by individuals carries a negative connotation from one context to another. Such associations have no legitimate basis or grounding. The spread phenomenon has been viewed in the literature as the association of imperfections with certain characteristics of an individual (Tripp & Sherrill, 1991). Originally used in discussions regarding people with disabilities, this can be carried over to the field of youth development. Youth workers should be careful not to adhere to this concept, for example, correlating overly aggressive behavior to the ethnicity of the youth. There is no significance in this relationship, but what occurs is a misassociation of one characteristic to others.

Ethnocentrism and Ethnorelativism

Youth workers often are confronted with actions, language, and behaviors that suggest that one individual feels superior to another. In fact, our society encourages such behavior. The encouraging of rivalries that are manifested in positive as well as negative ways contributes to this end. Feelings of superiority as evidenced in competition, creation of identity markers, as well as deprecating comments regarding others, all contribute to the establishment of ethnocentric behaviors. On the other hand, youth workers can work to lessen the impact of such behaviors and promote greater acceptance, tolerance, and value of others. This is the opposite of ethnocentric behavior and is referred to as ethnorelativism. Ethnorelativism promotes a more egalitarian perspective of others.

Ethnocentrism is the belief that one cultural group is superior to other inferior groups; that one group is the standard to which all other groups are measured (Spencer & Swanson, 2000; Wildemeersch & Redig, 1997). It is a belief that is rooted in negative attitudes towards others because of a desire to maintain one's own self-esteem. Youth and youth workers may use discriminatory actions to illustrate their preference of one culture as superior to others. Inclusion and the resulting exclusion of specific individuals in programming and activities, language and whether it is derogatory in nature, and favoritism can be signals of a preference in the youth development field. Avoidance of these actions may include training and education on the different facets associated with multiculturalism.

Ethnorelativism is the ability to understand individuals in the context of their own cultures—to not judge those individuals as inferior or superior based upon one cultural perspective, but to understand the social atmosphere that surrounds them and how they interact with it. Giroux uses the term "border crossers"—this means an individual going outside of the traditional mindset associated with his or her own cultural identity and attempting to relate to other cultural constituencies; to understand the partiality of his or her own views (Giroux, as cited in Banks, 2000). The enemy to multiculturalism is the inability to act in an ethnorelative manner and understand the various contexts in which cultures are witnessed. It is difficult for individuals to cease judging other cultures from their own natural perspective and to interpret actions in a multicultural manner (Pedersen, 1994).

WHAT IS CULTURE?

Why discuss culture and youth work? For a youth worker to operate in an effective fashion, he or she must have a deep understanding of the cultural context in which he or she operates. Further, knowledge of a youth's culture can help the youth worker in assisting other youth in understanding the various qualities and perspectives that exist in diverse social environments. An important role that youth workers play is creating understanding between individuals and providing informal learning environments that enable youth to gain greater awareness and tolerance of others. Youth workers often play the role of not only providing information to youth, but also serving as a pathway or conduit through which the culture of one youth is presented to another. This bridging of cultures becomes an integral part of youth work and helps promote greater understanding between individuals of different cultural contexts.

The term culture, according to Smith and Bond (as cited in Imam, 1999), is an organized system of shared meanings that are attributed to a certain group of individuals. The members who make up the culture give the meanings to that culture and pass those meanings on to subsequent generations (Peregoy & Dieser, 1997). The characteristics associated with culture are derived from the interactions of individual members of that specific group. Within the cultural context of youth development, there are certain meanings and interactions specific to that group. Knowledge of these meanings and interactions pave the way to greater understanding and appreciation of others and their cultures.

What is Culture Shock?

Youth workers and youth are both susceptible to culture shock. When we have encounters with other environments that carry different meanings from our own, we may experience culture shock. In an increasingly diverse society, the probability of culture shock occurring has increased. It is very likely that youth workers and youth will be placed in various social, cultural, economic, religious, and even political contexts that will be different or foreign to their current context. Most individuals operate comfortably within their own cultural context. However, inevitably there will be occasions when a youth worker or youth finds himself or herself outside of his or her cultural comfort zone. When this happens, culture shock may occur.

We can think of the concept of culture shock as a profoundly personal encounter with individuals from a different culture (Pedersen, 1994). Each person's experience with culture shock is unique and different. There are five stages that individuals pass through that characterize culture shock: initial contact, disintegration, reintegration, autonomy, and independence (Pedersen, 1994). Initial contact refers to the unique and exciting experiences a person has upon encountering a culture that is different from their own. Disintegration refers

to the "breakdown" of confidence of a person from the overwhelming nature of their encounter. Reintegration is the "fighting back" of the individual towards the culture they initially experienced. Autonomy is a reassurance of the person's confidence and identity, that the similarities and differences of the cultures are accepted and satisfactory. Finally, independence occurs in the form of a multicultural identity and an understanding of how to act in the different cultures experienced. From the first phase of initial contact with a different culture to the final phase of independence, there is a progressive change in the person rooted in their exposure to something wholly different than what they have experienced before in life. Some indicators witnessed during culture shock include anxiety, discomfort, helplessness, nostalgia for past comfortable experiences, and a loss of understanding how to behave.

Youth workers may experience culture shock as they transition between youth populations in the field. A worker may be accustomed to working with school-age children, and then move to a position working with youth. The characteristics of youth are different than young children, and this may cause a feeling of discomfort or anxiety in the worker as they interact. Techniques that may have worked with the former population may not work with the youth, and the worker may question his or her ability or future success. As indicated in the steps associated with culture shock, perseverance is vital to working with different cultures. Acknowledging and accepting the cultural characteristics will ease the transition for the worker, improving his or her understanding of the population in the field. There are several ways that culture shock may be experienced—between different age groups, ethnicities, ability levels, and geographic locales are just a few examples.

WHAT IS MULTICULTURALISM?

Increasingly, we live in a multicultural society. As indicated, the great American melting pot is giving way to a new perspective, calling for a greater recognition and valuing of individual cultures. In Canada, the metaphor of the melting pot is not employed but rather the notion of the separate ingredients that comprise a salad bowl is embraced. We are all together in the salad bowl, but each ingredient retains its individual identity, integrity and flavor. It is becoming important to think about the implications of the differences inherent in these two approaches to building our culture in America.

According to McFadden (1993), multiculturalism can be thought of as an ongoing awareness of all cultural and individual identities. Also, multiculturalism has been described as an attempt to stress and protect the cultural variety within a society, or to respond to the needs of everyone (Popple, 1997). Individuals experience the differences and similarities between themselves and others and how important each

person's culture is in the composition of society. The unique qualities each person has are embraced and recognized as important in their development. Individuals who are multicultural can improve their own well being by actively participating in various cultural activities and traditions, therefore expanding their knowledge base of the population that surrounds them.

What Are the Implications for Youth Development?

Youth workers can practice different techniques when working with youth representing multiple cultures. A multicultural perspective is useful and is readily applied in youth work. For example, if there are conflicts, difficulties, or actions among individuals that seem inappropriate, they may be analyzed from the worker and the youth's cultural perspectives. If there is resistance in behavior management, conflict resolution, or group dynamics issues with a youth, it is important to recognize that resistance may be due to the makeup or framework of their cultural group. The resistance may include a response towards the youth worker that may not be usual or expected. The worker should not interpret this negatively and react in a defensive manner; this is an opportunity for the individual to exhibit their multicultural attitude.

Youth often react in an honest, sometimes brutally honest, manner (Hansel, 1979). One method of reaction by the worker may include becoming defensive and being distracted from the discussion point.

The alternative is to recognize the youth may be reacting as he or she has learned from the other individuals in his or her cultural group, and that he or she is not attacking the worker on a personal level. Taking this stance will ease the tension and hostility a worker may feel towards a youth's comments or reactions.

How Can We Develop Multicultural Informal Education Strategies?

The initial step in educating youth development workers in multiculturalism is to encourage adjustment of negative or detrimental attitudes (Dattilo & Williams, 1991). The amount of interactions between workers and youth are just as important as the quality of the interactions. Youth workers who have stereotypical attitudes and beliefs hinder the development of themselves and the youth they encounter through stigmatized interaction and communication. Youth workers who understand and are open to diverse cultures provide youth with a strong support system to lean on in times of need (Lightfoot, Mukherjee, & Sloper, 2001).

Wildemeersch and Redig (1997) add that multiculturalism develops within youth work when there are lively (meaning active) social networks between youth development organizations and individuals. These networks help establish competence in youth development by introducing a variety of cultural characteristics to individuals within youth development. The interconnectedness of organizations and youth workers establishes a knowledge base to foster sensitivity, and to address injustices directed towards cultures, and to avoid a state of anomie.

Anomie is a state of normlessness in the environment, when individuals have goals but do not have the means to attain them (Durkheim, 1951). In social situations, there are conditions or norms that manage behavior and interaction. Youth may have certain goals they would like to accomplish, but if there is cultural intolerance that adversely affects them, the customary norms for success may be altered. Individual youth may have the same desires as other youth, but if they are discriminated against because of their characteristics, ability level, or ethnicity, this will alter their accomplishment of goals. This will in turn foster an environment that illustrates a deviation from the norms, which can lead to reactionary tactics by the youth that affects themselves and possibly others.

Lerner (1995) contends that for successful multicultural education to occur, youth development stakeholders should develop an agenda that incorporates research on multiculturalism gathered by scholars. Interdisciplinary efforts may occur between different schools of thought, such as leisure, youth and human services, and child psychology. Bringing together academicians may increase the amount of research that impacts youth development. This research should be coupled with the creation and implementation of policies and programs as discussed in Chapter 10, as well as involving collaborative efforts among agencies and individuals. Research related to youth development should have a pragmatic result; once the data is gathered, it is imperative that it be used to benefit the individuals that work directly with youth.

Kraus (2001) discusses the different programmatic options youth workers have to emphasize development of a multicultural attitude. Involvement in programs devoted to the arts can introduce youth to various cultural traditions. Opportunities such as choral groups, storytelling, theater, dance, festivals, and arts and crafts fairs expose youth and create an awareness of the history and cultural contributions many groups have to society.

The Minnesota Multicultural Youth Corps is an opportunity for youth to learn about different cultures, lead in a variety of settings, and develop an awareness of societal barriers that inhibit diversity (2001). Some of the activities facilitated by the Minnesota Multicultural Youth Corps include learning Native American dancing, going on trips to exciting and important cultural events, visiting community cultural centers, and conducting peer cultural awareness days. The goals of the Minnesota Multicultural Youth Corps include fostering an understanding of diversity and social change issues through interaction with other youth from diverse backgrounds and community members who are educators in these areas. Education can include team building, discussions on cultural issues, workshops, retreats, and training. The mission of the Minnesota Multicultural Youth

Corps is to empower youth to make a positive impact on communities through multicultural understanding and collaborations.

As discussed earlier in the chapter, one method to introduce and promote cultural awareness is to develop a "multicultural area" within the youth development organization (Nichols, 1999). This area should be a space that promotes tolerance and understanding of cultures evident in society. Characteristics of the area should include a welcoming, comforting environment, an opportunity for confidentiality if needed, trained workers who can interpret and understand cultural issues, and an up-to-date resource library stocked with educational materials. The multicultural area is a place for continual learning by youth as well as workers.

Terminology and Nomenclature Used in the Field

The language employed by youth workers is important in encouraging multiculturalism. For after all, it is through our language that we symbolically communicate our intentions, prejudices, biases, and even hope for the future. Dattilo and Williams (1999) discuss the appropriateness, courtesy, and accuracy of terminology or language when interacting with diverse populations. These authors suggest that it is important to use language that is respectful of others. Putting the youth before their identifying characteristics illustrates that the youth is not defined by a single attribute.

A youth worker who is Caucasian once had an experience at a historic and predominantly black university where he gazed out into an audience of 125 individuals, all but two of who were African-American. At first blush, his perspective was to identify an individual by his primary characteristic. In the context of his cultural experience, when encountering a person of a different race he often would identify the individuals by their racial color. In viewing his audience he could not point to that "black person". They were all black, and he was forced to change his perspective and look at the unique characteristics of each individual. For him this was a life altering experience, an epiphany that provided him with greater understanding of the importance of not identifying people by the color of their skin, but rather by the quality of their character (King, Jr., 1963).

By employing appropriate terminology and nomenclature, the youth worker may be able to interact with youth in a fashion that recognizes their intrinsic individual worth and value. Further, the youth worker models, through his or her communication, a way of embracing and recognizing the uniqueness of others. Through such actions, values are passed on to others that have the potential to influence their behavior. The youth worker who is respectful of youth is viewed by youth as a role model they can emulate and a standard by which they can pattern their own communication style and hence attitudes and actions towards others.

What is Multicultural Communication?

Multicultural communication helps us understand our differences and similarities. An understanding of the process of communication is essential in establishing mutually beneficial relationships between youth workers and youth. It is also critically important for youth to build such relationships among one another. As Jordan (2001) indicates, there are several components to the communication process: 1) the sender, or the initiator of the communication; 2) the message, or content of the communication; 3) the channel, or method of communication; 4) the receiver, or recipient of the communication; and 5) the feedback, or reaction of the receiving the communication. For effective communication to occur in youth development, the worker and the youth must be able to send and receive verbal and nonverbal messages accurately and appropriately.

What is the goal of multicultural communication? As indicated, multicultural communication helps the youth worker and youth embrace and understand the similarities and differences between cultures. Further, such communication provides channels of communication that are understood and link all parties involved. Sue and Sue (1990) illustrate several factors within the multicultural communication process. They include the following:

- **Nonverbal communication.** Youth workers should recognize the different meanings of nonverbal communication and how it may vary across cultures. Many cues, such as posture, body language, clothing, hairstyle, and time considerations differ between cultures.

- **Proxemics.** This is the study of personal and interpersonal space. The distance between individuals during communication may be greater or less than what the worker is used to in his or her culture.

- **Kinesics.** This describes the use of body movement as a communication tool. Certain body movements, including eye contact, facial expressions, posture, and gestures have been connected to specific cultures.

- **Paralanguage.** Paralanguage refers to vocal cues outside of language that are used to communicate. These cues include loudness of voice, pauses, hesitations, rate, pitch, and inflection (Jordan, 2001).

- **High/low context communication.** High-context (HC) communication is a verbal message that relies heavily on nonverbal cues and group understanding for successful interpretation. Low-context (LC) communication is a message that places strong emphasis on the verbal aspect.

The Mentor Training and Consulting Center of the United Way in Morris County, New Jersey facilitates an educational program involving how to mentor youth that addresses diversity and multiculturalism (personal communication, JoAnn Tsonton, May 2, 2003). The trainers work with the participants in the program in approaching the topic of diversity and multiculturalism as more than just race, ethnicity, age and gender. The discussions and educational sessions include other components of multiculturalism such as communication styles, interaction styles, family status, working style, and personal experiences. The program includes exercises illustrating the importance of strong personal values and how the topic of multiculturalism can influence the formation of those values. The mentors learn to not impose their values on youth, but to allow the youth to test their own values through exploration of why they act and feel in certain ways related to others. The mentor provides guidance for youth, but doesn't smother or inhibit the youth's opportunity to experiment and learn in a healthy manner related to growth.

Within the context of youth development, workers may need to adjust their communication styles to interact more constructively with youth (McFadden, 1993). Being flexible and moving outside the traditional methods of communication improves the opportunity to build successful relationships with youth. The aforementioned factors require a global examination of how workers send and receive information to colleagues and youth.

What are Barriers to Multicultural Communication?

There are a variety of assumptions and differences that can hinder effective communication between youth and youth workers. The "mosaic" composition of the youth population, of young people coming together with their unique individual qualities and together forming a group, affords workers the opportunity to either progress or remain stagnant in their development of multicultural communication. Pedersen (1994) illustrates several barriers that can affect multicultural communication and how youth workers can avoid these pitfalls:

- *Assumed similarity.* Assuming similarity between cultures is a method of diminishing the importance and unique differences in individual cultures. Sue & Sue (1990) define this as an assumption that different cultural groups operate and communicate in identical ways. Workers who investigate and learn about the cultures represented by the youth population they serve will be less apt to assume similarities. Understanding the important characteristics of each culture, enables workers and youth to build important relationships.
- *Language differences.* Not every worker speaks the same language as the youth they encounter. Some techniques to improving communication include learning the language spoken by the youth, asking for clarification if there is un-certainty about what was said, and, if it is not possible to learn the language, finding someone who does speak it to work with the youth.

- *Nonverbal communication differences.* Nonverbal communication techniques vary when analyzed across cultures. Something may be insulting in one culture, but not in another. Successful nonverbal communication includes an understanding of the different techniques used by all cultures encountered, including the youth worker's own culture.

- *Preconceived notions and stereotypes.* These consist of generalizations or assumptions with little relevancy about cultures. Avoiding quick judgments, reinterpreting behavior of youth from other cultures, and changing perceptions about cultures are ways to dispel these categorizations.

- *Evaluation and judgment of communication content.* This includes being subjective instead of objective about the communication received. Workers should remain objective and not judge the youth's actions verbally and nonverbally by what is considered proper in their own culture.

- *Anxiety related to unfamiliarity.* Many youth may encounter unfamiliar or foreign environments or customs during their development. It is imperative to allow the youth to grow accustomed to their surroundings without pressure or coercion. Pacing their immersion into a new environment, allows youth the freedom to familiarize themselves and establish their own boundaries.

- *Organizational constraints.* Youth development organizations have hierarchical structures that may regulate the worker's behavior and interactions with youth. Understanding the structure, policies, and procedures allowed in the workplace enables the worker to develop proper communication styles with youth from various cultures. Knowledge of diverse cultures, coupled with the appropriate actions, will help youth development workers construct healthy relationships with youth.

SUMMARY

Understanding the different components of multiculturalism provides the groundwork for proper multicultural education. We can think of a culture as an organized system of shared meanings between a specific group of individuals. Knowing what a culture is benefits youth workers greatly as they develop multicultural educational practices. Understanding the primary and secondary characteristics of youth enables workers to interact with more effective outcomes.

Youth work is a field where various social actions occur that may be detrimental to a youth's growth. Prejudice, discrimination, stereotyping, racism, and ethnocentrism are choices people make that divide individuals in an unfair manner. Youth may often be the targets of these choices, and the results can last long into their adulthood. Multicultural education is a device that can enhance the quality of life for not only youth, but also for the other individuals with whom they interact, including youth workers.

The implications of multicultural education to youth development include assessing the proper terminology, personal space, and nonverbal and verbal communication during interaction in the workplace. Proper assessment of these procedures enables youth workers to build healthy relationships with their peers and the youth they serve. Unfortunately, there are some obstacles to overcome in developing multicultural education, such as assumptions of similarity, differences in verbal and nonverbal communication, anxiety, and traditional constraints. It may require a significant amount of time to work through these obstacles in order to develop value systems that are open and welcoming to all individuals. Our goal throughout this chapter is to offer methods and ideas to encourage growth in a multicultural manner, with hopes of shedding light on issues that inhibit progress so that these issues may be addressed and remedied.

References

Banks, S. (1999). *Ethical issues in youth work*. London, England: Routledge.

Boys & Girls Clubs of America. (1999). *Tools for inspiring and enabling young people to realize their full potential our national programs* [Brochure]. Atlanta, GA.

City of Phoenix Parks, Recreation and Library Department. (2000). *Vision 2000: A 21st century journey for our children and youths* [Brochure]. Phoenix, AZ.

Dattilo, J., & Williams, R. (1999). Inclusion and leisure service delivery. In E. L. Jackson & T. L. Burton (Eds.), *Leisure studies: Prospects for the twenty-first century* (pp. 451-463). State College, PA: Venture Publishing.

Durkheim, E. (1951). *Suicide: A study in sociology*. Glencoe, IL: The Free Press.

Giroux, H. A. (1994). *Disturbing pleasures*. London, England: Routledge.

Hansel, T. (1979). *When I relax I feel guilty*. Elgin, IL: David Cook.

Hazekamp, J. L., & Popple, K. (1997). Racism, youth policy and youth work in Europe: A fragmented picture. In J. L. Hazekamp & K. Popple (Eds.), *Racism in Europe: A challenge for youth policy and youth work* (pp. 1-11). London, England: University College London Press.

Hirsch, E., Kett, J., & Trefil, J. (Eds.). (1993). *The dictionary of cultural literacy*. Boston, MA: Houghton Mifflin Company.

Imam, U. (1999). Youth workers as mediators and interpreters: Ethical issues in work with black young people. In S. Banks (Ed.), *Ethical issues in youth work* (pp. 125-144). London, England: Routledge.

Jordan, D. J. (2001). *Leadership in leisure services: Making a difference* (2nd ed.). State College, PA: Venture Publishing.

King, Jr., M. L. (1963). An American Dream. In C. Carson & P. Holloras (Eds.) *A knock at midnight: Inspiration from the great sermons of Reverend Martin Luther King, Jr.* (pp. 61-78) New York, NY: Warren Books.

Kraus, R. (2001). *Recreation and leisure in modern society* (6th ed). Mississauga, Ontario, Canada: Jones and Bartlett Publishers, Inc.

Lerner, R. M. (1995). *America's youth in crisis: Challenges and options for programs and policies*. Thousand Oaks, CA: Sage Publications.

Lightfoot, J., Mukherjee, S., & Sloper, P. (2001). Supporting pupils with special health needs in mainstream schools. In S. Riddell & L. Tett (Eds.), *Education, social justice and inter-agency working* (pp. 143-157). London, England: Routledge.

Loden, M., & Rosener, J. (1991). *Workforce America!: Managing employee diversity as a vital resource*. Homewood, IL: One Irwin.

McFadden, J. (1993). *Transcultural counseling: Bilateral and international perspectives*. Alexandria, VA: American Counseling Association.

McLoyd, V. C. (1994). Research in the service of poor and ethnic/racial minority children: A moral imperative. *Family and Consumer Sciences Research Journal, 23,* 56-66.

The Multicultural Association of Fredericton, Inc. (2001). *Rainbow of cultures summer camp.* Retrieved from http://mcaf.aloak.ca/rainbow/html

Nichols, S. L. (1999). Gay, lesbian and bisexual youth: Understanding diversity and promoting tolerance in schools. *The Elementary School Journal, 99*(5), 505-521.

Pedersen, P. (1994). *A handbook for developing multicultural awareness.* (2nd ed.). Alexandria, VA: American Counseling Association.

Pelled, L., Eisenhardt, K. & Xin, K. (1999). Exploring the black box: An analysis of work group diversity, conflict, and performance. *Administrative Science Quarterly, 44*(1), 1-28.

Peregoy, J. J. & Dieser, R. B. (1997). Multicultural awareness in therapeutic recreation: Hamlet living. *Therapeutic Recreation Journal, 31,* 3, 174-188.

Popple, K. (1997). Understanding and tackling racism among young people in the United Kingdom. In J. L. Hazekamp & K. Popple (Eds.), *Racism in Europe: A challenge for youth policy and youth work* (pp. 13-38). London, England: UCL Press.

Rodrigues, L. (2003). *The Minnesota Multicultural Youth Corps.* [On-line] Available: http://www.fourh.umn.edu/multicultural

Rosenthal, R., & Jacobson, L. (1968). *Pygmalion in the classroom.* New York, NY: Holt, Rinehart & Winston.

Shikwambi, S. J., & Randall, S. (2003). Gay and lesbian youth, youth programs and HIV/AIDS: Changing policy and practice to ensure the future of African youth. *Society for Research on Adolescence Newsletter.* [On-line] Available: http://www.s-r-a.org.nws.html

Spencer, M. B. & Swanson, D. P. (2000). Promoting positive outcomes for youth: Resourceful families and communities. In S. Danziger & J. Woldfogel (Eds.), *Securing the future: Investing in children from birth to college* (pp. 182-204). New York, NY: Russell Sage Foundation.

Sue, D. W. & Sue, D. (1990). *Counseling the culturally different: Theory and practice* (2nd ed.). New York, NY: John Wiley and Sons.

Tripp, A., & Sherrill, C. (1991). Attitude theories of relevance adapted to physical education. *Adapted Physical Activity Quarterly, 8,* 12-27.

United Way of Morris County. (2000). *Invest in your community.* [On-line] Available: http://www.uwmorris.org/mentoring/mentoringlearn.html

U.S. Department of Commerce, Economics and Statistics Administration. (2000). *Statistical abstract of the United States.* Washington, DC: U.S. Census Bureau.

Wallace, R. A. & Wolf, A. (1991). *Contemporary sociological theory: Continuing the classical tradition* (3rd ed.). Englewood Cliffs, NJ: Prentice-Hall.

Wildemeersch, D., & Redig, G. (1997). Towards multicultural and anti-racist youth work in Flanders. In J. L. Hazekamp & K. Popple (Eds.), *Racism in Europe: A challenge for youth policy and youth work* (pp. 123-145). London, England: UCL Press.

Wrenn, C. G. (1962). The culturally encapsulated counselor. *Harvard Educational Review, 32* (4), 444-449.

CHAPTER TEN

Ethics

INTRODUCTION

Like other human service professionals, youth workers are involved in ethical decision making on a day-to-day basis in their interactions with others. Youth workers reflect through their actions ethical behaviors that youth often model and draw on as guideposts for themselves. Thus, it is important for youth workers to understand how their ethical actions and behaviors influence their work with youth. A basic knowledge of what ethics are and the importance of behaving ethically is the focus of this chapter.

Acting ethically permeates all of the responsibilities of a youth worker. Youth workers are often bound to a code of ethics outlined within their work environment in which the consequences affect their interaction with the youth with which they serve, their co-workers, and other stakeholders within the

community. The violation of such a code of ethics may directly impact their relationship with youth, those with whom they work and even perhaps tarnish the image of the organization within the community, which they work. Youth workers wear many hats in youth development; all of these "hats" are roles they fill during their tenure with an organization. Disciplinarian, confidante, and motivator are a few examples of roles that require ethical behavior of youth workers in order for them to truly be effective with youth.

In this chapter, the topics of ethics within youth work will be presented. First, ethics will be defined to provide a foundation for the reader. Following, we will discuss why ethics are important in the practice of youth work. Next, we will present a discussion of the relationship of ethics and cultural diversity. Last, the chapter will discuss in-depth ethics and youth worker roles. Some of these roles have been previously discussed in chapter four; however, the information presented within this section of the book expands the roles to include ethical responsibilities.

WHAT ARE ETHICS?

When we think of ethics we think of terms such as morality, moral standards, moral philosophy, and standards of conduct. Such concepts are important as they provide a framework to guide the actions of youth workers. The ethical positions and resulting actions of youth workers have great influence on the development of youth. Having knowledge of such terms and concepts, as well as how ethics influences our lives, is the focus of the introductory portions of this chapter and are intended to provide a basic foundation for the reader.

Ethics Defined

The Blackwell Dictionary of Twentieth Century Social Thought (Outhwaite & Bottomore, 1994, p. 202) provides an inclusive definition of ethics. They suggest that ethics in its broadest sense "refers to the normative appraisals of the actions and character of individuals in social groups." This means that ethics can be thought of as the obligations and duties that govern the actions of individuals and groups. In other words, we can think of ethics as a system of moral standards or values. Jordan (2001, p. 219) writes, "ethics are characterized by high-standards based on morals. However,

she points out that "ethics are not the same as morals; they are a product of morality."

Priest and Gass (1997) have suggested that there are two categories of ethics in decision making—principle and virtue ethics. Principle ethics can be thought of as a "set of impartial rules, often determined by a governing professional organization or by the current professional standards of behavior" (Priest & Gass, 1997, p. 285). On the other hand, virtue ethics involves "examination of particular factors and influences of each act, asserting that correct behavior is defined in each specific situation and that you cannot link any decisions made in other situations" (Priest & Gass, 1997, p.285).

A youth worker's approach to interacting with others may be predicated upon the system of moral standards or values underlying his or her beliefs. Each youth worker and each youth organization seeks a set of ethics to guide their actions. For example, a perennialist ethic suggests that an individual is guided by a set of external truths provided by some divine being. A humanistic ethic would suggest that humans are of supreme value in the universe and that the attention of youth workers should be toward the development of human potential. Either of these two orientations provides a standard upon which judgments are made in interacting with youth and in the planning, organizing, and implementation of programs and services.

Sarah Banks, writing in *Ethical Issues in Youth Work*, provides a perspective of professional ethics as related to the efforts of youth workers. Banks suggests that professional ethics can be thought of as "the study of ethical issues arising in the context of people doing their work." (1999, p. 5). In the human service professions, we often talk about ethics in terms of our relationship with those receiving services. The term "ethic of care" is often used by youth workers. A youth worker "who follows the ethic of care would respond to moral and ethical issues and develop a personal philosophy out of caring and concern for others (Edginton, Jordan, DeGraaf & Edginton, 2002, p. 100).

How do Ethics Influence Our Lives?

Ethics are the actions or behaviors that result from an individual's values or beliefs that are considered the proper social expectations (Pollock, 1994). If a youth strongly adheres to the value of honesty in life, he or she should act in an honest manner—not lying or cheating and telling the truth when asked for it, are a few examples. Honesty is considered moral as a result of society's acceptance of the positive results of acting in an honest manner. Dishonesty is considered immoral and the resulting actions unethical due to the negative results. A youth may cheat and escape capture one time; this can have a negative affect on that person. There are consequences that are detrimental to the youth's development if they are dishonest—the cheating and subsequent results may become grander or more serious as they age.

When working with youth, workers may encounter ethical dilemmas. The ethical choices youth workers make affects themselves as well as others around them. Youth workers are challenged to adhere to an ethic of rights and justice and an ethic of care in their professional lives (Jordan, 2001). An ethic of justice includes actions that originate from the standards or laws of the youth development organization. An example of adhering to an ethic of justice would be enforcing the sign-in policy at the youth center for accountability purposes with youth. An ethic of care centers on actions based upon the needs in relationships. A youth worker who acts under the ethic of care believes in the health and welfare of youth. An example could be a youth worker sharing his or her lunch on an outing with a youth who forgot his or her lunch. The worker does this because he or she want the youth to not go hungry and to continue their enjoying on the outing. There may or may not be a policy regarding this situation within the youth center, but the worker is motivated to act because he or she cares about the youth.

Griffith (1999) outlines several points emphasizing the importance of ethics with youth work. Whether the youth worker is a manager of a facility or an hourly program assistant, the following points are solid foundations to adhere to when working:

• ***Moral leadership is essential.*** In order to have an organization that promotes moral and

Exhibit 10.1
Cheaters Don't Belong in 4-H

How sad that rules must be toughened to prevent fraud in the show ring.

Holy cow! News of the State Fair champion steer's I.D. being questioned made the Sunday Register's front page. It's almost funny to learn that contestants are nose printed to be sure they are who their owners say they are—until you think about it.

Cheating apparently is enough of a problem in 4-H that identification checks are somewhat routine. The organization that 135,000 young Iowans belong to really does promote integrity. Yet some families whose children show animals face temptation to break the rules because of the money involved and the sheer desire to win.

It's a rule, for example, that the animal must be in the owner's possession from May until the county fair and, if it wins, the Iowa State Fair. One concern is that the project really is the work of the youngster; another is tampering by outside interests with a stake in the outcome.

Livestock fraud at fairs in recent years has led numerous states, including Ohio and Missouri, to crack down.

A recent New York Times story described such practices as injecting corn oil into steers to fill out their hind ends.

In Iowa, the 4-H program already is looking into changes for next year's State Fair, said Joe Kurth, state director of 4-H youth programs at Iowa State University Extension.

One possibility is DNA testing, he said, because ear tags aren't foolproof. 4-H also will reinforce existing education about the purpose of raising animals for show—such as the discipline involved in care and feeding—and ethical responsibilities.

In the controversy over this year's Iowa State Fair champion steer, officials said a nose print taken at the fair didn't match one taken earlier. The family of 16-year old Jenna Sievers, whose 1,295 pound crossbred steer is under scrutiny, won a temporary court order overruling the Iowa State Fair Board's decision to prevent him from going to auction.

The steer, named Pickles, sold for $16,000 at the Sale of Champions on Saturday. (The owner gets 80 percent of proceeds, with 20 percent going to 4-H scholarships.)

Then on Monday, more troubling news. The fair board announced that both the grand and reserve champion 4-H market lambs had been pulled from Saturday's Sale of Champions. Questions about their histories supposedly led their owners to withdraw the animals.

4-H is a fine program for young people. Most wouldn't dream of cheating when they show animals at the fair. What's most disturbing is that any who do are probably influenced, if not coerced, by their parents.

How sad.

Source: Cheaters don't belong in the 4-H [Editorial]. (2002, August 21). *The Des Moines Sunday Register.*

ethical behavior, the highest administrators need to establish the pattern for what is moral and ethical in the environment. The administrator acts as the rudder on a ship, and the other workers are the various sections of the boat, all following the direction of the rudder. If the rudder goes awry, so does the boat.

- *Sound systems and procedures encourage ethical acts.* The verbal and nonverbal actions of youth workers can indicate the importance of morality and ethics in the workplace. These actions often originate from policies and procedures of the organization. In order for the proper action to occur and for continued success, the policies and procedures need to be maintained and kept up-to-date.

- *Behavior that is not ethical must be identified and discouraged.* A youth organization must adhere to its mission and philosophy in all aspects both in public and within its own walls. If there is unethical behavior occurring within the youth development organization, the workers in charge should be proactive and highlight the importance of ethics and address the unethical behavior immediately. Failure to address the unethical behavior may create a domino effect regarding unethical actions—if one worker does something

unethical and the action is not addressed, what keeps the other workers from doing it?

- *Workers should be empowered to the greatest extent possible.* Empowering youth workers can include active involvement from all levels of work in creating and implementing programs. Other empowering acts include creation of disciplinary strategies with youth and ad hoc committees run by workers for special event planning.

- *The organization should offer moral counsel and support.* If there are moral or ethical dilemmas that arise within the youth worker, there should be an individual or group of individuals (committee) that the worker can go to for ethical and moral guidance. Informal moral counsel or support should also be available; an example would be a youth worker who confides in another worker. That person may not be a designated member of an ethics committee, but as a worker who believes in the philosophy of the organization and his or her coworkers, he or she should be able to give sound advice or guidance.

- *The organization's visible incentives—nonmonetary and monetary—should be based on reward rather than blame.* If a youth organization is going to use incentives, those incentives should be associated with hard work and success. Administrators of youth development agencies will get more out of their staff if they motivate positively, highlighting successes and growth, instead of motivating by fear and punishment.

- *Standard methods of persuasion should be used for moral issues.* When dealing with issues of morality such as honesty and integrity, it is beneficial to be forthright and state exactly what is needed. Youth organizations with philosophies based on such issues should have workers that practice them daily. Youth that see this obvious practice can then understand the issue and incorporate it into their lives.

- *Leadership should be selected and promoted for moral and nonmoral competence.* In order to be a successful youth organization, workers should practice moral behaviors. It is also important, but difficult at times, to retain the youth workers that are positive moral and ethical role models. Offering competitive wages and benefits is a primary method for retention, but if that is not possible, alternatives need to be developed.

WHY ARE ETHICS IMPORTANT IN THE PRACTICE OF YOUTH WORK?

With the above foundation in mind, two important questions for youth workers are required to be addressed: 1) Why are ethics important to youth workers? and 2) What are the consequences of unethical behavior in youth work? Why are these two questions important? Simply stated, youth workers must understand ethically what they do, and most importantly, must understand the consequences of their actions. Such consequences not only affect the youth worker, but also the youth they serve and the communities in which they operate.

Reasons Why Ethics Are Important to Youth Workers

There are numerous reasons why ethics are important in the practice of youth work. The ethical actions and behavior of youth workers is reflected in many different outcomes. For example, when we view the power relationships that may exist between youth and youth workers, there are a myriad of ethical considerations that must be addressed in establishing such a relationship. Some of the areas in which ethical actions and behaviors must be considered include the following: Accountability, professionalism, confidentiality, developing trust, integrity, and social welfare. The following is a discussion of these areas and their importance in ethical decision making for youth work.

Accountability. A youth worker who is accountable is an individual who takes responsibility for his or her actions. According to Edginton, Hanson, Edginton, and Hudson (1998), accountability requires an understanding that the youth workers are going to be responsive and provide relevant opportunities and services to youth to meet their needs. It is important for youth workers to recognize the need for the programs they provide and to provide those programs in a manner that does not compromise the values of the youth development organization. Presently, if there is an unethical situation that occurs in youth work, the corporation is usually held accountable for the actions (Minkes, Small, & Chatterjee, 1999). Traditionally, the accountability fell to all youth workers who were willingly involved with the unethical situation.

Professionalism. Professionalism has a myriad of descriptions when discussing youth work. There is a group of general guidelines regarding professionalism in the youth organization. The first component is a commitment to self-assessment. As a youth worker, we are constantly bombarded with new programs to implement, new youth to guide, and new policies to follow. Self-assessment enables a youth worker to identify areas in his or her work that need improvement. Witt, Crompton and Baker (1995) describe self-assessment or self-evaluation of the goals, content, leadership, management, or facilities as a method to determine if the program character-

istics are achieving the desired results. Youth workers can provide information for self-assessment through evaluations, interviews, and interaction with coworkers. A youth worker can measure his or her performance against organization, agency, or national standards to see if he or she is are providing adequate guidance. The second component is a continual accruement of knowledge related to the youth population. Ideally, as a youth worker, an individual accepts the commitment to work with youth that are continually changing physically, emotionally, and mentally. It is the worker's responsibility to access training, knowledge, and skills that will help him or her evolve. Methods to expand the knowledge base of the youth worker can include joining and participating in local and international, professional youth development organizations (e.g., NSACA, IYL, ACYS, etc.) reading youth development books or articles, attending training seminars or conferences, and developing short and long range plans for professional development. A growing part of professional youth development involves sharing information through coalition or group websites. As Robertson (1997, p. 580) points out,

> staff development is a structured and thoughtfully planned organizational approach designed to support service standards and program effectiveness. It expects the skill sets, knowledge, and

performance outcomes of staff members to increase beyond their entry employment expectations. It is a long-term and proactive commitment to quality of service, innovation, expectation of change, internal promotion whenever possible, high levels of staff retention and job diversity.

The third component is an application of professional ethics at all times in the workplace. A youth worker is an advocate for a portion of the population who otherwise may not be heard. There are issues with youth that may require intervention by the worker such as abuse, neglect, and violence. If the youth worker does not speak up in a professional manner, those issues may go unnoticed and can affect youth. Speaking out can be verbal as well as written. Methods include accurate documentation and recordkeeping, consultations with other professionals, or a combination of both. In the workplace environment, youth workers are obligated to maintain an unbiased rapport with all portions of the population they serve.

Confidentiality. Morgan and Banks (1999) define confidentiality in the youth development arena as the ability to maintain trust and understand the privacy of youth. The youth worker has the duty to maintain confidentiality unless the youth involved is in harm or danger. Issues that often remain private, such as sexual abuse or rape, may remain private but the youth worker can discuss these issues with youth in an open environment, not illustrating personal stories but discussing the important facts. Introducing support groups, resources or activities that can benefit the youth may dissolve the feeling of helplessness that youth workers face in regards to confidentiality.

The issue of confidentiality in youth development can create dilemmas. Some of the questions regarding confidentiality circle around who should have access to private files and gossip between workers about youth in the workplace (Morgan & Banks, 1999). In other cases, an opportunity may arise to discuss youth with individuals other than their parents. These encounters should be handled in a way to not violate the privacy of the youth.

Developing Trust. Malekoff (1997) notes that confidentiality is important in the youth-worker relationship, but trust is also a necessary cornerstone if there is going to be a productive dynamic. Skills needed to build trust with youth include amplifying subtle messages ("Are you wondering if what we do and talk about is going to reach your parents?") and reaching for a feeling link ("It's not easy doing that activity. Are you sure you want to do it? If not, why?") (Malekoff, 1997). The youth worker may realize that it is important to verbalize subtle messages with one youth but not with another. This is part of the developmental process of building trust with youth—understanding when to say something and when to simply observe and hold back.

Establishing a relationship with youth means understanding each youth and not categorizing youth. Youth like to discuss their interests and share those interests with others. Youth workers can build a trusting relationship by allowing the youth to share their interests. When youth share their interests, they are in a vulnerable position. They are exposing themselves, allowing others into their world. Establishing trust involves listening and individualizing the youth, even if there are others who have the same interests. Stating the importance of what the youth is doing, celebrating successes, and downsizing failures, are ways to build a trusting relationship. As funny or different as something sounds, the youth worker should actively listen and encourage positive growth. Mocking or teasing the youth will erode trust and could have negative effects on the youth.

Knop, Tananehill and O'Sullivan (2001) illustrate that trust is built if the youth has more involvement in the planning process of activities. Youth workers need to incorporate this style of organization into their work and follow through with it. If the youth are given the opportunity to establish regulations and rules for activities or behavior, and the youth worker does not implement them, then trust in the decisions made by the worker will decline. The youth worker should follow through with his or her agreement to share in the decision making process and reserve time to reflect with the youth on the outcomes of their decisions. By doing this, trust

remains intact; and the youth are exposed to methods of managing and evaluation.

Rauner (2000) discusses acceptance as a tool in building a trusting relationship between a youth and a youth worker. Youth are not carbon copies of each other; each one is unique in his or her psychological, sociological, biological and emotional makeup. Youth workers encounter different interactive styles when working with youth; these styles are ways by which the youth tests to see if a youth worker can be trusted. The youth worker should understand this and accept each youth as an important individual. Actively listening to youth and engaging them in conversations about their lives is a stepping stone to building trust.

Integrity. Jordan (2001, p. 228) defines a person with integrity as someone who "knows their own values, takes a stand for what they believe in, and profess their own standards." Maintaining integrity in youth development originates with understanding the mission when working with youth and trying to accomplish it. How the youth worker attempts to succeed in following the mission is how his or her integrity is measured. The development of trust between youth and youth coworkers is a central tenet to integrity. Other qualities associated with integrity include the following:

- Responsibility.
- Realizing that each person lays the groundwork for what she or he will be.

- Awareness that one has the freedom to choose.
- Faithfulness to one's convictions.
- Putting all of oneself into little as well as big things.
- Being accountable for decisions and their consequences.
- Realizing that one can be accountable for inaction as well as action.
- Admitting mistakes and correcting them (Mattison, 2000; Minkes, Small, & Chatterjee, 1999)

Youth workers must maintain integrity within the hierarchy of the organization. In order to convey a message that an employee is a person of integrity, that individual must follow the code of ethics that is outlined by the organization. A code of ethics can be written and formalized, informally understood, or a combination of both styles. A youth worker who does not follow the code of ethics of the organization will fall into contempt with others. The higher the status of the person who violates the code, the more dissension will result with other coworkers. As Kouzes and Posner indicate (as cited in Minkes et al., 1999, p. 330), "leaders who could not personally adhere to a firm set of values, could not convince others of the worthiness of those values. . .leaders without integrity were only putting on an act."

Social Welfare. The definition of welfare includes a state of happiness, prosperity and good fortune related to a person's well-being (Random House College Dictionary, 1980,

p. 1493). Social welfare is working towards a harmonious state with members in society. It also includes helping others when needed, and taking care of not just biological family members, but social family members as well (Ehlstain, 2002). Youth workers should convey to youth a sense of "civic housekeeping," or taking care of the "house" or community in which their "family" members live. This "civic housekeeping" should have no boundaries when discussing the diversity of residents in a community and who might need aid.

Banks (2001, p. 197) states that youth "need knowledge of their social, political, and economic worlds, the skills to influence their environments, and humane values that will motivate them to participate in social change to help create a more just society and world." Many youth will get this knowledge from school, but the implementation of this knowledge goes beyond the walls of the classroom. Youth workers should encourage the implementation of concepts, ideas, or theories that youth hear through education. Many youth development programs include service learning or citizenship components in their structure. Within youth development, workers should also include the opportunity for youth to develop critical thinking skills—how knowledge is constructed, assumptions that go with the knowledge, and how to develop thoughts and knowledge on their own (Banks, 2001). As youth develop the ability to think critically, this enhances the "filtration system" of eliminating stereotypes and biases. This filtering process aids in maintaining the social welfare of the community and builds competent youth.

Consequences of Unethical Behavior in Youth Work

In order for behavior to be unethical, judgment and accountability need to be examined (Worthley, 1997). Who is judging the behavior? "What are the accountability standards for the youth development agency? If the behavior in question violates the judgment of an established ethical individual and/or compromises the accountability standards of a youth development agency, then it is unethical. Unfortunately there are occurrences of individuals abusing their authority in youth development and compromising their actions.

Examples of unethical behavior in youth work may include rudeness, profane language, promise breaking, deception, dishonesty and withholding important information (Hofmann, 1999). There are consequences to unethical behavior in youth development:

- **Tension among youth and coworkers.** When unethical behavior occurs, individuals may be unsure of how to act or respond. This confusion can add unwanted stress to the youth development agency, affecting the communication between the unethical individual and others.

- **Erosion in the vision and mission of the youth development** agency. By not addressing the unethical behavior when it initially occurs, one indirectly condones it. This could adversely affect the mission of the youth agency, fostering a belief in other coworkers or youth that it is okay to act unethically.

- **Loss of trust with coworkers, youth and the community.** When unethical behavior occurs, other youth development workers may be hesitant to interact with the individual committing the actions. Youth may be dissuaded by the worker's actions, affecting their trust in that person. The community may see the unethical behavior as an organizational component, affecting the reputation of the youth agency.

To insure that unethical behavior does not occur in youth development, agencies can take steps to promote quality actions when interacting with youth. Some steps include ethics training, peer reviews, and a code of ethics. All of these examples should emphasize the importance of trust; without trust, youth development cannot occur.

ETHICS AND DIVERSITY

In most communities, youth workers serve diverse populations. Not only diverse in the sense of race, culture, ethnicity, socioeconomic class, and gender, but also as diverse in the sense of the developmental characteristic of youth, which is just as important. In a given situation youth may possess some consistent developmental characteristics, however, youth are more likely characterized by their divergent patterns of family life, peer relationships, individual interests, wants, needs, and desires. Such dynamics require tolerance, understanding, compassion, and trust between youth and youth workers. Therefore, supporting the diverse developmental needs of youth becomes an ethical responsibility of youth workers. In this part of the chapter, a focus on the ethical responsibilities of youth workers to promote diversity will be presented.

What Are the Ethical Responsibilities of Youth Workers in Promoting Diversity?

Before a youth worker can promote diversity while working with youth, the individual needs to examine his or her own beliefs, knowledge, and actions. This examination includes:

- **Becoming aware of one's own attitudes and beliefs.** Understanding one's own cultural heritage and background, as well as recognizes cross-cultural competencies. Parts of this include acknowledgment of discomfort of the youth worker with other cultures.

- **Understanding of one's knowledge.** Simply having

knowledge about one's cultural heritage is not good enough; a youth worker should understand the knowledge he or she has and how important it has been to the development of their culture. This comprehension includes understanding oppressive practices, communication, and how one's own culture can influence other cultures.

- **Articulating cross-cultural skill levels.** This includes education and training regarding cross-cultural issues and understanding multiculturalism when interacting with individuals from other cultures.

Once an examination has been made, youth workers may then address their own beliefs, knowledge, and skill levels regarding other cultures. This includes:

- **Becoming aware of attitudes and beliefs.** A youth worker needs to realize his or her negative and positive reactions towards other cultures, as well as stereotypes regarding other cultures.

- **Understanding of one's knowledge.** A youth worker must interpret the knowledge acquired regarding other cultures and sociological, political, and economic influences that can affect people in other cultures. This also includes recognizing the knowledge distributed regarding diversity and youth development and how it affects working with youth.

• *Articulating cross-cultural levels.* A youth worker should become familiar with relevant research regarding youth development and other cultures, and be actively involved in groups addressing issues of diversity within youth development (Peregoy & Dieser, 1997; Dieser & Peregoy, 1999).

It is a youth worker's obligation to address diversity in youth development. The youth worker's objectives should include 1) an understanding by youth of how different ethnic, racial, and religious backgrounds affect behaviors and attitudes and 2) a sensitivity to similarities and differences among people (Malekoff, 1997). There are several ways that workers can discuss diversity when working with youth. Youth workers should encourage an open forum to talk about diversity. Interaction about identity, discrimination and the resulting prejudices, and group dynamics are important discussion points. Highlighting current issues that relate to diversity globally (e.g., Matthew Shepard murder, Tibetan independence) or locally could invoke a sense of responsibility in youth regarding the care for others. The youth worker should model appropriate and effective actions and language when discussing diverse populations. This means recognizing personal discomfort around certain issues. Attending cultural awareness rallies, presentations, or celebrations expose youth to different traditions, practices, and customs that can augment their existing knowledge of diversity.

ETHICS AND YOUTH WORKER ROLES

Ethical decision making is pervasive in all of the roles and actions of youth workers. As indicated in the introduction to this chapter, a number of these roles have been previously discussed in Chapter 4. The discussion in this portion of the chapter expands upon the previous discussion, and more specifically, links youth worker roles directly to ethical responsibilities. Specifically, youth worker roles such as authority figure, controller, disciplinarian, mentor, friend, overseer, confidante, motivator, collaborator, and facilitator, will be included. Many times, maintaining our ethical stance can be a difficult situation, as seen in Exhibit 10.2. A number of the roles have been clustered into similar categories. Within each section, an explanation and discussion of the benefits and/or results of youth workers carrying out their responsibilities in an ethical fashion are provided.

Youth Worker as an Authority Figure/Controller/Disciplinarian

When the role of the youth worker is disciplinary, the goal should be to aid youth in developing self-discipline (Jordan, 2001). As a worker is interacting with youth, the idea of maturity and growth should always be kept in mind. A youth worker should not look at his

Exhibit 10.2
Youth Advocate Resigns to Avoid Conflict

The director of Des Moines' Youth Law Center resigned Wednesday to spare the firm the loss of 850 child-welfare cases because of a perceived conflict of interests.

Still unclear Thursday was whether Martha Johnson's resignation will eliminate the appearance of a conflict and lift a judge's order last week stripping the firm of most of its legal work with abused and delinquent children.

"Given the position of the court, the board determined, and Martha Johnson agreed, that resignation was in the best interest of the Youth Law Center and its advocacy mission," said Victoria Herring, the center's board president.

Staff attorney Michael Sorci will be interim director.

Johnson, who was an assistant Polk County attorney for almost four years, took over the helm of the 25-year old center last fall, even though employees complained of a possible conflict. State ethics rules prohibit lawyers from acting as both public prosecutor and private attorney on the same case.

Johnson's resignation during a meeting with the center's board of directors came after employees learned the firm would lose most of its existing caseload because Johnson had been involved as a prosecutor in many of the law center's cases.

The employees said the loss could cripple the center financially and disrupt progress in cases involving at-risk children, many of whom are placed in shelters, group homes and foster care.

The Youth Law Center handles more than half of all child-welfare cases in Polk County. In recent weeks, private attorneys had begun to challenge Johnson's involvement in cases, saying her prior knowledge created a conflict for her and the employees she managed.

Johnson did not respond to a request to be interviewed.

Source: Rood, L. (2003, June 6). Youth advocate resigns to avoid conflict. *The Des Moines Register*, p. 3B.

or her role as a "me vs. them" situation; rather, he or she is encouraging youth to succeed. Youth are interested in trying new things, experimenting to see the results—this is curiosity. Being curious is okay, unless it can bring harm to the individuals involved. Once the youth worker realizes that harm could result, he or she needs to intervene and guide the situation. Intervention may require a discussion with the youth of the risks of certain actions, or it could include removal of the youth from an activity altogether.

There are many options for discipline. If the youth does not develop the ability to control their actions after the worker's intervention, the discipline is ineffective. Effective discipline techniques include the following:

- Showing respect through correction—not talking down to the youth, but talking with him or her about the need to adjust their behavior.
- Preaching—not emphasizing the incorrect behavior, but rather the values associated with proper behavior.
- Attribution—offering youth reasons for their actions. Giving reasons for why a youth needs to do something aids in intrinsic motivation, or the desire from within the person to do something.
- Modeling and instruction—when youth workers "practice what they preach" it is easier for youth to understand why they are being corrected (Rauner, 2000).

As illustrated in Exhibit 10.3, when an ineffective approach to youth work is taken, there can be disastrous results. These techniques highlight a theme that aids in the development of self-discipline with youth competence. Competence is a tool in building self-esteem and self-confidence within youth. Youth strive to be viewed as adults, as individuals who can make good decisions. Using the techniques listed above are ways youth workers can show they believe the youth is competent. Youth who recognize workers who treat them as competent will engage in behaviors to maintain that perceived competency.

Youth Worker as Mentor/Friend/Overseer/Confidante

Today's youth are faced with many challenges that threaten the development of their identities. When a youth worker decides to be a mentor or friend to a young person, he or she is are making a choice that will cause a chain reaction of events that will long outlive him or her. That choice of mentoring carries a significant commitment on the mentor's part towards the youth. The commitment is towards the person, the process and the purpose (Group, 1998).

Being committed to the mentee is something that involves in-depth relationship building and an understanding that there will be moments of angst and pain, as well as joy and elation. To maintain that commitment to the youth means understanding the investment that goes with mentoring. This investment is not something that may be taken lightly; if the choice to mentor is half-hearted in effort, we are not being true to the youth as a caring individual. It is a difficult decision to make, but if a youth worker commits to mentoring, he or she needs to be honest in how much time and effort he or she can give to the youth.

A mentor should be committed to the process of mentoring. This process does not proceed linearly, moving from stage to stage without revisiting previous stages. Distractions and obstacles in daily life may

Exhibit 10.3
Little League Coach Resigns after Scuffle

He is charged with assault after being accused of grabbing a player. Two others face possible charges.

A post-game scuffle that involved a 14-year old Perry boy, two Little League coaches, and a father ended with a criminal complaint against one coach and possible charges against the other.

Police allege that coach Ricky Pentico, 39, grabbed and shook Jeff Kirchoff Jr., 14, after a game at Pattee Park on Tuesday. Pentico said Kirchoff, a member of the opposing team, displayed poor sportsmanship and was "prancing around like a dancer" after he drew a walk. Pentico also said the boy refused to shake hands after the game.

"He had no right to play like that," Pentico said. "It's not called for."

Pentico admitted that he grabbed Kirchoff by the shirt. Kirchoff's coach, Russ Moore, said he threw his arms around Pentico to pull him away from the teenager.

"What is a guy supposed to do in a situation like this? I did the right thing," Moore said. "I subdued him and I kept the situation under control."

More than 20 players witnessed the incident.

At least two people called police. Pentico was charged with assault.

Police continue to investigate. Charges could also be filed against Moore and Kirchoff's father, Jeff Kirchoff Sr., who was also involved in the fray, Lt. Ray Uric said Thursday.

Kirchoff Sr. could not be reached for comment.

Pentico, coach of the Osmundson Dodgers, resigned Wednesday at a meeting with the league's president, Daryl Harker. Harker, Pentico's longtime friend, said he would have asked for the resignation if Pentico hadn't stepped down.

"I don't care what took place afterward or what took place first," Harker said. "Ricky was wrong when he grabbed a baseball player. Period."

Still, Harker said, he wants to see charges against Pentico dropped.

"Anytime anything like this happens, it isn't good," he said. "It hurts the program."

The two teams play again Thursday at Pattee Park.

Source: Little league coach resigns after scuffle [Editorial]. (2002, June 14). *The Des Moines Sunday Register.*

affect the mentoring process, but the youth worker should maintain a sense of genuineness and integrity when working with the youth. Truthful interaction and diligence are hallmarks of a sincere mentoring relationship—the same qualities that can be found in friendship. These qualities are part of the process that helps maintain an ethically sound mentoring program.

Finally, a mentor should be committed to the purpose of mentoring. Youth workers who are friends or confidantes to youth understand that there is "hidden treasure" in a youth, and part of the mentoring process is for that treasure to be found and celebrated with others. There may be instances of guidance and tutelage that are painful to the worker and the youth, but that is the role that the youth worker plays as a mentor. If a youth worker is truly a mentor, they will oversee the growth of the youth, observe the actions of the youth, and provide guidance when needed. This guidance may come in the form of a private conversation with only the youth, or in front of the youth's peers. The important component as a mentor, friend, overseer, or confidante is that the youth worker understands his or her obligation and commitment, and that the guidance he or she provides is sincere. If the youth worker is not truly invested in the mentoring relationship, he or she cannot fulfill the roles listed above.

Youth Worker as a Motivator

According to Edginton and Griffith (as cited in Edginton,

Hudson, & Lankford, 2001, p. 151), motivation is defined as "the process whereby an environment is created that enables individuals to be stimulated to take action that fulfills the goals of the organization." Motivation includes anything that moves youth toward action. Youth workers can motivate extrinsically or intrinsically. Extrinsic motivation involves something outside of the individual to inspire him or her to perform. Examples of extrinsic motivation with youth may include

- certificates, medals, or trophies;
- extra time doing their favorite activities; and
- opportunities to choose activities.

The drawback to this type of motivation is commonly referred to as the carrot-and-stick or reward theory (Edginton, Hudson, & Lankford, 2001). This theory states that youth will only act appropriately as long as the reward or extrinsic motivator is in front of them. Once the reward is removed, the appropriate behavior will cease as well. Youth workers could also run out of rewards, or the youth may not be motivated by the particular rewards the worker is using.

Extrinsic motivation may also occur through fear of punishment. Threatened removal of equipment or activities can motivate youth to perform as needed. Unfortunately, this can erode the level of trust needed to develop a healthy collaborative relationships with youth.

Intrinsic motivation is the preferred and most effective way to encourage youth to perform. When something is intrinsically motivating, it comes from within the youth. This requires an understanding of how and why youth make their decisions, and an understanding that each youth is a unique individual with his or her own needs. Techniques to intrinsically motivate include

- creating an environment encouraging achievement and success;
- empowering youth so they can test their decision-making skills;
- valuing their input and showing it is useful;
- collaborating with youth on activities and in discussions; and
- respecting youth and communicating with them, not at them.

It is not a simple process; rather, it requires time and caring on the worker's part to gain insight into the interests and desires of the youth. It is very simple to say, "Do this, and you will get this reward," but how beneficial is that to the youth? As youth mature and age, there will be opportunities to get involved in activities that are beneficial to others. One goal of youth work is to develop youth who care for others or are altruistic, and to do this requires youth to be moved to perform not only for themselves. Altruism originates from a desire to help someone else, and not receive anything in return. Youth workers should examine their techniques for motivation and assess if they are useful in achieving this goal.

Youth Worker as a Collaborator

Youth workers encounter youth who are unique and special with desires, goals, and aspirations. On occasion, the youth worker may not be able to create an environment that is conducive to what the youth needs to succeed. To aid in the growth of the youth, the worker should collaborate with other individuals or groups within the community. These individuals or groups could include people who live in the neighborhoods near the youth development organizations, schools, churches, working groups, government representatives, and special interest groups (Shields, 1995). The benefits of collaboration are as follows:

- **Enhanced availability of community resources.** A youth *development* agency may not own a rock-climbing wall for activities, but if the local recreation center has one, the two agencies could work together to provide rock-climbing activities for youth. Subsequent collaboration could include clinics or demonstrations for the agency youth, given by recreation center employees who possess the knowledge.
- **Enhanced enrollment of youth.** If more agencies are collaborating, there are more opportunities for activities. This could attract more youth, depending on the diversity within

the collaboration (Beck, Reynolds, & Gavlik, 1995).
- *Healthier communities.* As more individuals are invited to join in the vision of the youth development agency, their contributions will improve the health and well being of the generation of individuals that will succeed them.

Collaboration can also occur between youth workers and youth; and this is a successful technique in motivating a youth. In order to collaborate on an activity, the worker has to empower or relinquish some control to the youth. Empowering the youth gives him or her opportunities to try new skills and experience the emotions that go with working on an activity. This is an excellent way to learn and grow, for the youth as well as the worker. As the collaborative activity is completed, the youth can claim ownership for his or her work. If the effort was enjoyable, it may motivate the youth to get more involved with other activities. If the result was not enjoyable, at least the youth has gained insight into working on an activity and having responsibility. The worker experiences teamwork and may learn new techniques for working with youth. He or she may find qualities in the youth he or she didn't know existed and also learn more about the youth, strengthening their relationship.

Youth Worker as a Facilitator
Youth workers are often the facilitators, or initiators, of encouraging growth within youth. A youth

worker often takes the first steps to developing programs, creating an environment, or facilitating discussions aimed at improving the well-being of youth. An example occurs with a youth worker who is a counselor in a summer camp setting. If some of the goals at summer camp are to facilitate positive interactions between youth, healthy play during activities, the development of social skills, and self-discipline, then the counselor creates an environment conducive to these goals. The counselor may design colorful banners with positive rules stated on them and hang them around camp, or he or she may introduce games that stress the importance of teamwork and group problem solving. When the counselor gives encouraging feedback, this may signal success to a youth that is striving to achieve one or more of the goals. The counselor is serving as a facilitator by encouraging continued action by youth that will aid in their growth. This encouragment may include active involvement or participation by the youth worker. Leading by example is a method youth workers use to illustrate the importance of a thought or point. Youth workers can "drive a point home" with youth if they promote through their actions the importance of what they are discussing or stressing to the youth.

Rauner (2000) describes facilitation by youth workers as a method of creating a sense of acceptance in the youth. Wherever youth work occurs, a feeling of belonging should occur within the youth. Feeling that his or her input is important, being recognized for success, and being appreciated for what he or she can do are examples of belonging. It is imperative for youth workers to create this "familial" environment, because many youth may not experience this sense of belonging or acceptance anywhere else.

According to Merriam-Webster, a secondary definition of "facilitate" is to make something easier (*Random House Collegiate Dictionary*, 1980, p. 473). To make something easier does not always mean reducing the level of difficulty of a situation or problem. Youth workers may provide insight, guidance, or wisdom to youth by discussing important topics and getting involved with youth in activities. Injecting new views or thoughts into conversations with youth may create decision dilemmas for youth. Initially, these dilemmas could cause a youth to flounder around in frustration, searching for the decision that suits him or her best. But, if his or her final decision on a topic includes the positive views and thoughts introduced by the youth worker, the long-term affects may ease further difficult decisions. The youth may look back at what the worker said or did with him or her and use that as guidance in the future.

SUMMARY

In the first part of this chapter, the definition of ethics was discussed, as were the different views that can be incorporated into ethics. Ethics refers to the obligations and duties to which an individual should adhere when interacting with others. Ethics influence youth work-

ers' lives through relationships and policies. An ethic of justice has its foundation in the policies formalized by a youth development organization. Ethics of care are associated with youth workers' actions in relationship to others.

The importance of maintaining an ethical approach to youth work involves several factors including accountability, professionalism, confidentiality, trust, and integrity. Youth workers who are unethical will reduce or completely wipe out some, if not all, of these factors. Once a youth worker has acted unethically, there are different consequences that result. If the youth worker attempts to reverse his or her unethical behavior, it can be difficult due to the number of individuals directly and indirectly affected by the actions. As youth development continues to expand, workers are challenged with incorporating multiculturalism into the organization. Before youth workers can do this, they need to examine their knowledge, understanding, and skills related to their own culture. Once they have a grasp on their own culture, they should analyze interpretations of other cultures. Only after these two steps are taken, can youth workers guide youth about multiculturalism.

The chapter closes with descriptions of the many roles youth workers have in an organization. The spectrum includes a disciplinarian or authority figure, mentor, motivator, friend, collaborator, and facilitator. Several of these roles are in conjunction with community organizations or individuals; all are directly related to working with youth.

REFERENCES

Banks, J. A. (2001). *Cultural diversity and education: Foundations, curriculum, and teaching.* Boston, MA: Allyn and Bacon.

Banks, S. (1999). *Ethical issues in youth work.* London, England: Routledge.

Beck, T. M., Reynolds, J., & Gavlik, S. (1995). Partnership for civic change. *Journal of Physical Education, Recreation and Dance, 66*(4), 38-39.

Cheaters don't belong in 4-H [Editorial]. (2002, August 21). *The Des Moines Sunday Register.*

Delgado, M. (2002). *New frontiers for youth development in the twenty-first century: Revitalizing and broadening youth development.* New York, NY: Columbia University Press.

Dieser, R. B. & Peregoy, J. J. (1997). A multicultural critique of three therapeutic recreation service models. *Annual in Therapeutic Recreation, 8,* 56-69.

Edginton, C. R., Hanson, C. J., Edginton, S. R. & Hudson, S. D. (1998). *Leisure programming: A service centered and benefits approach.* (3rd ed.). Dubuque, IA: WCB-McGraw Hill.

Edginton, C. R., Hudson, S. D. & Lankford, S .V. (2001). *Managing recreation, parks, and leisure services: An introduction.* Champaign, IL: Sagamore Publishing.

Edginton, C. R., Hanson, C. J., Edginton, S. R. & Hudson, S. R. (2002). *Leisure and life satisfaction: Foundational perspectives* (3rd ed.). New York, NY: McGraw-Hill.

Elshtain, J. B. (2002). *Jane Addams and the dream of American democracy.* New York, NY: Basic Books.

Emerging Young Leaders. (1998). *Successful youth mentoring.* Loveland, CO: Group Publishing.

Griffith, J. R. (1999). Can a manager be a moral leader? In P. B. Hofmann & W. A. Nelson (Eds.), *Managing ethically: An executive's guide* (p. 7-9). Chicago, IL: Health Administration Press.

Hofmann, P. B. (1999). Abuse of power. In P. B. Hofmann & W. A. Nelson (Eds.), *Managing ethically: An executive's guide* (pp.21-23). Chicago, IL: Health Administration Press.

Jordan, D. (2001). *Leadership in leisure services: Making a difference.* State College, PA. Venture Publishing.

Kleiber, D. A. (1999). *Leisure experience and human development: A dialectical interpretation.* New York, NY: Basic Books.

Knop, N., Tananehill, D., & O'Sullivan, M. (2001). Dead end: Making a difference for urban youths. *Journal of Physical Education, Recreation and Dance, 72*(7), 38-44.

Little league coach resigns after scuffle [Editorial]. (2002, June 14). *The Des Moines Sunday Register.*

Logan, R. D. (1986). A reconceptualization of Erikson's theory: The repetition of existential and instrumental themes, *Human Development. 29,* 125-136.

Malekoff, A. (1997). *Group work with adolescents.* New York, NY: Guilford Press.

Minkes, A. L., Small, M. W. & Chatterjee, S. R. (1999). Leadership and business ethics: Does it matter? Implications for management, *Journal of Business Ethics, 20* (4), 327-335.

Morgan, S., & Banks, S. (1999). The youth worker as confidante: Issues of welfare and trust. In S. Banks (Ed.), *Ethical issues in youth work* (pp. 145-163). London. England: Routledge.

Outhwaite, W., & Bottomore, T. (1994). *The Blackwell dictionary of twentieth century social thought.* Cambridge, MA: Blackwell.

Peregoy, J. J. & Dieser, R. B. (1997). Multicultural awareness in therapeutic recreation: Hamlet living. *Therapeutic Recreation Journal, 31*(3), 174-188.

Priest, S. & Gass, M. (1997). *Effective leadership in adventure programming.* Champaign, IL: Human Kinetics.

Rauner, D. M. (2000). *They still pick me up when I fall: The role of caring in youth development and community life.* New York, NY: Columbia University Press.

Robertson, R. (1997). Walking the talk: Organizational modeling and commitment to youth and staff development. *Child Welfare, 76*(5), 577-589.

Rood, L. (2003, June 6). Youth advocate resigns to avoid conflict. *The Des Moines Register,* p. 38.

Shields, C. (1995). Improving the life prospects of children: A community systems approach. *Child Welfare, 74*(3), 605-618.

Stein, J. & Su P. T. (Eds.). *The Random House college dictionary.* (1980). New York, NY: Random House.

Walker, G. (2001). The policy climate for early adolescent initiatives. In P. L. Benson & K. J. Pittman (Eds.), *Trends in youth development: Visions, realities and challenges* (pp. 77-90). Norwell, MA: Kluwer Academic Publishers.

Witt, P., Crompton, J., & Baker, D. (1995). Evaluating youth recreation programs. *Journal of Physical Education, Recreation & Dance, 66*(4), 27-34.

Worthley, J. A. (1997). Reporting unethical behavior. In P. B. Hofmann & W. A. Nelson (Eds.), *Managing ethically: An executive's guide* (pp. 105-107). Chicago, IL: Health Administration Press.

CHAPTER ELEVEN

Formulating Youth Policy

INTRODUCTION

The formulation of social policies to assist in establishing the rights of youth, as well as the provision of programs and services for youth, is the focus of this chapter. Such policy requires the active attention of all of the stakeholders who are committed to the welfare and well-being of youth. Parents, educators, community workers, business leaders, government officials, legislators, and most importantly, youth and youth workers all have a responsibility to assist formulating strategies to assist youth in their development.

Youth rights and the formulation of youth policy is the focus of this chapter. First, the concepts of the rights of youths will be presented. Included is a discussion of how the rights of youth are connected with social policy. Following,

will be a discussion of the importance of policy in the field of youth development. Next, the effects of policy on youth work will be presented. The chapter concludes with an interpretation of the effects of youth policy on the professional practice of youth work. The primary goal of this chapter is to expand the practical application of information currently available on youth rights and policy. It is the intention of the authors to add to the professional body of knowledge that formulates youth policy. Our goal is one of positively influencing youth development by creating a greater understanding of this topic and its application to youth work.

WHAT ARE RIGHTS?

Rights are commonly thought of as lawful power or privilege. Further explanations of a right include a claim that is virtuous, just, morally approved, or suitable (Franklin, 1995). The rights of youth are addressed when discussing how to formulate policies for youth. Many policies pertain to what is suitable for youth physically, mentally, and emotionally. The foundation of youth policy is built upon an acknowledgment that youth have rights in society. How these rights are interpreted and subsequent actions related to them depends on the structure of the policy.

Bandman (1999) defines the function rights play in society related to youth. These functions are 1) to provide just and equal distribution of benefits and responsibilities; 2) to resist abuses; 3) establish standards of what is acceptable and what is not; 4) to provide a basis for disputing claims between individuals; and 5) to guide behavior. These functions monitor interactions related to youth and elevate awareness of the importance that youth have in society.

WHAT IS YOUTH POLICY?

A starting point in defining a policy is to think of it as a guideline or set of guidelines that assist individuals and organizations in achieving their goals. Lerner (1995) indicates a more specific definition, suggesting that a policy is a standard or rule outlining the conduct or actions of individuals, institutions, or organizations. Policies often are associated with rights because they are the agreements or plans made to emphasize or categorize rights. Youth policy addresses the conduct of the aforementioned groups related to youth development and youth work. Youth policies are structured to let all people involved know how to act and react when working with youth. They reflect what is at stake when interacting with youth and what community members care about regarding the lives of youth.

Youth policy, in some cases, may be under the umbrella of an organization's or even a community's broad set of social policies. Governing bodies recognize a need for policy affecting youth, but at times it is not classified as a separate entity of needs (Hazekamp & Popple, 1997). Some of the areas of social policy that affect youth include education, juvenile justice, housing and employment.

Crimmens and Whalen (as cited in Banks, 1999) point out that youth policy is not only the legalized documentation protecting youth, but also the unwritten values that youth workers uphold in the workplace. The basic tenets, such as treating all young people with dignity and respect, listening to youth, and acknowledging their input, are examples of such policies. These unwritten policies of youth development are equally as important as the ones documented on paper and should carry the same value. Part of the success that youth workers experience includes the adherence to the written and unwritten policies involving youth development.

WHY IS YOUTH POLICY IMPORTANT IN THE PRACTICE OF YOUTH WORK?

The above definitions and functions of youth rights and policy provide a foundation for understanding these concepts. The significance of these two terms and applicability to the broader concept of youth development is the focus of this section of the chapter. In working with youth, the establishment of policies can assist in the quest to help youth develop into contributing members of society. Youth policies serve as a foundation for youth workers mentoring or guiding youth.

Current Issues Related to Youth Policy

Understanding how youth policies are formulated requires viewing the main issues discussed in chapter one, which affect youths' rights, their families, and the communities they live in today. There is quite often an interrelation between the different issues. For example, there is a significant relationship between youth that were abused or neglected and their tendency to engage in serious or violent behavior (Rochester Youth Development Study, 1999). As previously stated, adolescent pregnancy and academic deficiency tend to be related. As policymakers, youth workers, and other community members address these issues, they need to be cognizant that multiple concerns may manifest within a single youth.

As policies are developed discussing these issues, youth workers are also competing with other factors that may influence youth. Media outlets such as television, radio, magazines, and the Internet provide exposure to these topics, and in some cases, are the only tools for guidance in a youth's development. Other pressures affect their growth, such as their peers and school, home and work environments. Still another environment exists that can influence youth—this is the environment outside of school, work, and home (Caldwell, Smith, Shaw, & Kleiber, 1994, as cited in Kleiber, 1999). This is an environment, such as a mall or skatepark, where the adult control is limited and there is the opportunity for exposure to influential factors in development. This environment also provides space for experimentation and the chance to incorporate the results into life.

Within the United States, achieving a national consensus on what should be governed by youth policy has been an issue in several cases; at the moment, there is no overall children's policy (Walker, Brooks, & Wrightsman, 1999; Cohen, as cited in Franklin, 1995). The diverse feelings regarding sensitive issues, such as the ones listed above, has led to a lengthy national debate and prolonged inception of youth policy.

The Purpose of Youth Policy

We can think of policies as having three primary functions. First, they enable individuals and organizations to pursue goals or ends that they would not be able to pursue if such policies were not in place.

Second, they are regulatory in nature. Such policies govern routine activities that occur within organizations. Last, policies inhibit behaviors. In other words, policies exist to prohibit or discourage certain types of behaviors. The following is a description of each of these functions.

Enable. Policies serve to enable organizations or individuals to pursue goals or ends that would not be possible without them (Edginton, Hudson, & Lankford, 2001, p.124). Opportunities for youth in all facets of development are expanded due to policies that enable or empower. The following is an example of an enabling policy illustrated in the YMCA of Black Hawk County's (in Iowa) policy regarding youth development. "Y's Kids Before and After School programs are designed to provide working parents with a quality childcare option for their school-age children in the hours before and after school" (YMCA of Black Hawk County, Iowa, 2002). This policy enables parents to drop off their children and feel comfortable knowing that their children are in the care of trained youth workers.

Regulate. Edginton, Hudson, and Lankford (2001, p. 126) state that policies "are regulatory in nature; that is, they regulate routine behaviors." Youth policies regulate the behaviors of youth and workers; they steer societal development in the desired direction that is beneficial for youth "(Flekkoy & Kaufman, 1997). The following examples outline the importance of professionalism and leadership while working with youth.

Camp Chief Ouray of the YMCA of the Rockies, Colorado, issues to potential staff members a policy regulating dress code. "The YMCA of the Rockies dress code, for men only, allows mustaches (neatly trimmed), no beards and hair no longer than dress shirt collar length" (YMCA of the Rockies, 2002). This policy is designed to illustrate professionalism in the workplace and the importance of good hygiene. The administration of Camp Chief Ouray realizes the importance of good role models through actions, as well as image.

The American Camping Association issues skills verification guidelines that regulate the behavior of counselors that work with youth in a camp setting. These checkpoints include counselors demonstrating

- proficiency in an activity;
- ability to assemble, use, maintain, and store non-hazardous and hazardous equipment;
- ability to set up and maintain course or program areas;
- ability to give clear and accurate directions for programs;
- ability to problem solve and find appropriate solutions;
- ability to understand and implement operating procedures;
- ability to monitor safety of youth; and the
- ability to respond to emergency situations. (American Camping Association, 2003)

The criteria listed above monitor the quality of counselors interacting with youth at camp. An organization wants to make sure that they employ skilled individuals to shape and mold youth at camp. Periodically, these guidelines are reviewed over camp sessions between a counselor and an administrator. Using them as a checklist helps the person grow in his or her role and become a better leader for youth.

Inhibit. Policies also limit the behaviors of individuals or organizations (Edginton, Hudson, & Lankford, 2001). Many youth policies are implemented with the youth's welfare in mind. The following is an example of an inhibitory policy constructed by the Athletics Program of the Boys and Girls Clubs of the Lewis-Clark Valley in Idaho:

> The Boys & Girls Clubs of the Lewis-Clark Valley in Idaho has adopted a no tolerance policy for disturbing behavior at all games and practices related to our athletic programs. This includes, but is not limited to, vulgar language and unsportsmanlike conduct. Such behavior will result in expulsion from the current game and/or future games. If needed, a meeting will be set up with the athletic director to discuss further action. Decisions made by the Boys & Girls Clubs of the Lewis-Clark Valley will be fair and keep the best

interests of the children in mind. This policy will be strictly enforced and all decisions will be final (Boys & Girls Clubs of the Lewis-Clark Valley, Idaho, 2000).

This policy clearly states what the participants of athletic events associated with the Boys and Girls Clubs of the Lewis-Clark Valley are permitted to do. It delineates what is appropriate behavior and the repercussions if the participant chooses not to follow the policy of conduct. Youth are the focus of the athletic programs, and the Boys and Girls Clubs are attempting to maintain an environment conducive to growth within the events.

Camp Waziyatah in Waterford, Maine constructed inhibitory policies illustrating what behaviors are not acceptable or permitted for all campers. The policies presented in Table 11.1 inhibit certain actions with the goal of encouraging positive growth and development among the youth attending summer camp. The different standards are in place to ensure that each camper who attends Waziyatah enjoys his or her experience and is able to interact with others in a positive manner. Inhibitory policies for youth are methods to encourage growth and development of certain skills that hopefully will be attributed to future success. The core of inhibitory policy development is the mission of each youth development organization and the values to which workers adhere when interacting with youth.

Table 11.1
Camp Waziyatah Standards of Behavior

Our goal is that every Waziyatah camper will have a memorable and fulfilling experience. Nothing is more important to the accomplishment of that goal than that each person abide by the following standards of behavior. Any deviation from these principles will be cause for disciplinary action, and any serious deviation will be cause for expulsion.

- Each member of the Waziyatah community shall treat every other member with respect.
- There shall be no bullying.
- There shall be no physically, verbally, sexually or emotionally hurtful or abusive behavior.
- There shall be no use of, possession of, or association with illegal drugs, alcohol, or tobacco products.

Source: Camp Waziyatah (2002). *Camp Waziyatah standards of behavior.* East Walpole, MA: Peter Kerns, Patricia Kerns, Heather Kerns & Holly Kerns.

At times, each of the three categories related to policy development may overlap with each other. In the example of Camp Waziyatah, the administration is not only inhibiting certain behaviors but also regulating how the campers treat each other—with respect. The Boys and Girls Clubs of the Lewis-Clark Valley inhibit disruptive behavior by regulating the actions of participants and observers at the athletic events. The construction of potent youth policies will incorporate one or more of these categories into the statement design.

Finn and Checkoway (1998) developed a list of points to consider when structuring youth policies. The following benchmarks should be considered when developing youth policies and programs that will spring from them:

- An active level of involvement from youth who are targeted through the policy.
- A capacity to contribute to the personal development of youth, the organizational development of all agencies involved, and the development of a strong community.
- Partnerships between organizations and individuals regardless of gender, race, class, and generation.
- Awareness on the part of participants and youth workers of the diverse cultures involved in development.

Following the points listed above will help guide the process of policy development, creating an inclusive environment for all individuals who are affected. Youth workers can learn the value of diversity and group dynamics during the creation and implementation of policies through multiple channels of input; and youth will begin to receive the recognition that their input justly deserves.

HOW DOES POLICY AFFECT YOUTH WORK?

The establishment of policies effecting youth development may have great influence on not only the behavior of youth, but also on the actions of youth workers. A review of the various approaches and/or orientations to youth work as identified in Chapter 5 suggests that these strategies may be very influential in the types of regulations that come into being within a youth setting. In this section, the remedial, prosocial, and integrative approaches to youth work are discussed. The different approaches outlined below include a discussion of how various stakeholders, including a given target population of youth, may be drawn into the policymaking process.

Who is involved in the Policies Affecting Youth Work

There can be several groups of individuals involved in youth policy design and implementation. The number of different groups, organizations, or individuals who participate in the process depends on the approach taken when operating under the criteria related to youth development. Neighborhoods are groups of people who live or work in communities where youth policies are implemented. Coalitions within the neighborhoods can raise the awareness of issues pertaining to youth that live there. Often, neighborhood watch groups, open forums, or block meetings are methods to discuss and evaluate youth policy. Work groups or nongovernmental groups are citizens who represent public, private, special interest, nonprofit, or voluntary organizations in and out of the business sector. These individuals are visible leaders within the community who can use their status as a method of persuasion during the process of policy development. Government groups, such as city councils, are representatives from the local, state, and federal branches who are committed to creating youth policy.

Each group can influence the policymaking process, either singularly or together. For example, a neighborhood watch group may realize that in their town many youth do not have a place to spend their time after school and end up hanging out in front of local establishments. A few of the business owners may become displeased with the youth in front of their stores and complain to city council members about the situation. The watch group may approach the local business owners to help solve the crisis. These two groups, together with city council members, may come up with a solution to develop an area in town for youth to spend time after school. Together, the groups may create an opportunity for the youth.

Traditional Policy Design towards Youth Work— Remedial Approach

As shown in Chapter 3, the remedial approach (sometimes referred to as a traditional or clinical approach) to policy design sees the purpose of youth development programs as incorporating youth with problems into a purposely structured environment and to have experts solve those problems. The image of the youth development organization is that of an "agency."

A successful youth development program under the remedial approach is one in which the youth, or clients, change their behaviors due to their participation in the program. There is an adherence to a standard way of programming with youth (Yowell & Gordon, 1996). Youth are categorized into specific "classes" or groups, diagnosed with a specific behavioral problem, and the youth worker assumes the responsibility to adjust the problem (Malekoff, 1994).

Finn and Checkoway (1998) state that the issues listed in Chapter 1 are reasons why the remedial approach is used in youth development. As workers look at the youth, they see victims or potential victims of these issues. In order to protect the youth, the workers act to "save the children" or to intervene and address the problems the youth may have or encounter. Instead of addressing crime or delinquency on a community or societal level, the behaviors related to these issues are addressed on an individual level.

Challenges to the Remedical Approach

As Shields (1995) outlines, there are certain tendencies that hinder the success of youth development programs. These methods are approaches that have been used repeatedly by workers with youth. They are as follows:

- To organize resources around reducing problems instead of accentuating dreams and aspirations.
- To analyze the success of a youth development program around how much service they provide instead of the desired outcomes from the services.
- To avoid the reality that the amount of resources for youth development is dwindling and that alternative sources need to be sought.
- To give the authority for allocation of resources to someone who is not directly involved with youth development.
- To consider the field of youth development as a separate field with no connection to other youth related fields such as education, health, and recreation.

Yowell and Gordon (1996) illustrate the detrimental affects that these programs cause in the development of relationships between youth workers and youth. The youth workers are dependent upon the youths' problems to maintain their status as a professional. They focus on individual remedies for the specific problems of the youth, instead of looking at the "larger picture", which is the community where the youth lives. The importance is to build and maintain an authoritarian structure within the agency, instead of eliminating "expertism" and to create strong, trusting relationships with learning, occurring both in the worker and the youth.

Hancock (1994) highlights that the remedial approach fails to recognize that youth development may include addressing problems with youth and their families. Too often, the agency or organization spearheads the effort to address the problem youth may have, without asking parents for their input. The lack of familial involvement perpetuates the belief that the problem can be solved by experts focusing on the behavior, instead of looking at the environment and seeking others' assistance to develop effective youth policies (Dryfoos, 1997). An unfortunate consequence of the agency assuming sole responsibility in the development of youth is the agency may replace the family as the source for significant relationships (Yowell & Gordon, 1996). If this occurs, the youth could encounter conflicting thoughts and ideals when involved in a decision-making process.

Present Policy toward Youth Work—Prosocial Approach

The prosocial approach to youth development often results in policy frameworks focused on building the resilience or positive assets of youth. As previously indicated, this approach is built on the assumption that youth are inheritably good and the aim of youth workers is to assist them in their positive development. Youth work in this context is focused on attempting to insulate or protect youth from the ills of society. As Witt (2002) has suggested, youth development can be thought of as a process, which prepares youth to meet the challenges of adolescence and adulthood. Policy formulation would focus on building a coordinated and progressive series of supports and opportunities (Witt, 2002). Witt likens this to a building, which needs scaffolding or support during its construction.

The Carnegie Corporation of New York (1992, p.13) discussing the growing crisis in youth development has made a number of policy recommendations, which embrace the prosocial approach as defined above. They suggest that 1) funders of all types—private and public, national and local—should work in partnership with youth development organizations and with one another to identify and address the pressing needs of youth in communities across the country; and 2) local, state and federal policies should be coordinated, focused on increasing support for basic youth development services, and targeted to areas with the greatest need. Table 11.2 presents some of the broad policy initiatives that can be undertaken by various stakeholders.

Challenges to the Prosocial Approach

As the different organizations outlined in Table 11.2 begin to build the support structure for youth, there are potential challenges that surface (Carnegie Corporation of New

Table 11.2
Potential Stakeholder Initiatives in
Youth Development

Community-Based Organizations	• Expand work with young adolescents, especially those living in low-income urban and isolated rural areas. • Engage in joint planning, share training resources, and collaborate in advocacy with and on behalf of youth.
Schools	• Construct alliances with community agencies that recognize common goals, combine strengths for maximum effectiveness, and respect inherent differences.
Parents and families	• Help young adolescents make wise choices about the constructive use of their free time. • Direct energies to youth organizations as program leaders and advisers, board members, or fund-raisers.
Health Agencies	• Increase adolescents' access to health care services, as well as information about disease prevention and health promotion by combining forces with youth organizations and schools.
Higher Education Institutions	• Help community agencies identify what works in youth programs, improve capacities for evaluation, strengthen professional development, and conduct joint programs that serve youth.
Researchers and Evaluators	• Expand efforts by forming partnerships with community-based youth organizations on program development and evaluation.
Funders	• Strengthen and stabilize the funding base for youth development programs by moving from categorical funding to core support of youth agencies, combining public with private funds, and facilitating collaboration among fragmented youth and community organizations and the schools. • Target new resources to low-income neighborhoods. • Establish as funding priorities the professional development of youth workers, evaluation of programs, replication of programs that work, and vigorous advocacy with, and on behalf of youth.

(continued)

Table 11.2 (continued)

Media	•	Expand coverage of positive youth activities and success stories by increasing publication and broadcasts of material created by young people, encouraging high-quality programs that feature youth in key roles, and publicizing available youth activities to adolescents and their families.
Local, State and Federal Governments	•	Articulate a vision for youth of all communities by coordinating policies for youth at all income levels, intensifying support for youth development programs, targeting services to youth in low-income areas, and devoting special priority to locally generated solutions.
Young Adolescents	•	Become involved in designing and implementing youth programs.
	•	Serve communities as volunteers.

Source: Carnegie Council on Adolescent Development. (1992). *A matter of time: Risk and opportunity in the nonschool hours.* Report of the task force on youth development and community programs. New York, NY: Carnegie Corporation.

York, 1992). The first challenge is how to modify an organization's offerings without adversely affecting the youth involved. The preferred arrangement is for stakeholders concerned with youth development to actively engage different groups of youth within their means. Organizations want to avoid working with one portion of the youth population to the detriment of another.

To complicate this challenge, there is the shrinkage of funding for youth programs on a national level. Many organizations are attempting to work with other stakeholders, but may not be able to bring much "to the table" financially. Low funding can inhibit the organization's ability to educate, guide, and mentor the workers, as well as the youth. There may be innovative conferences, tools, or technologies that can positively affect the youth development organization, but if the ability to acquire these options is related to financial means, there may be a delay or absence of them in the workplace.

An even bigger dilemma is that communities may not have an organization or person who is in charge of planning and organizing youth services. The funding sources may exist, but there may not be someone who initiates the creation of services or programs for youth. Before the prosocial approach can be instituted, the community needs an individual, organization, or group to step forward and assume the responsibility of guiding initiatives positively affecting youth.

Emerging Policy towards Youth Work—Integrative Approach

Emerging policy in youth development emphasizes relationship building and collaboration between everyone involved in youth work (Jarvis et al., 1997). The integrative approach has a very strong emphasis on collaboration. Collaboration defined by Reilly and Petersen (1997, p. 21), is the "organizational and interorganizational structures where resources, power and authority are shared and where people are brought together to achieve common goals that could not be accomplished by a single individual or organization independently." The main assumption is that youth can contribute positively to shaping community life and are to be viewed as contributors, not problems. The focus of the integrative approach is one of providing an environment encouraging positive growth by youth, and a realization by youth workers that they are not experts, but rather individuals who should be open to continual learning. As Dettmer (as cited in Keys, Bemak, Carpenter, & King-Sears, 1998) states, a person's title or position within a collaborative style does not dictate immediate seniority or expertise; rather, within each collaborative effort, the participants learn together and make group decisions. The nature of the youth development programs and issues dictates who is a participant.

According to Friend and Cook (as cited in Keys et al, 1998), there are certain features that create a successful collaboration. These features are as follows:

- **Collaboration is voluntary, without coercion or force.** The individuals or organizations involved are free to act, because they care about youth. They realize the importance of youth development, and are proactive in developing policy that enhances the rights of youth.

- **All components of collaboration are viewed as equal in value and fundamentally essential.** Within collaboration, the different participants and their input is valuable to the overall success. This includes youth and their families; the feedback they give is essential to understanding their needs. Jordan (1996) defines this as synergy—when different participants or groups come together, and the results are more effective than if each group or individual was acting alone.

- **All participants involved with the collaboration must have the same goals.** As Kemper, Spitler, Williams, and Rainey (1999) discuss, there needs to be a shared vision between all the groups or individuals involved. Jordan (1996, p. 75) defines this shared vision or prioritizing group goals as collectivism: "elements such as loyalty, trust and cooperation within group members are considered paramount. Members perceive achievement as group rather than individual accomplishment."

- *The responsibility for the collaborative effort needs to be shared among all participants.* The participants involved should have an active part in planning, implementation, and evaluation. This does not always have to be shared equally among participants, but rather should be based upon what each group or individual feels comfortable or capable of doing.

- *The resources involved with the collaborative effort must be accessible to all.* Regardless if the organization or individual owns or controls the resources, resources should be available to all involved. In some cases, specialized plans for use of resources may need to be developed.

- *All participants involved are held accountable for the outcomes achieved.* Once collaboration is underway, the participants should understand they are responsible for the results. If there is something that does not go according to plan, or a result occurs that was not expected, the participants should evaluate the collaboration and discuss whether to continue on the same path or adjust for different results.

Lerner (1995) emphasizes the importance of collaboration by discussing the effect needs assessment has in youth development programs. Providing programs in controlled environments, as discussed in the clinical approach, does not allow for real-world experiences and the natural relationships that result, to occur. The collaborative approach gives everyone in the community, including the youth and their families, the opportunity to voice their needs and create a plan of action. Inclusion of youth and their families fosters a sense of ownership and value in the program. Emphasis should be placed on the importance of research, policy development, and the variety of institutions involved in the planning process. No component is less valuable than another, and all components are essential to success. Each time community members rally in an effort to develop a youth development agenda and program, there may be structural differences in the plan. This is a significant point with a collaborative effort—that each program can be unique and specific to the needs of the community.

A successful program using the integrative approach has several results that are beneficial for everyone involved, including youth. The first is the development of an environment of trust and caring for the youth through partnerships between multiple organizations. This environment is welcoming to all and could include goal setting, social issue discussions and decision making between youth workers and youth. It is important to realize the collaborative approach stresses the value of the youths' input, involvement, strengths, and aspirations, not just their weaknesses and problems.

The second result is a renewed sense of citizenship within individuals involved in youth development. The active participation of youth is essential to reenergizing and sustaining the civic spirit of communities (Hancock, 1994). Youth who are included as an integral part of the planning process and implementation of programs have a direct effect on their generation and the future of their communities. This involvement allows youth to become proactive in addressing issues, such as the ones listed earlier is this chapter, that can affect their development.

The third result is the opportunity for older generations to help develop the future generations. Hancock (1994) defines the older generation as the "stakeholders," the individuals who hold the finalization of youth policy in their hands. It is extremely important to collaborate with everyone who could potentially be affected by youth policy. The legalization or enforcement of such policies falls to the generation of adults who are in charge. This could be the program director of a local YMCA or Boys and Girls Club, the executive director who oversees several youth development organizations, or a congressman representing his state in Washington, D.C. The "stakeholders" realize they have the ability to shape and mold their communities, for the benefit of the younger generations who will follow them.

The fourth result is the opportunity to individualize attention to specific youth (Dryfoos, 1997). The collaborative approach includes each person's input in the policy-making process. These people may verbally give their opinions, or it may be passed on through group representatives. Regardless of the method, the youth worker may then learn how to positively affect youth in a personal manner. Instead of a blanket policy or program, individualized attention illustrates to youth an element of caring. By taking the time to listen and ingest input from youth, workers show youth they are tuned in to their needs. Youth also recognize this and realize they are considered important in the policy-making and programming process. This importance and caring often translates to youth taking ownership of the policy or program and actively supporting it.

The Voices of Youth in Creating Policy

Youth can play a strong role in the development and implementation of policies concerning their rights. Age appropriate involvement can have lasting effects on the population. Adults who recognize the importance of youth in creating policy acknowledge that youths' rights are important to their growth as citizens. There is also recognition of the potential to contribute actively to society. Their participation can assume many forms: organized forums for discussions, advisory groups consisting of youth members, initiatives addressing rights, consultation with adults and collaborative decision making (Martineau, as cited in McGillivray, 1997; Franklin, 1995;

Alexander, as cited in Franklin, 1995). The repercussions of involving youth in the creation of policy can have lasting effects on their communities. Aside from the immediate youth involved, subsequent generations of young people can benefit from having their voices heard through the youthful representatives.

Importance of Reflection in the Integrative Approach

Ogden and Claus stress that reflection is a fundamental approach to turning what is experienced into learning (1997). Traditional reflection occurs after the conclusion of the youth development program, with a specific time set aside for discussion and thought between participants and the adults leading the activities. This compartmentalizing of reflection time is detrimental to learning because much of the learning occurs during the program, not afterward.

Participants involved with collaboration learn during the planning process, the implementation of the program, and when outcomes are reached. Reflection is a concept that encourages thought about an individual's involvement and an understanding of the importance of the actions being done. For youth workers, there is a constant realization that what they are doing with youth is impacting lives, and at times, that realization occurs at the moment they are working with youth. Reflection of this nature can be free flowing, informal and can occur in different capacities. For example, it may happen between agency repre-

sentatives during the activity, or it may happen between an organization representative and a participant who are on a break between activities.

Challenges to the Integrative Approach

As with any positive, high-quality program or event, there may be drawbacks and constant challenges. Youth workers who recognize and are aware of these concerns can develop options for dealing with them so they do not adversely affect the program. Some of these challenges are identified below, although this is not an exhaustive list.

- ***All community members need to recognize themselves as effective, contributing partners in community youth development.*** Workers who are involved in the development of youth are taking the first step towards positively affecting youth, regardless of their background experience or education. If they are the only individuals involved in youth development within a community, the ideal of youth development may seem overwhelming. As more people become involved through collaborative means, the task of guiding youth in the community becomes more realistic. In many cases, the fact that the person is taking part in guiding youth is a major factor in positive development.

- *Addressing understaffed organizations and undertrained workers in the youth development field.* "In the year 2000, the world population was an estimated six billion, half of who were under the age of twenty" (Delgado, 2002, p. 21). While everyone has an active role in the healthy development of our youth, the profession suffers without leaders dedicated to research and constant development of best practice. In addition, we need youth workers at the level of delivery dedicated to the informal, social interaction with youth. Unfortunately most of these positions do not compensate employees well enough to retain them in the profession for long periods of time, at least not at the level of delivery. Finally, there is a growing share of children in the youth development area whose first language is not English. In order to provide adequate programs for youth, multilingual youth workers, properly trained, are required (Danziger & Waldfogel, 2000).

- *The need for creative programs, unique ideas, and new arenas for expansion and opportunities for youth.* Most practitioners are comfortable operating programs in youth centers or in after-school settings, but there is tremendous opportunity outside the comfort zone of centers and schools (Delgado, 2002). Youth professionals need to stretch beyond their comfort levels, take programs to unique geographic locations, and ask for the involvement of other professionals and community members. One of the reasons creativity can be so challenging is the lack of funding, particularly the reservations of people to fund programs that don't fit a widely understood mold.

- *Lack of funding.* This challenge will become greater as youth professionals push for unique programs, unfamiliar to funding agencies. While it is not likely to subside, this drawback should only push us toward creative funding options, rather than discourage our energy for continuous improvement in the development of healthy, productive youth.

Batavick (1997) illustrates the difficulty that youth workers and organizations may have in releasing much of the traditional "power" to form collaborations for youth development. In the past, many organizations were the sole providers for youth development, with little or no assistance from other organizations in the community. Empowering others with responsibilities, including the youth and their families, may require a different plan of action for the organization—one that may be difficult to "digest" in the beginning, but is beneficial in the end.

YOUTH POLICY AND THE ROLE OF THE YOUTH WORKER

Youth workers are involved in multiple ways in formulating and implementing youth policy. In this section of the chapter, the various roles of a youth worker will be explored. These roles were previously discussed in Chapter 9. More specifically, the intention in this section is to elaborate on three important roles within a youth workers scope of responsibility—the role of the youth worker as "protector" of rights of youth, ethical and moral guide for youth, and mentor for youth. The following discussion provides a brief description of each of these roles, as related to the formulation and implementation of youth policy and the intended results.

"Protector" of Rights of Youth

Workers can act as the "protector" of the rights of youth in different ways. They can listen to youth for warnings of abuse or trouble in their lives, and they can provide input or guidance. As indicated earlier, there are several issues related to youth development that can adversely affect a youth's growth. These issues can be traumatizing, rendering a youth helpless psychologically, physically, or emotionally. Often, workers are the individuals who provide shelter from the storm of traumatic events impacting a youth's life. As this occurs, there is a validation of how important a youth's rights are, and that these rights should be acknowledged and upheld. By not protecting youths' rights, workers inhibit their opportunities to grow and mature into active community members. Analogously speaking, youth and their livelihood is the flame of a candle. With a candle, the flame will blow or flicker out if it is not protected from forces around it. This is true for youth—if workers don't protect the rights of a youth from external forces affecting him or her, the young person's energy and potential could diminish or disappear, just like the flame.

Ethical and Moral Guide for Youth

Spencer and Swanson (2000) illustrate the importance of the youth worker as a guide for youth through their encouragement and support. As a person the youth looks to, the worker needs to exercise sound morals and ethics, as discussed in Chapter 9. A youth worker who does this plays an essential role in the development of the youth, providing emotional stability, advice, knowledge, and assistance. With a positive role model, the youth can identify and carry out beneficial life choices.

Young (as cited in Banks, 1999) describes youth workers as guides who adhere to a policy of social education. Youth are searching, at times floundering, to find themselves and navigate through the path of growth and maturity. Workers who serve as the "rudder" in this navigation process believe youth are proactive, assume responsibility, and develop an identity for themselves.

Mentor for Youth

Erikson (as cited in Edginton, Jordan, DeGraaf, & Edginton, 2002) characterizes a component of middle adulthood as the years when individuals are prone to concern for family, as well as other members of their community. This concern for subsequent generations of citizens translates to a feeling of generativity. Generativity is the desire to be productive; with middle adults, the desire for productivity lies in developing a positive community. This development can take shape in the molding or building of a community that will endure once they are gone (Logan, 1986). The importance of the youth worker as a mentor is also discussed in Chapter 9.

SUMMARY

An awareness of the importance of the rights of youth provides an underpinning for this chapter's focus on formulating youth policy. We can think of a right as a lawful power or privilege. An understanding of the privileges, which are established for youth in the context of any community, has great implications in the formulation and implementation of policies. Such policies often prescribe or govern expected or intended behaviors and support the establishment of programs and services. Written or unwritten, policies have a significant impact on the welfare of youth and the way in which a community organizes and distributes its resources in the support of youth needs and concerns.

Policies can be thought of as guidelines that assist individuals and organizations in achieving their interests, ends, or goals. Youth policies are those that have been established to address the concerns of this age grouping. They are often related to helping youth in society understand expectations, as well as to assisting other individuals in understanding how to act and react when working with youth. As mentioned, youth policies often deal with such topics as drug and alcohol use and abuse; physical, psychological, emotional and sexual abuse or neglect; child labor; unsafe or unprotected sex; teenage pregnancy and parenting; school failure, underachievement, and drop-out; and delinquency, crime and violence. Policies serve to enable, regulate, and inhibit youth workers in structuring programs and organizations that are beneficial to the overall development of youth. These policies may include a variety of stakeholders, such as community groups, private business organizations, government officials, and public educators.

In this chapter, a presentation of the relationship of policy formulation and implementation of three basic approaches to youth development—remedial, prosocial and integrative—has been included. Each of these approaches will have great influence in the types of policies that are established. For example, the remedial approach often finds policies that are directed toward solving the problems of youth. In the prosocial orientation to youth development, policy formulation often focuses on building structures to insulate youth from societal concerns or ills. Building individual and community assets are often the cores of policy activity. The integrative approach to youth development finds policy activities directed toward establishing and nurturing collaborative efforts with all community stakeholders. Each of these approaches provides a unique context for the efforts of youth workers.

References

Alexander, G. (1995). Children's rights in their early years: From plaiting fog to knitting treacle. In B. Franklin (Ed.), *The Handbook of children's rights: Comparative policy and practice* (pp. 131-146). London, England: Routledge.

American Camping Association. (2003). *American Camping Association, skills verification guidelines* [On-line]. Available: http://www.acacamps.org/accreditation/skillsguidelines.htm

Bandman, B. (1999). *Children's rights to freedom, care and enlightenment.* New York, NY: Garland Publishing, Inc.

Banks, S. (1999). *Ethical issues in youth work.* London, England: Routledge.

Batavick, L. (1997). Community-based family support and youth development: Two movements, one philosophy. *Child Welfare, 76*(5), 639-663.

Beck, T. M., Reynolds, J., & Gavlik, S. (1995). Partnership for civic change. *Journal of Physical Education, Recreation and Dance, 66*(4), 38-39.

Brown, K. H. (1995). Alternatives through interagency collaboration. *Journal of Physical Education, Recreation and Dance, 66*(4), 35-37.

Browning, L., Thornberry, T. P., & Porter, P. K. (1999). *Highlights of the findings from the Rochester youth development study* (Fact Sheet #103, Office of Juvenile Justice and Delinquency Prevention). Washington, DC: U.S. Department of Justice.

Caldwell, L. L., Smith, E. A., Shaw, S. M., & Kleiber, D. A. (1994). *Development as action: Active and reactive leisure orientations among adolescents.* Paper presented at the Leisure Research Symposium, Minneapolis, MN.

Camp Chief Ouray. (2002). *Camp Chief Ouray YMCA of the Rockies: Summer staff information* [Brochure]. Granby, CO: Trueman E. Hoffmeister.

Camp Waziyatah. (2002). *Camp Waziyatah standards of behavior* [Brochure]. East Walpole, MA: Peter Kerns, Patricia Kerns, Heather Kerns & Holly Kerns.

Carnegie Council on Adolescent Development. (1992). *A matter of time: Risk and opportunity in the nonschool hours.* Report of the task force on youth development and community programs. New York, NY: Carnegie Corporation.

Cohen, C. P. (1995). Children's rights: An American perspective. In B. Franklin (Ed.), *The handbook of children's rights: Comparative policy and practice* (pp.164-176). London, England: Routledge.

Conley, J. (2000). Child Labor: Robbing children of their youth. *Pediatric Nursing, 26*(6), 637-638.

Crimmens, D., & Whalen, A. (1999). Rights-based approaches to work with young people. In S. Banks (Ed.), *Ethical issues in youth work* (pp. 164-180). London, England: Routledge.

Danziger, S., & Waldfogel, J. (2000). Investing in children: What do we know? What should we do? In S. Danziger & J. Waldfogel (Eds.), *Securing the future: Investing in children from birth to college* (pp.1-15). New York, NY: Russell Sage Foundation.

Delgado, M. (2002). *New frontiers for youth development in the twenty-first century: Revitalizing and broadening youth development.* New York, NY: Columbia University Press.

DeVries, R., & Zan, B. (1994). *Moral classrooms, moral children: Creating a constructivist atmosphere in early education.* Williston, VT: Teachers College Press.

Dryfoos, J. G. (1990). *Adolescents at risk: Prevalence and prevention.* New York, NY: Oxford University Press.

Dryfoos, J. G. (1997). Adolescents at risk: Shaping programs to fit the need. *Journal of Negro Education, 65*(1), 5-19.

Edginton, C. R., Jordan, D. J., DeGraaf, D. G. & Edginton, S. R. (2002). *Leisure and life satisfaction: Foundational perspectives* (3rd ed.). New York, NY: McGraw-Hill.

Edginton, C. R., Hudson, S., & Lankford, S. (2001). *Managing recreation, parks and leisure services: An introduction.* Champaign, IL: Sagamore Publishing.

Elshtain, J. B. (2002). *Jane Addams and the dream of American democracy.* New York, NY: Basic Books.

Finn, J. L. & Checkoway, B. (1998). Young people as competent community builders: A challenge to social work. *Social Work, 43*(4), 335- 345.

Flekkoy, M. G. & Kaufman, N. H. (1997). *The participation rights of the child: Rights and responsibilities in family and society.* London, England: Jessica Kingsley Publishers.

Franklin, B. (1995). The case for children's rights. In B. Franklin (Ed.), *The handbook of children's rights: Comparative policy and practice* (pp. 3-22). London, England: Routledge.

Hancock, M. (1994). Collaboration for youth development: Youth action programming. *National Civic Review, 83*(2), 139-146.

Hazekamp, J. L., & Popple, K. (1997). *Racism in Europe: A challenge for youth policy and youth work.* London, England: UCL Press.

Jarvis, S. V., Shear, L., & Hughes, D. M. (1997). Community youth development: Learning the new story. *Child Welfare, 76*(5), 719-743.

Jordan, D. J. (1996). *Leadership in leisure services: Making a difference.* State College, PA: Venture Publishing.

Kemper, K. A., Spitler, H., Williams, E., & Rainey, C. (1999). Youth service agencies: Promoting success for at-risk African-American youth. *Family and Community Health, 22*(2), 1-13.

Keys, S. G., Bemak, F., Carpenter, S. L., & King-Sears, M. E. (1998). Collaborative consultant: A new role for counselors serving at-risk youths. *Journal of Counseling and Development, 76*(2), 123-133.

Kleiber, D. A. (1999). *Leisure experience and human development: A dialectical interpretation.* New York, NY: Basic Books.

Lerner, R. M. (1995). *America's youth in crisis: Challenges and options for programs and policies.* Thousand Oaks, CA: Sage Publications.

Logan, R. D. (1986). A reconceptualization of Erikson's theory: The repetition of existential and instrumental themes. *Human Development, 29,* 125-136.

Malekoff, A. (1994). A guideline for group work with adolescents. *Social Work with Groups, 17*(1), 5-19.

McGillivray, A. (1997). *Governing childhood.* Brookfield, VT: Dartmouth Publishing.

Ogden, C., & Claus, J. (1997). Reflection as a natural element of service: Service learning for youth empowerment. *Equity & Excellence in Education, 30*(1), 72-80.

Reilly, T., & Petersen, N. (1997). Nevada's university-state partnership: A comprehensive alliance for improved services to children and families. *Public Welfare, 55*(2), 21-28.

Robertson, R. M. (1997). Walking the talk: Organizational modeling and commitment to youth and staff development. *Child Welfare, 76*(5), 577- 589.

Shields, C. (1995). Improving the life prospects of children: A community systems approach. *Child Welfare, 74*(3), 605-618.

Spencer, M. B., & Swanson, D. P. (2000). Promoting positive outcomes for youth: Resourceful families and communities. In S. Danziger & J. Waldfogel (Eds.), *Securing the future: Investing in children from birth to college* (pp. 18-204). New York, NY: Russell Sage Foundation.

Substance Abuse and Mental Health Services Administration. (2000, March). *Patterns of alcohol use among adolescents and associations with emotional and behavioral problems.* Rockville, MD: Janet C. Greenblatt.

Walker, N. E., Brooks, C. M. & Wrightsman, L. S. (1999). *Children's rights in the United States.* Thousand Oaks, CA: Sage Publications.

Witt, P. A. (2002, October). *Youth development: The importance of intentionality.* Paper presented at the meeting of the National Recreation and Park Association, Tampa Bay, FL.

YMCA of Black Hawk County. (2002). *Fall/Winter Session: September-December 2002* [Brochure]. Waterloo, IA:

YMCA of the Rockies. (2002). Staff handbook [On-line]. Available: http://www.coolworks.com/ymcarock/sm/handbook/default.htm#APPEARANCE

Yowell, C. M. & Gordon, E. W. (1996). Youth empowerment and human service institutions, *Journal of Negro Education, 65*(1), 19-29.

CHAPTER TWELVE

Professional Development

INTRODUCTION

The quality of youth development programs is largely dependent upon the effectiveness of the youth workers leading programs. It is the youth worker who sets the stage for the type of culture and environment in which young people and adults will interact and go about the business of "doing life together" within a youth-serving agency or out in the field of play; and it is this culture that most significantly impacts a young person's developmental experiences (DeVries, 1994). However, ensuring that a program is being led by an effective youth worker is more often than not a "hit-or-miss" proposition (Magnuson & Randall, 2002).

In part, this is due to the diversity among youth workers in the field. They may come from any one of a smorgasbord of professional fields (e.g., education, social work, criminology) and may or may not be familiar with the philosophies, beliefs, and assumptions that traditionally guide practice within the field of youth work. Youth workers traditionally focus their work with young people on a different set of goals and processes than do professionals in other fields. For example, youth work is usually interested in issues of identity, voluntary participation, education, autonomy, and relationships. Whereas those in working with youth in schools, juvenile courts, and counseling centers find it difficult to avoid a focus on conformity to social norms and training young people in the ways that will lead them to a life of productive citizenry—lessons usually learned in programs where participation is compulsory.

The effectiveness of youth workers is also impacted by the amount of professional support available to them within, as well as outside, youth-serving agencies. Youth work is a demanding, and at times, stressful career; the quality of the professional network that is in place to support youth workers is a critical factor in preventing turnover and burnout (Madzey-Akale & Walker, 2000). Without access to mentors, resources, in-house support from program directors, and continued educational opportunities, youth workers can easily find themselves isolated and frustrated, which ultimately impacts the quality of the programming being delivered to young people.

Continued professional development and professional support can help increase the probability that effective youth workers are leading programs in ways that positively impact the development of young people. It can also help decrease turnover and burnout within youth serving agencies, thus creating a more stable environment for children and youth. Higher education and apprenticeship programs can ensure that those practicing under the title "youth worker," are indeed, leading programs and experiences for young people that are true to the philosophical roots of the field. This chapter will seek to define career

development, discuss what career development in youth work should look like, as well as offer some insights into preparing for a successful career in youth work.

YOUTH WORK IS A PROFESSION?

Hahn and Raley (1998) have posed the fundamental question, "Is there a youth development field?" Noting the varying knowledge, skills, and competencies as well as settings within which youth development is practiced, they asked the basic question "Is there a youth development profession or simply a convenient organizing concept describing the field of specialized workers who have deeper and clearer ties to other professions?" In answering this question, they suggest there is uncertainty and lack of clarity. They suggest that in light of the field of youth developments, "heterogeneity and its resulting difficulty in collecting standardized information poses barriers to professional recognition." As Hahn and Raley write, youth "workers define themselves and the work they do in vastly different ways. Many identify with the settings in which they work rather than the field of youth development (1998, p. 393).

Nonetheless, Hahn and Raley point out that promising advances have been made toward the professionalization of youth work. Using Earnest Greenwood's (1957) classical framework for defining the "attributes of a profession" they suggest that distinguishing forces of a profession include:

1. a systematic body of theory that informs the profession's practice;
2. practitioners who have a monopoly of judgment over their clients based on their knowledge and expertise;
3. training centers and accreditation, curriculum, admissions, and licensing systems that regulate and control who can be a member of the profession; and
4. a professional culture that is promoted and sustained in institutional settings, educational and research centers, and professional associations.

In analyzing these components, Hahn and Raley (1998) suggest that the process of professionalizing the career of youth development has received momentum. They note that many external bodies have suggested that youth work is worthy of professional designation. In addressing the core components of a profession, they suggest that there is a need to continue to find ways of strengthening the identity of the field as a legitimate professional occupation. However, they point out that there is a need to continue to develop uniform definitions to define the titles, work performed, educational requirements, and other activities of youth workers.

Hahn and Raley (1998) point out that there have been efforts to define the core competency, skills, attitudes, and behaviors for youth workers. They note that many of the developed frameworks are focused on the creation of a common in-service training curriculum. Core competencies identified by these authors include:

1. knowledge of youth and adult development;
2. learning strategies for youth development;
3. organizational systems for youth development;
4. partnerships for youth development; and
5. volunteerism for youth development.

Extending this discussion to include not only youth work organizations, but also nonprofit organizations, American Humanics, Inc. (1996) has identified the following competencies:

1. career development and exploration;
2. communication skills:
3. employability skills;
4. personal attributes;
5. historical and philosophical foundations;
6. youth and adult development;
7. board and committee development;
8. fundraising principles and practices;
9. human resource development and supervision;
10. general nonprofit management;
11. nonprofit accounting and financial management;
12. nonprofit marketing;
13. program planning; and
14. risk management.

With respect to the establishment of educational programs, they note that many in-service training programs are in place. They also suggest that a number of academic programs to prepare youth development workers have been established at colleges and universities. For example, the program in Youth and Human Service Administration in the School of Health, Physical Education and Leisure Services at the University of Northern Iowa prepares individuals at all degree levels—bachelors, masters, and doctorate-for professional careers in youth development and/or youth and human services management. American Humanics, Inc. identifies nearly 100 college and university affiliates that participate in the preparation of youth and human service professions. Currently, American Humanics, Inc. is the only national organization that is exclusively focused on the preemployment preparation and certification of individuals attending colleges and universities in the United States.

The crafting of the culture of youth work and the promotion of professional identification among individuals practicing youth work is lacking. Again, although progress has been made in this area, there is a need to continue work in this area. As Hahn and Raley point out, there have been many promising strategies including: "support for self studies, professional associations, new journals, organizational renewal projects, opportunities for exchange of information through clearing houses and electronic forms, and peer to peer practitioner networks" (1998, p. 398).

Using the various ways of identifying occupations as professions, it appears as if youth work is emerging as a professional entity. It is hampered by a lack of a coherent framework underpinning the efforts of youth development workers, a lack of common definitions and terms, as well as a lack of public support and awareness for the efforts of youth workers. Nonetheless there have been numerous attempts at defining youth development, identifying core professional competencies, establishing numerous mechanisms to exchange information including journals, and most importantly, establishing academic programs to prepare individuals for the field. It remains to be seen if the heterogeneous nature of the profession and the commitment to an individual's work setting can be subsumed under a broader ideal. Such a transformation would result in the creation of a professional context for youth work practice that would transcend one's commitment to a specific agency or institution. This would assist in the elevation of youth work to professional status and perhaps provide greater recognition for the importance and efforts of youth workers. On the other hand, professionalization of the occupation may very well deprive youth work of its contextualization, which currently provides meaning for its primary efforts and connection to youth.

WHAT IS PROFESSIONAL DEVELOPMENT?

Professional development is a continuous process of developing and maintaining the skills and knowledge of theory and practice necessary to enhance one's professional performance. This process can take many forms, including attending formal classes for credit at an institution of higher learning, attending conferences or workshops, working closely with a mentor, participating in informal reading or study groups, or some combination of all of the above. The aim is to be constantly learning and growing in ways that help one enhance professional practices and contribute to the mission of one's organization, program, or institution.

Professional development also relates to the manner in which one plans to accomplish individual career goals, as well as measuring one's progress toward the attainment of those goals. This is not to say that career development is to be pursued in isolation. To the contrary, it is a process best pursued in collaboration with others—colleagues, established experts within one's chosen field, or even those outside one's field. However, the goals one sets out to pursue, as well as the motivation for attaining those goals, must come from within, if one is going to truly own one's career. Others can provide valuable insights and guidance, but it is up to each individual to choose his or her own career path according to his or her own calling within a chosen career field.

It is the merging of these two areas—professional knowledge and skills and individual career goals—that is the essence of career development. The purpose is not only for each individual to engage in activities that will help him or her learn and grow in his or her chosen fields, but to also help one find him or herself and calling within the field. Combining these two areas of professional development is not always an easy task. Outside forces within one's career field can often serve to extinguish the individual self, but it is establishing and maintaining a balance between one's profession as a whole and the one's self that allows for meaningful learning and effective practice to take place.

Importance of Professional Development in Youth Work: The Meaning-Work Connection

Especially after the events of September 11, 2001, many Americans have placed an increased emphasis on finding meaning in their lives. For many, the search for meaning prompts a critical review of the work to which they have dedicated their lives; and for some this search has encouraged change in professions all together (Cannon, 2002). "Many individuals are no longer satisfied with working for living but instead want to work at living" (Imel, 2002, p. 1).

This work-meaning connection makes sense when one considers the nature of work in the twenty-first century. Personal identity is much more closely attached with what one does for a living today than it was before the industrial or technological revolutions. We certainly live in an era where "who you are is what you do" (Warshaw, 1998).

Youth workers, if genuinely connected to the young people they are working with, typically do not have to search very hard for meaning in their careers. The very nature of youth work "gives youth workers the opportunity to make a difference in the lives of young people—the kind of job satisfaction that money can't buy" (Vanneman, 1995, p. 1). Youth work, more so than other career fields, attracts individuals who inherently understand the connection between meaning and work. Youth workers are "people who do not put salary first, who are motivated by a sense of commitment" to the work they do with young people (Vanneman, ibid). As Chris Kwak at the Kellogg Foundation has stated, "If you want to keep them, you should play to their special needs. These people are lifelong learners. They believe in personal development, for kids, but also for themselves. Give them opportunities for both professional and personal development on the job" (Vannenman, 1995, p. 1).

This is not to say that basic elements of a professional position, such as a competitive salary and benefits, are not important. Youth agencies should always have the best interest of young people at heart, and the old adage that "you get what you pay for," is as true for youth work as it is in any other field. Low salaries and/or low staff-youth ratios lead to poor programming and staff burnout. However, that stated,

youth workers are generally individuals who place a high value on being engaged in activities that contribute to the continuous improvement of their professional performance and the advancement of their professional knowledge. Opportunities for career development, for the youth worker, are clearly embedded in the connection between meaning and work.

PROFESSIONAL KNOWLEDGE IN YOUTH WORK

How can one locate the body of knowledge in youth work? Youth work is a combination of theory and practice. Its body of knowledge is located at the juncture of these two constructs. One must not only understand the underlying theories or principles that influence the application of youth work, but the successful youth worker also finds the body of knowledge in the practical application of his or her efforts. Thus to understand the body of knowledge of youth work, one must have a firm grounding in both the theory which supports youth work and also its actual practice.

Professions often refer to their body of knowledge as "professional knowledge." Professional knowledge can be differentiated from scientific knowledge. We can think of scientific knowledge as the facts or the understanding that we derive from the process of empirically, scientifically verified research. Scientific knowledge results from systematized observation and experimentation. The process of producing such knowledge results in the creation of theory, which is used to describe the relationships or underlying principles of some observed phenomena, which has been verified through the scientific process.

On the other hand, we have professional knowledge which can usually consist of three elements: theory, professional values, and applied or engineered skills. First, is the theory that we draw from various scientific disciplines. For example, our understanding of behavior is largely drawn from the theories that are used to explain the complex nature of human interaction. This is drawn from such disciplines as psychology, sociology, social psychology, anthropology, history, and philosophy. Scientific knowledge influences how we communicate with youth and each other, our historical and philosophical foundations, our notions of youth and adult development, our understanding of how others learn, as well as many other concepts that influence our work with youth. For example, we often use the work of Abraham H. Maslow to explain human behavior. Maslow (1987) suggests that human needs are arranged in a hierarchical fashion with lower order needs such as one's safety, security, and physiological desires attended to, prior to addressing one's higher order needs such as self-esteem and self-actualization.

Second, our values as a profession are an important part of our body of knowledge. In the area of youth work, we value relationship building, informal education, trust, respect, promotion and protection of human rights, ethical decision making, empowerment, and other important elements. These values attach meaning or worth to our work. In youth work, we favor these ends and seek them in our work. Professional values are important as they provide a beacon and a compass to guide our efforts. Such professional values are so powerful that they may actually bend or modify our interpretation in the way in which we apply the scientific knowledge base.

Third, applied or engineered skills can be thought of as those abilities or proficiencies that are required to practice the profession, such as organizing and delivering a program, interacting with youth, managing a budget, generating funds for a program, supervising other employees, marketing experience, preparing a professional portfolio, assessing risk, evaluating events, and many skills. Applied or engineered skills are often acquired on the job. The context of a youth worker's efforts may call for the application of very unique and specific skills. Often, the youth worker will gain these skills through on-the-job training or some type of in-service staff development. One may learn the general principles to be applied, but the actual application in a given setting may vary, requiring additional development on the part of the youth worker.

The integration of the knowledge found in professional practice with scientific theory and the values we espouse, creates the opportunity for praxis. In this sense, we can think of praxis as the integration of theory with practice. In most youth work settings, we follow a framework of the creation or application of some ideology to guide our work. We then plan the program and then through some form of interaction with youth, intervene to promote learning, growth, development, fun, and/or some other outcome. To fully complete our efforts, we then reflect on what has happened, not only in terms of changes to the youth we serve, but also the processes that we use to bring about the change. Our reflection provides an opportunity for continuation, modification, and/or maintenance of our efforts. This can be thought of as "reflective professional practice." We use the elements of our professional practice as the underpinning for our efforts in principle and application, and then we reflect on the extent to which we have achieved the desired goals or ends.

BALANCING KNOWLEDGE AND SELF

In the pursuit of one's vocation in life, one's calling, the blending of a profession's body of knowledge and one's awareness of one's own personal attributes is paramount. As educator Parker Palmer (2000, p. 16) has written, "true vocation joins self and service," and as Buechner (1993, p. 95) notes, it is ". . .the place where your deep gladness meets the world's deep needs." The notion of one's calling in life or vocation comes to us from a theological perspective. Edginton

Table 12.1
Education Levels Among Youth Workers

Some high school	2%
High school diploma	11%
GED	4%
Some college	29%
College degree	39%
Graduate school	13%

Source: BEST strengths youth worker practice: An evaluation of building exemplary systems for training youth workers, National Training Institute for Community Youth Work, 2002

Table 12.2
Proposed School Age Child Care and Youth Worker Basic Competencies

Categories	Proposed Basic Competencies For The Child Care And Youth Worker
1. **Professionalism**	Understanding the worker's job and role in the organization, professional boundaries, and professional self-care.
2. **Diversity**	Understanding differences and inclusion principles and techniques.
3. **Stages of Development for Children and Youth**	Understanding the stages of development for children and youth, including both expected and atypical behavior.
4. **Managing Behavior**	Understanding how to prevent and deal with behavior.
5. **Structuring Activities**	Understanding how to plan, carry out, and assess activities.
6. **Safety Issues**	Understanding how to maintain personal health safety.
7. **Child Care and Youth Workers as Community Resources**	Understanding the importance of empowering children, youth, and families as members of their community.
8. **Building Caring Relationships**	Understanding trust, communication, respect, empathy, and identifying assets.

Source: Adapted from NYC Voluntary Agency Training Consortium (2002). Council of Family and Child Caring Agencies.

(2001) suggests that the notion of a calling comes from the Christian religion where individuals are called to serve God in all aspects of their lives. Further, Edginton (2001, p. 136) writes, "one's calling can also be thought of as one's visions or dreams."

Youth workers often make a deep commitment to the service of others. It is this fundamental calling to serve others that is the *raison détre*, or reason for being, or doing for youth workers. Youth workers do not seek engagement with youth because it provides handsome financial rewards, status, or prestige, but often their strongest motivation comes from their deep, deep commitment to influencing in positive ways the lives of youth. It is in acknowledging this aspect of one's self that one's purpose in life and in the pursuit of youth work is fully understood. It is only when one embraces this commitment that awareness of their actions is understood and fully appreciated.

The youth worker must effectively merge the professional knowledge that is gained through the mastery of theory, a commitment to the values and ideals of working with youth, and the thoughtful, reflective application of skills. This professional knowledge must in turn be linked with a deep commitment to serving others. When these are joined, true professionalism occurs. Such a commitment requires ongoing and continuous reflection to enable the youth worker to maintain an up-to-date understanding of the basic body of professional knowledge. As Edginton (2001) has indicated, there is no substitute for competence. Parallel with maintaining one's professional knowledge is the critical importance of reaffirming one's commitment in service to others on a continuous basis. A youth worker's spiritual journey is an ongoing quest. It is important to reaffirm one's commitment to the service of others. As a youth worker, a continuous reaffirmation of one's desire and drive, one's passion and commitment, and one's purpose in the field is essential.

The most successful youth workers we know are ones who have combined these elements. These individuals maintain a high level of competence, organization, and self-control when interacting with youth. Successful youth workers are active listeners and communicators, promote multiculturalism, anticipate the needs of youth, and believe and support youth's abilities. Finally, they grow with youth and aspire to create an environment that provides opportunities for personal achievement and learning. Successful youth workers understand the scope of influence their calling has in a youth's life and how deep and long-lasting their work is with youth.

MANAGING YOUR CAREER

Developing as a professional also means finding one's place in the field, identifying one's professional interests, goals, and talents, as well as learning how to use those professional attributes to secure a job and to contribute to the mission of an organization, program, or institution. These tasks are not easily negotiated. They require a good deal of thought, planning, and training.

Getting Started: Finding Your Place in the Field

Youth work, by nature, is a field concentrated on developing practices that will benefit the development of youth and their families. Thus, youth workers spend a good portion of their time investing in the lives of others. They are continuously involved in helping young people negotiate their own personal life projects. However, before one can adequately help others, one must first complete the work of discovering one's self. One must concentrate on what the educator Parker Palmer has called "inner work" (Palmer, 2000, p. 91).

It is this "inner work," the work of discovering who one is meant to be, that is the essence of professional development. Being a professional means, discovering what one is being called to do and who one is being called to be, not simply achieving certain goals or a specific professional status. The answers to these questions can only come from within, and until they are found, one cannot, to the fullest of one's potential, go about the business of helping others discover who they are. "If people skimp on the inner work, their outer work will suffer as well" (Palmer, 2000, p. 91).

Getting started down the road toward finding one's place within the field of youth work, or any other field for that matter, needs to begin with spending some time focused on one's inner work. Before sending out resumes, it is important to ask yourself some questions that will help identify your own unique calling within the field. Youth workers need to spend some time asking themselves, "Who am I?" for it is this question that "leads inevitably to the equally important question Whose am I?" (Palmer, 2000, p.17). They need to ask themselves who they are, what type of work do they enjoy doing, in what types of settings do they really enjoy working, and with whom they want to work—both colleagues, as well as the types of young people. Without a clear understanding of who one is, it will be impossible to identify an answer to the question, "Whose am I?"—rather, to which area of youth work am I being called to serve?

Developing a Plan of Action: Determining What, Where, and How

After one has identified one's calling in the field, one can then move on to developing a plan of action for placing one's self in a position to answer that calling. This plan could include developing a time line, outlining where one would like to be in a year, five years, or even ten years; whatever feels comfortable for each individual person. The plan should include the types of skills or the knowledge that need to be gained or developed, where this knowledge or those skills could be obtained (e.g., formal schooling, apprenticeship), the types of experiences that would be helpful toward one's professional development, where these experiences might be gained, as well as any number of other questions that appear to be personally relevant to one's professional journey (e.g., where do I want to live, what is best for my family, do I want to pursue a degree, is graduate school right for me, etc.).

Self-Assessment: Identifying the "What." It is important, before setting out to search for a position in one's chosen career field, reflect on the skills one possesses, as well as the knowledge one has developed, as might be required by a potential employer. This can be a self-educating task, but it is also one that many professionals are uneasy about undertaking. This is because "many find it difficult to objectively evaluate their own skills and level of professional knowledge" (Bernstein, 1999, p. 123). Regardless, successfully completing an objective self-assessment of one's professional skills and knowledge can go a long way in helping one determine the type of positions that might be a good personal fit, as well as helping one discover which areas could use some development.

Target Areas: Identifying "Where" to Apply. After one has spent some time considering one's skills and levels of professional knowledge, one can begin to identify which positions or areas in the field of youth work seem like a good personal fit. It is at this time that it is important for one to determine which types of positions and/or organizations match one's talents, skills, level of knowledge, and personal values. Finding the right position is not just a matter of having an employer decide that one is the right person for their organization, it is also a matter of finding the right position, organization, and mentor that match one's philosophical, practical, and personal beliefs and values.

There are a variety of online resources available to youth workers seeking the right type of career opportunity for them, including the National Youth Development Information Center (www.nydic.org/nydic), Youth and Family Assistance (http://www.yfa.org/jobs.htm), Youth Work Central (http://www.youthworkcentral.org/

job_resources.html), as well as websites that have been created by any of the national youth-serving agencies (e.g., Boys and Girls Clubs of America, YMCA, YWCA, Boy Scouts, Girl Scouts). Each of these sites includes descriptions of openings in the field, as well as links to other job search resources.

Implementing Your Plan: "How" to Get a Position in the Field. Once one has identified potential employers, it is then time to look more critically at the descriptions posted outlining job requirements, and consider how one's individual skills and competencies can help those employers strengthen their organizations and better achieve their professional missions. No youth serving agency is going to hire someone who cannot strengthen the team of individuals they already have in place. One should familiarize one's self with the goals, practices, and services of the program, institution, or organization with which one is seeking employment. Doing so can help determine where one fits into the mission of the potential new employer and demonstrates a high level of professionalism.

Demonstrating Your Skills and Competencies: Creating a Professional Portfolio
Demonstrating one's competencies and skills to a potential new employer can sometimes be difficult to do, especially during a job interview, when the "time to shine" is limited, and the discussion is generally guided by the individual or

group conducting the interview. Even when submitting a resume, cover letter, and several references, much of what one has accomplished professionally, may not be adequately presented. Creating a professional portfolio is one way for youth workers to present their skills, knowledge, training, and professional growth; and they can help a potential employer see what one can do, as opposed to reading a description of past experiences and professional responsibilities.

Reasons for Using a Professional Portfolio. If prepared correctly, a professional portfolio can provide direct evidence of one's professional growth, including the experience one has obtained, the skills one has developed, and the type of work one has produced. A portfolio captures the type of worker one has been in a way that a simple resume and cover letter cannot. It allows a potential employer to gain a more complete understanding of the type of person applying for employment, as well as the specific ways in which that person might strengthen the organization (Marquand & Weiler, 1994).

How to Use a Professional Portfolio: Selling Yourself. A professional portfolio should be used to sell oneself to a potential employer. There are not necessarily any traditional rules for submitting one's portfolio. It could be presented at the time of an interview, or it could be sent along with one's resume so that the employer has time to review as he or she is deciding whom

to invite in for an interview. However, one thing is certain—the portfolio should be high quality and should include a description of the work one has accomplished to date, as well as examples of one's work (e.g., newsletters, professional reports, publications) relevant to the position for which one is applying. The idea is to sell oneself to the employer by presenting them with the best and most complete picture of who one is, as well as what one can do for the organization one hopes to join (Marquand & Weiler, 1994).

Putting the Professional Portfolio Together. There is no set formula for constructing one's professional portfolio. In fact, no two professionals have shared the exact same experiences, and so no two portfolios should be exactly alike. There are a variety of items that may be included; it is only important to remember that the portfolio should be put together so that it is relevant to the position one is applying for. Potential components of a portfolio include letters of college transcripts, certifications, examples, projects completed, reports prepared, presentations developed, letters of recommendation, awards, grants, and scholarships received (Marquand & Weiler, 1994).

SUMMARY

It is through continued professional development and support that the youth work field can advance its knowledge-based practices and developmental opportunities for young people. This effort should be a collaboration between educators and practitioners in the field, as well as others invested in field of youth work. It is important that youth workers be given opportunities for continuous professional development, within the context of a supportive professional network of individuals and agencies, committed to improving services for young people.

Trends in the field of youth work, including the development of professional competencies, certification, and higher education programs, are positive advancements in the effort to advance the field toward continued recognition as a useful profession. These same developments can help those interested in the positive development of young people create effective youth services for young people and improve the quality of youth work practices. The field has a way to go in terms of developing and maintaining a productive and informative body of knowledge, and working toward the development of professionals in the field will go a long way in accomplishing this goal.

References

American Humanics, Inc. (1996). *Certification competency requirements for youth and human service nonprofit entry-level professionals*. Kansas City, MO: Clevenger & Company and American Humanics, Inc.

Becker, H. (1962). *Education for the professions*. Chicago, IL: National Society for the Study of Education.

Bernstein, G. S. (1999). *"Human Services? . . . That must be so rewarding." A practical guide for professional development* (2nd ed.). Baltimore, MD: Paul H. Brooks Publishing Co.

BEST Training Institute. (2002). *BEST strengthens youth worker practice: An evaluation of building exemplary systems for training youth workers*. Boston, MA: National Training Institute for Community Youth Work.

Buechner, F. (1993). *Wishful thinking: A theological ABC*. San Francisco, CA: Jossey-Bass.

Cannon, A. (February 18, 2002). Left a good job for meaning: Some have responded to September 11 by trading stability for fulfilling careers. *U.S. News and World Report*, 44-45.

Center for Childcare Workforce (2002). Current data on childcare salaries and benefits in the United States [On-line]. Washington DC: Author. Available: http://www.ccw.org.pubs/2002Compendium.pdf

Council of Family and Child Caring Agencies (2002). Proposed School Age Child Care and Youth Worker Basic Competencies. NYC Voluntary Agencies Training Consortium. New York.

Edginton, C. R. (2001). *A profession as one's calling: A personal reflection*. Revista do Instituto PolitÈcnico de Macau. 4(1), 131-153.

Friedson, E. (1972). *Profession of medicine: A study of the sociology of applied knowledge*. New York, NY: Dodd, Mead & Company.

Greenwood, E. (1957). Attributes of a profession. *Social Work, 2,* 45-55.

Hahn, A. B. & Raley, G. A. (1998). Youth development on the path toward professionalization. *Nonprofit Management & Leadership. 8*(4), 387-401.

Imel, S. (2003). *Career development for meaningful life work* [On-line]. Columbus, OH: ERIC Clearinghouse on Adult Career and Vocational Education. Available: http://www.ericfacility.net/databases/ERIC_Digests/ed467240.html

Madzey-Akale, J., & Walker, J. (2000). *Training needs and professional development interests of Twin Cities youth workers summary.* Minneapolis, MN: University of Minnesota Extension Service, Center for 4-H Youth Development.

Magnuson, D., & Randall, S. (2002). *ECHOES after school learning programs: A first report.* Unpublished manuscript, University of Northern Iowa Institute for Youth Leaders.

Marquand, E., & Weiler, M. (1994). *How to prepare your portfolio: A guide for students and professionals* (3rd ed.). New York, NY: Art Direction Book Company.

Osei-Hwedie, K., Mwansa, L. K., & Mufune, P. (1990). *Youth and community work practice.* Zambia: Mission Press.

Palmer, P. (2000). *Let your life speak.* San Francisco, CA: Jossey-Bass.

Pittman, K. (1999). The power of engagement. HYPERLINK "http://www.youthtoday.org"\t "_blank" *Youth Today, 8,*(8), 63.

Randall, S. (2002). *Situated learning in youth development programs: Investigating a youth ministry program as a community of practice.* Unpublished manuscript, University of Northern Iowa, Cedar Falls.

Smith, M. (1988). *Developing youth work: Informal education, mutual aid and popular practice.* Berkshire, UK: Open University Press.

Sub-Committee for Children and Families of Boston Coalition. (1999). *Boston school-age child care and youth worker basic competencies.* Boston, MA.

Vanneman, A. (1995). The best youth workers money can't buy [On-line]. *Illinois Parks and Recreation, 26*(6). Available: http://www.lib.niu.ed/ipolip951127.htm

Warshaw, M. (June-July, 1998). Get a life [On-line]. *Fast Company,* 15. Available: http://www.fastcompany.com/online/15/getalife.html

CHAPTER THIRTEEN

Challenges and Issues

INTRODUCTION

As is the case with any emerging movement or profession, there are enumerable challenges and issues which must be addressed. Youth work in America is very fragmented. There is no distilled focus that unifies youth work as a movement or as a profession. A lack of clarity in terms, definitions, and concepts provide challenges in communicating not only among youth workers, but perhaps even more importantly to the public at large, the intentions, ideals, and values of youth work. Further, there is no basic perception as to whether or not youth are important contributors to change within community life or whether or not they present challenges to the existing norms, customs, and community expectations.

In addition, as a culture we are frequently concerned with the issues that surround youth today. The ways in which concerns regarding youth issues are manifested in society often serve as a barometer of the well being of society as a whole. We see youth as a reflection of our own well-being. Youth behaviors are often scrutinized with great detail. Such examination often leads to inappropriate characterizations that frame youth and youth issues as problematic. Clearly there are concerns that must be addressed both from the context of the role of youth in society and the response of those involved in youth work.

In the past several years a significant number of commissions have advanced a variety of reports addressing youth challenges and issues. In 1988, the William T. Grant Commission's report *The Forgotten Half* suggested that youth need contact with adults to assist them, opportunities to participate in community activities, support for special problems, and opportunities to develop their vocation. Following came the Carnegie Council's Report *Turning Points: Preparing American Youth for the 21st Century*. This report focused on concerns related to education for youth. In particular this report postulated several questions related to the educational and school-related experience of youth and suggested that a typical 15-year-old youth will be "an intellectually reflective person, a person en route to a lifetime of meaningful work, a good citizen, a caring and ethical individual, and a healthy person" (Carnegie Council on Adolescent Development, 1989, p. 15). The challenge forwarded was one of defining and creating structures of teaching and learning for adolescents that will yield mature young people of competence, compassion, and promise (15). In 1992, the Carnegie Corportation of New York produced a landmark report entitled *A Matter of Time: Risk and Opportunity in the Nonschool Hours*. This report suggested that not only were youth in need of support within their family lives and schools, but also a third side to the triangle also was essential to youth development, that is community support in the nonschool hours. Last, in 2000, the Forum for Youth Investment published a significant report entitled *Unfinished Business: Further Reflec-*

tions on a Decade of Promoting Youth Development. We have drawn on these documents to frame our discussion of various challenges and issues.

In this chapter, our effort is focused on identifying several selected issues that will be discussed briefly. By no means is the discussion comprehensive, but rather reflects a random smattering of a number of areas. One of the major challenges to youth work is the need to bring greater public attention toward concerns confronting youth today. The idea of youth work has not been clearly understood nor embraced because of the lack of clarity of mission and the fragmentation of community efforts to meet the needs of youth. In addition, we have included a discussion related to extending the practice of care in youth work. In particular, the venues in which youth work is occurring is shifting, modifying the context within which youth are engaged. We have also included in this chapter a discussion of situated learning. The ways in which youth workers assist youth in learning and in their development varies. The philosophical position of youth workers, relative to their work as it relates to how youth learn and develop, is an ever increasing issue to be considered. Further, considerable attention has been paid in recent years to the ways in which youth use their nonschool hours. These and other challenges and issues deserve focus and attention.

PROVIDING AN OVERARCHING FRAMEWORK FOR YOUTH DEVELOMENT

One of the major challenges facing individuals involved in youth development is in distilling a broad focus for the movement. Youth work lacks a consistent overarching framework for practice. Although youth development is increasingly viewed as being an essential element of the services found in any community, the movement lacks coherence. Youth work is fragmented and splintered, often reflecting fragmented agency or institutional goals. There is little that connects one youth worker with another, outside of their commitment to serving youth.

Securing Youth Development as a Powerful Public Idea

Pittman, Irby, and Ferber (2000, p. 14) suggest that the primary focus of the emerging youth development profession should be ". . . to secure youth development as a powerful public idea." Building on the ideas presented in Mark Moore's chapter in *The Power of Public Ideas,* these authors suggest that the overarching goal of youth work must be to establish itself securely in the minds of the public. They suggest that when the concept of youth development has permeated the consciousness of policy makers, public and private actors, and the general population, movement will occur which will result in greater action. Further, they note that a great deal of emphasis in recent years has been placed on the provi-

sion of services for youth in after-school hours by nonprofit organizations. However, they suggest that there is an important need to move the dialogue to a broader public forum. They write that, ". . . while there have been successes, it is clear that the overarching vision of the youth development approach "the public idea" has not been sufficiently honed and promoted" (2000, p. 12).

Citing Moore's discourse, Pittman, Irby, and Ferber suggest that there are many ways that youth development can become a public idea with impact. As Moore (1998, p. 75) has indicated, "when ideas become dominant in public policy debates, when an organization develops a strong sense of mission, or when a social norm mobilizes private actions on behalf of public purposes and suppresses other possible approaches, ideas demonstrate their power to provide a context for public debate and action."

Again, borrowing from the work of Pittman, Irby, and Ferber (2000, p. 15), there are a number of issues regarding youth work and youth development that require discussion as we move into the twenty-first century. They have clustered ten categories of emerging and recurring issues as presented in Figure 13.1. It is interesting to note that these authors have suggested that there has not been a clear message that has been disseminated to the public regarding youth work and youth development. They use the term "fuzzy or shoveling fog" to define the efforts thus far at clarifying the intent of youth development. In order to overcome this, they suggest

Figure 13.1
EMERGING AND RECURRING ISSUES

- **Clarifying the Message**
  What: Getting to the specifics of youth development.
  Why: The necessity of a publicly understandable message.
  How: Engaging the public systems to consistently help the majority of youth.
  For Whom: The populations served by youth development efforts.
- **Counter Negative Public Perceptions of Youth and of Youth Development Principles**
  Understand and accommodate public opinion.
  Correct public misconceptions.
  Engage the communication professionals.
- **Build Vocal Constituencies**
  Support youth organizing, governance, and leadership.
  Create grassroots citizen constituencies.
  Expand professional associations and unions.
  Nurture unlikely supporters.
- **Connect to Popular Issues, Institutions, and Strategies**
  Link with established "development" efforts.
    - Community development.
    - Economic development.
    - Family support and development.
    - Early childhood care and development.
  Link with hot issues.
  Link with emerging change and reform efforts.
  Close the loop between prevention and development.
- **Strengthen and Interpret the Evidence Base**
  Conduct strategic evaluations.
  Foster university-based research and teaching.
  Engage the established research disciplines.
  Create an interdisciplinary cadre of "translation" professionals.
- **Encourage Monitoring and Assessment**
  Improve national indicators.
  Strengthen and diversify local monitoring and assessment tools.
- **Define the Full Range of Roles and Actors**
  Define the actors.
  Specify their responsibilities.

(continued)

Figure 13.1 (continued)

- **Strengthen and Link Public and Private Support Systems for Youth**
  Strengthen the nonprofit youth development sector.
  Engage the "remedial" public systems in promoting youth development.
  Link to schools, museums, libraries, primary health care, and recreation.

- **Build Sustainable Local and Regional Infrastructures for Funding, Planning, Training, Advocacy, Network Development**
  Build to the capacity of local capacity-building intermediaries.
  Support regional advocacy and coalition building.
  Create and strengthen institutions that do cross-system planning and funding.

- **Saturate Neighborhoods with Solid Supports**
  Effectiveness: Youth are provided with high-quality services, supports, and opportunities.
  Scale/Saturation: Opportunities and supports are available for youth that need and want them.
  Sustainability: Services are available from year to year and sibling to sibling.

Source: Pittman, K. J., Irby, M., & Ferber, T. (2000). *Unfinished business: Further reflections on a decade of promoting youth development.* Takoma Park, MD: The Forum for Youth Investment.

that greater focus occur which results in promoting concrete deliverables, which can be understood by the public. These authors also note that there are many misconceptions that need to be countered regarding youth work and youth development. Youth are often characterized from a negative or troublesome perspective rather than being viewed as contributors to society. Correcting these public misconceptions can help to frame young people as positive contributors and be a way of more effectively connecting to the public.

Pittman, Irby, and Ferber (2000) also advocate for the building of constituencies to support youth development, which according to these authors, starts with assisting youth in speaking and representing their needs on their own. This often requires building opportunities for youth leadership, as well as for organizations that bring youth and others together on an intergenerational basis. The continued organization of professional groups and societies can also serve as a powerful, positive voice for youth. Also, they strongly recommend that it is important to link youth work and youth development to other concerns that command the public's attention. Issues related to community building, economic development, family initiatives, and child care are mentioned by the authors as areas where linkages may occur. Further they note that it is important to link with issues that reflect emerging societal changes and reform activities.

Further, Pittman, Irby, and Ferber (2000) note that one of the most challenging issues to be dealt with is that of insuring that the public and decision-makers understand the benefits that occur as a result of youth development programs. There is a need to place greater emphasis on scientific evidence in support of the efforts of youth workers and the programs and services they offer. Little is known regarding the impacts of such programs, and further there is a lack or rigorous valuation activities that are a part of the program process. They suggest that there is a need to establish positive social indicators that reflect the status of youth. Many, if not most, social indicators are framed in a fashion as to emphasize negative rather than positive types of behaviors. There are opportunities to create such quality indicators in many areas such as health, education, leisure, and economic well-being.

From the perspective of these authors, youth development requires the contributions of many different individuals in different settings, acting in varying and diverse roles. Youth work and youth development requires a commitment of many different segments of society. Clearly the family, religious institutions, schools, government, and nonprofit organizations all have important roles to play in establishing quality youth development strategies.

They also strongly recommend the strengthening of ties to various support systems. In particular, they focus on the importance of linking to schools, museums, libraries, health care, and parks and recreation systems. As many of the programs for youth are found in the nonprofit sector, they also recommend the importance of strengthening nonprofit organizations. As they note ". . . while not true of every individual organization or network, as a group, these organizations are in desperate need of funding, accountability, and marketing." (Pittman, Irby, & Ferber, 2000, p. 23). Building the professional capacity of nonprofit organizations, as well as increasing accountability is recommended. They also note that it is important to strengthen the relationship between the public and private sectors. Reporting that tensions have emerged between the private and public sector in certain areas such as before- and after-school programs, they recommend that such interaction should be reviewed. Along with building the capacity of nonprofits, they also recommend that there is a need to focus the energy of the effort at the local and regional levels for that is where programs and services are provided. Closer articulation between various segments of our society and government, nonprofit and private, is called for.

Ultimately they recommend that there is a need to "saturate" the local level with "high quality services, supports, and opportunities" for youth (Pittman, et al., 2000, p. 24).

Refocusing Assumptions

From a historical perspective, youth work has been guided by many different assumptions. As indicated in Chapter 3, youth work emerged as a "child-saving" activity at the turn of the century. Great concern was expressed that children and youth were victimized by an economic system that demanded their insertion into the labor market at an early age. Such a set of assumptions viewed youth as being in trouble, and youth work provided an avenue of social reform wherein individuals were exempt (often by law) from the abuses that can come from such environments.

The development of the play movement in the United States was an effort aimed at providing safe places for youth to play. As the play movement developed, safe spaces also included opportunities for adult supervision and programs and services that were construed to be a wise use of youths' time. The assumption was that if youth were not working and fully engaged, their free time could be misused, which could lead to delinquent behaviors and crime. Therefore, there was a need to create alternatives for youth activities were wholesome and contributed to the development of the individual. A parallel was the establishment of character-building organizations. Initially such organizations, such as the Boy Scouts, were established to promote greater physical fitness as well as to promote the acquisition of a "trustworthy" character. Further, these types of organizations promoted self-reliance, citizenship, and leadership development.

In the middle years of the twentieth century, guided by new views of the psychology of youth, a strong effort was made to placate youth. It was thought that youth would not engage in deviant or antisocial behavior if they had had a happy childhood. The assumption was that deviance or counter-cultural behaviors occurred as a result of a dysfunctional family life. This set of assumptions gave way to the notion that if youth were happy, they would not be in or get into trouble. What emerged from this set of assumptions is what is illustrated in Chapter 2 as the "fun morality." If only we could provide youth programs and services that made them happy, they would not get into trouble. Everything had to be fun! In pursuit of this goal, the educational and developmental opportunities of youth programs and services were often set aside.

In the latter part of the twentieth century, concern arose for the welfare of youth. Social indicators suggested that teens were plagued by drug and substance abuse, inappropriate sexual behavior (often leading to teenage pregnancies), and a lack of achievement within the school environment. Youth had become viewed as being "at risk." The assumption was that youth were in trouble and needed to be fixed. Such a perspective gave way to the establishment of a number of services targeted toward problem youth. As Witt (2002) has suggested, viewing youth at risk created a cyclic phenomena wherein viewing some youth as being at risk led to the assumption that all youth are at risk and that some youth are more at risk than others. Operationalizing these set of assumptions suggested that youth workers should reduce problem behaviors and clean up environments that place youth at risk. As Witt (2002) points out, "youth can be problem-free and not grow up to be a fully functioning adult."

The Carnegie Corporation of New York's report, *A Matter of Time: Risk and Opportunity in the Nonschool Hours,* (1992) distills the concern for youth who may face risk. They write:

> Early adolescence has always been a challenging time, but youth today face far greater risks than did their parents or grandparents before them. Many young adolescents first experiment with tobacco, alcohol, illicit drugs, and sexual activity during early adolescence, several years earlier than their predecessors. Many drugs that tempt them are far more hazardous and addictive than those available just a generation ago. The number of young adolescents who use alcohol, either on an experimental or abusive basis, is at least equally significant: 77% of eighth graders (most of them aged 14 and 15) report having used alcohol, and 26% say they have had five or more drinks on at least one occasion within the past two weeks.

Approximately 30% of young adolescents report having had sexual intercourse by age 15 (27% of girls and 33% of boys), with nearly six in ten reporting that they did not use any contraception at first intercourse. Of all sexually active adolescents, fully one fourth will contract a sexually transmitted disease before graduating from high school. The threat of AIDS adds a new deadly dimension to their risks.

Dryfoos (1990) has suggested that high-risk behaviors among youth are often associated with substance use, adolescent pregnancy, juvenile delinquency, and school failure and/or dropping out. She notes that at least 25% of youth are at risk. In attempting to identify some of the antecedents of at-risk youth, she concludes that a number of factors contribute to making youth vulnerable and in jeopardy. They are

- early age of initiation of the behavior;
- poor achievement in school and low expectations for achievement;
- acting out, truancy, antisocial behavior, and conduct disorder;
- low resistance to peer influence;
- lack of parental support; and
- living in an economically deprived neighborhood.

As a result of these and other documents and reports, a great deal of attention has been focused on programming for youth at risk. Certainly, there are some youth who are placed in challenging situations, and there is a need to develop targeted programs and services. Further, there is often a need for direct intervention on the part of youth workers to extend youth programs and services that are focused on providing assistance in overcoming prevailing conditions. However, the youth services field has rethought its basic assumptions in casting all youth as being at risk.

Contrary to viewing all youth at risk has been the emergence of the idea that we should embrace youth as a positive and contributing factor in any community. This led to a set of new assumptions that resulted in the idea that the role of youth work is to take good kids and make them better. The term that emerged to define this concept was prosocial youth development. This concept has provided the basis for most contemporary youth development programs and resulted in the creation of many new programs and services. In fact, there has been a resurgence in the establishment of programs, especially those focused on the before-and-after school programs. Prompted by the work of the Search Institute in Minneapolis, Minnesota, there also has been attention paid to assisting communities in identifying assets and deficits that contribute to healthy development. Also, attention to the concept of youth development as a prosocial force has been highlighted in the work of the Boys and Girls Clubs of America, 4-H, 21st Century Learning Grants, and America's Promise.

As we journey into the twenty-first century, the "fun morality" has given way to a new set of assumptions. Today, youth development is increasingly viewed as an important aspect of community life; and significant strides have been made in terms of defining strategies, as well as programs and services to meet the needs of youth. Pittman, Irby, and Ferber (2000, p. 4) suggest that there is a need to move beyond the descriptive or predictive youth development models that currently exist. In fact, these authors strongly suggest that a commitment be made to broadening the goals of youth development. They suggest that youth workers should:

> promote not only problem reduction but also preparation for adulthood; increase the options for instruction and involvement by improving the quality and availability of supports, services and opportunities offered; and redefine the strategies in order to ensure a broad scale of supports and opportunities for young people that reach far beyond the existing status quo. (2000, p. 4)

These authors suggest that to broaden goals, a new set of underlying themes to guide youth work must be embraced. They are as follows:

Problem-free is not fully prepared. There is something fundamentally limiting about defining everything in terms of a problem. In the final analysis, we do not assess people in terms of problems (or lack thereof), but potential. "Problem-free" does not represent the full range of goals most parents have for their children. And it does not reflect what young people want for themselves.

Academic competence, while critical, is not enough. Success in adolescence and adulthood requires a range of skills. It includes intellectual competence, but it does not stop there. Numerous commissions, organizations and reports on employability skills, have defined a generic set of competencies that go beyond academic or cognitive competence to include vocational, physical, emotional, civic, social and cultural competencies.

Competence alone, while critical, is not enough. Skills may go unused or be used in unproductive, antisocial ways if not anchored by confidence, character, and connections. Gang members, for example, are often extraordinarily competent, confident, and well connected. Their characters however, are seriously questioned by adults and youth with a strong sense of social responsibility (Pittman, Irby, & Ferber, 2000, p. 4).

Thus one can discern that there is a new set of assumptions emerging regarding youth work. Obviously, it is suggested that youth issues should not be viewed primarily from a problem orientation. Rather, youth should be viewed for their potential contributions, including the new and fresh perspectives that they bring to our culture. Further, it is evident that academic success alone is not enough. There is a need to address youth from a more holistic perspective. A broader view of youth includes not only their in-school activities, but also their discretionary time. Further, it is important to address not only the cognitive needs of youth but also their social, physical, spiritual, and cultural needs. Last, the competence frameworks that have been employed in guiding youth work may not satisfy the need to fully promote citizenship, social responsibility, moral decision making, and a greater sense of being connected to the broader welfare of the community. A focus on character development is re-emerging in youth work. There is an increasing recognition of the importance of the need to assist youth in acquiring a moral compass to guide their actions.

DESCRIBING THE NATURE OF YOUTH WORK

One of the problems in conducting fruitful conversations about youth work is that the term itself is so broad that it could easily be labeled all-encompassing; or worse yet, meaningless. In this way, the field reflects its focus—young people. While youth are at once the criminals of today, the hopeful leaders of tomorrow, and everything in between, youth work, at least in America, is being described as everything from bully prevention programming to nature-hike-trip leading. Yet, as Murphy has pointedly expressed, "efforts to include everyone within the definition of youth development work . . .will undermine efforts to define the field" (1995, p. 13).

We have not been clear about what it is we do with young people or about the outcomes we hope to achieve. Bully prevention programming and nature-hike-trip leading could, in fact, be adequate examples of youth work; but then again, they could easily represent something completely outside the realm of philosophy of the field. Because the boundaries of what can be considered youth is ever expanding (Delgado, 2002), we need to work toward a description of what is, and what is not youth work—from a philosophical standpoint.

Youth Work: An Endangered Service?

This may not be an easy task to accomplish, because it is a task that requires more than defining youth work activities and youth program settings; it requires identifying and describing the core values and processes that set youth work apart from other forms of work with young people. However, as Young has pointed out for the youth service field in Europe, "The future of youth work rests on the clear articulation

of its own core purpose" (1999, p. 120). This same notion holds true in the U.S., without a clearly defined core of philosophical and ethical principles that help those within and outside of field, the youth service fields in Europe, as well as in the U.S., run the risk of losing their sense of purpose and identity as an approach to working with young people—apart from others working with youth, such as the juvenile justice, social work, psychiatric, and counseling fields.

We are not calling for a clearly defined model of youth work, for we concur with Jeffs and Smith (1996) when they describe the field comprising of a variety of competing models within the youth work framework. What we are suggesting is that without a clearly defined philosophical core, the field will eventually fail to exist, having been swallowed by other fields now interested in incorporating youth work as an approach within their own institutionalized practices (e.g., compulsory schools, juvenile justice). We need to work toward describing, not defining, the nature of the work we, as youth workers, engage in with young people. We need to, as Murphy (1995) has stated, define "youth development work as exclusive . . . distinct from teaching, child care, counseling, social services . . . in comparison to (these) other major professions."

What is Youth Work: An Art or a Science?

In describing the nature of youth work, a starting point may be whether the practice of youth work characteristically follows one of the traditional lines of thought-science or art. It may be that neither or both of these areas of knowledge organization and construction capture the essence of youth work. The important point is that exploring youth work within these frameworks will help youth work educators, practitioners, and researchers more fully develop a description of the nature of youth work itself.

A Scientific View of Youth Work. The rush toward professionalization within the field of youth work suggests that some within the field sense the existence of identifiable principles and generalizations in theory and practice that can be applied across the varied settings where youth workers interact with young people. These principles and generalizations, whatever they may be, then would make up what could be described as the scientific knowledge of youth work—knowledge that could be applied by practitioners to ensure the healthy development of youth. This way of thinking about youth work is consistent with those that tout the effectiveness of a certain brand of intervention (e.g., suicide prevention, drug-abuse prevention), as well as the asset-building model of positive youth development, which claims to have identified the forty "building-blocks" for healthy adolescent development (Leffert, 1997).

From this point of view, youth work, and the knowledge needed to conduct it are static and can be implemented in a uniform fashion toward the benefit of young people. In essence, if you provide the needed intervention or cultivate the needed developmental asset, then a young person will benefit from those efforts. Young people are individuals in need of treatment or support in order to become fully healthy adults; providing such treatment or support, helps youth realize their potential. This is not to say that such interventions or supports are characteristic of scientific law; however, what those who support scientific youth work are suggesting is that it represents specific generalizations in the processes toward helping young people overcome specific challenges to their healthy developmental journey toward adulthood.

An Artistic View of Youth Work. In contrast, an artistic view of youth work believes that the effectiveness of a particular approach to working with young people rests solely on the ability of youth workers to develop and sustain positive relationships with young people, that youth workers encourage young people to question the world around them in a critical manner, and that they assist youth in the process of "moral philosophizing" (Young, 1999, p. 93). This model of youth work suggests, along the lines of Plato, that this "moral philosophizing" is not an exact science, that it "involves not only an intellectual understanding but also acting in ways which enable young people to participate" (Young, 1999, p. 93). Artistic youth work is not an exact process, rather it is an approach that requires both intuition and perception on the part of the youth worker interacting with the youth.

From this point of view, youth are "people," able to participate in healthy and productive ways when given the opportunity; and artistic youth work is something that can stimulate the natural process of socially maturing. The artistic youth worker challenges the young person to reflect and feel, pushing them toward moral and virtuous decisions and behaviors. The goal is to get the young person to judge for him or herself the worthiness or value of making certain decisions or behaving in particular ways; in essence, encouraging the young person to mature and develop in his or her own unique manner.

It is important to consider the implications, positive as well as negative, of these varieties of youth work; and to ask whether these notions are true to the nature of youth work that one believes will most benefit young people. It is also important to ask whether or not these ways of thinking about youth work are consistent with the essence of what youth workers do with young people. The field of youth work is rich with examples of descriptions of the work being conducted by youth workers within a variety of settings. We should work to apply these descriptions to the philosophical questions we have about the nature of youth work.

Youth Work as Practice

Another perspective for viewing youth work it to see it as professional practice. In this sense, youth work is an occupational activity at which one works. Similar to other occupations, one can practice youth work just as one can practice law, medicine, or some other professional occupation. In a sense, engaging in the professional practice of youth work finds individuals carrying out an action in concert with or on behalf of youth. Such action requires specialized education and the possession of a unique body of professional knowledge that may include theoretical understandings, knowledge of applied or engineered skill, as well as the application of a distinct set of values.

Is youth work a practice or is it art or science? From the above, one might conclude that youth work may indeed reflect the qualities that would identify it as a professional practice. There is an emerging body of knowledge. This body of knowledge is eclectic in nature, drawing from a number of disciplines and professional areas. It is contextualized around not only adolescence, but it is also focused on various settings and/or organizations in which youth are served. Further, youth work is built around values that focus on such themes as recognizing or supporting the unique worth of individuals, assisting youth to seek their full potential as individuals, promoting ethical behaviors, and the protecting and promoting of human dignity. Character development has long been the focus of many youth service organizations, promoting caring, civic virtue, citizenship, justice and fairness, responsibility, and trustworthiness.

The practice of youth work can be thought of or referred to as the articulated actions between the youth worker and youth. Such practice often involves providing youth with opportunities for action and guided reflection. As a result, development, learning, and growth opportunities, which are facilitated or provided by the youth worker, work together to meet the overarching needs of youth in the broader context of societal conditions. Also, professional practice refers to methods and procedures used by youth workers, including strategies for building relationships with youth, as well as advocating for them. Seeking the most effective methods and procedures in working with youth often results in what is known as "best professional practice."

ENCOURAGING AN INTERDISCIPLINARY APPROACH TO YOUTH WORK

For youth work to become more effective in the twenty-first century, practitioners and educators from various professional areas and disciplines need to come together and pool their resources to build the profession. Connell and Kubisch have suggested that "social scientists, policymakers and program staff need to work together to define the paths that individuals, communities, institutions, and programs should be encouraged to follow towards improved well-being" (2001, p .183). It seems evident that theories of change aimed at institutional and community levels should blend both theory and practice. Our professional knowledge should be an integration of what we know and learn from pro-

fessional practice and the theories, frameworks, and ideas drawn.

Still further, it is evident that there is a need to blend not only elements of professional practice with theoretical ideas, but perhaps, also find ways of blending theoretical concepts together to create new blends of knowledge that can influence professional practice as well as scholarly endeavors. For example, Bronfenbrenner's (1979) conceptual work in the education field has been analyzed in relation with Putnam's (1993) concept of social capital. Bronfenbrenner's work (1979) suggests that each of us lives inside a system of close and distant relationships that influence who we are and how we behave. Family, peers, school, work, religion, and culture are part of our microsystem; neighborhood, career opportunities, local political environment, and so forth are part of our mesosystem; and economic conditions, national issues, and environmental concerns are part of our macrosystem. Bronfenbrenner's work may be used to support the youth and family and maximize the beneficial relationships available to them and to increase the youth's effectiveness, happiness, and hope by coaching him or her to understand the mutual influence process that occurs. Still further, Putnam's ideas of social capital can be thought of as "features of social organization, such as networks, norms, trust, that facilitate coordination and cooperation for benefit" (1993; as cited in Sampson, 2001). Social capital includes a sense of community, and strong informal associations in maintaining the overall well-being of the community and its residents (Connell & Kubisch, 2001, p. 179). The result for youth work has been the influx of two theories—one from education and the other from social science. The blending of these two theories has had a significant impact on both professional practice and research within the field of youth work.

Investing in an interdisciplinary approach provides youth workers more avenues for evaluation that may be beneficial to their programs. Each discipline brings opportunities for growth that may improve not only the youth program, but the worker as well. As youth workers absorb the various techniques from other disciplines, they improve their capacity as workers, constantly growing and learning.

Connell and Kubisch (2001) emphasize the complications involved with this decision. An interdisciplinary approach to youth work includes the recognition by workers and educators that they are continually learning. Active involvement of workers and educators also educates others in the process, expanding the field of knowledge for youth work. But, to achieve an interdisciplinary approach to youth work involves an alignment of short-and-long term goals.

As youth work programs are introduced in communities, policymakers, funders, workers, and educators should recognize the immediate importance and long term effect the programs will have with youth. It may be extremely difficult to justify a program's existence without quantitative results for funders

or policymakers. At this point, the educators and workers from various disciplines may use their research, skills and knowledge to show the importance of sustaining programs, even if the results or goals desired are not readily evident. Leisure, youth, and human service professionals, sociologists, psychologists, and curriculum educators are a few individuals who can support evidence of long-term growth in youth from various positions, which may provide encouragement for policymakers and funders to continue with a program. As Connell and Kubisch (2001) state, the inclusion of various disciplines with the infusion of practical knowledge from various youth workers may demonstrate the importance of short-and long-term goals to politicians, to funders who may have difficulty accepting a long term view, and to community residents who are eager for evidence of a successful program.

EXTENDING THE PRACTICE OF CARE

A challenge heading into the twenty first century is extending the practice of care to include the various community members that are stakeholders within youth development. During the latter part of the twentieth century, youth development agencies began to adjust their methods. Youth workers realized that working with youth included much more than an analyzation of the individual youth. Other factors began to play integral parts in the youth development process—school, family, environment, and peers are a few examples. Youth workers have long recognized the influence of these factors, but the direction of youth development changed in addressing these factors. Instead of interacting with the youth in an artificial environment, which then affects the authenticity of the situation, youth workers went out into the field, interacting with youth on youths' "turf".

Interaction with youth on their "turf" allowed youth workers to witness the relationships youth built and how those relationships affected their development. They began to realize that the larger environment was an essential factor in how to interact with youth to facilitate positive long-term growth. Spending significant amounts of time with the family is becoming a common way to learn about the most precious interactions and how they affect youth.

Extending the practice of care is a challenging method to integrate into a shifting paradigm of youth development. Traditional youth work consists of "clinically diagnosing" a youth and solving his or her problem through individualized intervention techniques of the worker, who is considered the expert. Extending the practice of care requires youth workers to reevaluate their methods and techniques, and look at the youth not as a problem, but as someone with an enormous amount of potential who needs guidance. That guidance may come from the worker, but also from other stakeholders in the community. Individual community stakeholders can provide resources and avenues

for growth within the youth that the worker may not be able to provide. Involvement of community stakeholders increases the self-worth of not only the youth, but also the community as a whole.

Youth workers who extend the practice of care for youth to community stakeholders are admitting the importance of collaboration and continual learning. This may prove challenging to some youth workers who maintain a significant amount of control in their programs. Relinquishing methods of guidance to community stakeholders and collaborating for successful youth development is a unique opportunity. Youth workers may have learned their methods from earlier generations of workers, and changing the delivery can disrupt programs, causing tension among workers. Youth workers who are leaders will recognize the advantages of collaboration and begin to adjust their programs to incorporate the many positive components within the community.

Extending the practice of care and incorporating youths' input into methods of youth work is crucial to successful long-term growth. Too many years have been spent neglecting the input of the target of interaction and growth. Embracing the population we work with and guide, and acknowledging the value of their words and actions, are truly extensions of the practice. They represent, in the most basic form, what Jane Addams states are the simplest human foundations to growth in society, and by doing this we are taking care of our "social family."

SITUATING YOUTH WORK IN THE EVERYDAY LIFE OF YOUNG PEOPLE

Youth workers face numerous challenges today as they strive to penetrate the everyday worlds of adolescents. Various models have been developed to assist youth workers in their efforts to positively impact the lives of young people (e.g., Positive Youth Development, 40 Development Assets). However, these models have been rightly criticized for being largely ineffective in identifying effective youth work practices (Randall, Coleman, Magnuson & Stringer, 2003; Magnuson, 1999).

Such models offer lists of traits, skills, beliefs, and assets to describe what "positive youth development" should look like, but they do little in the way of helping youth workers understand the practices that help adolescents arrive at the doorstep of healthy adulthood. In doing so, these models make acquiring healthy attributes the end result of development; however, as Dewey (1916) has pointed out, such characteristics are only a means for maintaining reciprocity and relationship, not ends in and of themselves. Conceptualizing learning and development in this way tells us nothing about how young people learn and develop adult attitudes and beliefs, or how youth programs should be designed in order to nurture such learning. They leave youth workers guessing as to which practices are most effective, and, in essence,

leave them to reinvent the wheel whenever one practice proves unsuccessful.

In order to understand the value of youth programs in the lives of young people, we need to focus our efforts on establishing justification (both philosophical and moral) for the goals of these programs. This way, we do not rely on a set of arbitrary words to define what the "product" of normal development should look like, but instead, begin to view the process and the product as integrally connected.

Focusing only on the outcome of development causes us to make instruction (for lack of a more relevant youth work term) a priority over learning and the content of that learning a priority over youths' life projects (Lave, 1996, p. 159). In other words, by focusing on the presence or absence of certain assets to define development, we overlook the importance of "the opening of identities—exploring new ways of being that lie beyond our current state" (Wenger, 1998, p. 263). Rather than the product, we need to start with the process of youths' participation and their identity-opening experiences.

What we need are not implicit descriptions of the value of youth programs, rather we need explicit descriptions of the locations in which the processes of learning and identity formation take place. This means rejecting current conceptions of youth development in favor of pursuing discussions of the developmental benefit of the experiences youth workers help create for young people. What we need to address are questions about learning and development that are focused on understanding what youth are learning as they participate in the everyday life within youth development programs, as well as who they are becoming as a result of this learning.

Doing so will help youth workers create a different framework through which to interpret the ways in which young people become competent adults. Instead of focusing on individualistic ideals and developmental pathways, that serve as a means to create a definition of "normal" development (the movement away from labeling one subnormal or "at-risk"), we could begin to conceive of learning and development in terms of a generative social practice. Our focus would be placed not on issues of more or less positive development, or the comparison of such issues across groups of individuals, but rather on the ways in which a "novice" member of a community, or young person, becomes an active participant, or an adult, in society.

In this way we move the question of youth development away from the accomplishment and accumulation of individualistic traits and abilities to also include the relationship of youth to the goals of social life and practice, from the protection and preservation of the social order to shared participation in the goals that create and revise the social order. This point of view focuses our attention on questions of access, of resources, of experimentation with identity, of cooperative social relationships, and of participation

through apprenticeship, rather than on mental and behavioral exercises in preparation for the future.

We need to criticize trait-centered theories of youth development and youth work, because of their individualistic assumptions and their misunderstanding about the relationship between those traits and skills and identity in learning. First, we need to begin by recognizing that youth are members of our communities, not individuals in training waiting to develop the required traits for participation, and then we must consider how it is we can best assist young people in the journey toward adulthood.

In order to understand the value of having young people participate in youth development programs, "we need" justification (philosophical and moral) for the goals of our programs; doing so helps us avoid the problem of treating youth as objects rather than as persons" (Randall, Coleman, Magnuson, & Stringer, 2002). This way we do not rely on a set of arbitrary words to define what the "product" of development should look like; instead we begin to view the process and the product of development as integrally connected.

THE NONSCHOOL HOURS

There has been considerable discussion in recent years regarding the use of out-of-school or nonschool hours. This period of time represents the largest block of time available to youth. The Carnegie Corporation of New York has suggested that there are several interesting points of analysis from their study. They are as follows:

- About 40% of adolescents' waking hours are discretionary—not committed to other activities (such as eating, school, homework, chores, or working for pay).
- Many young adolescents spend virtually all of this discretionary time without companionship or supervision from responsible adults. They spend the time alone, with peers, or—in some cases—with adults who may exert negative influences on them or exploit them.
- Positive opportunities available to young adolescents in their free time vary widely, from interesting and challenging activities in some communities to virtually none at all in others.
- Negative opportunities, which lead youth into risky behavior such as criminal activity and early sexual activity, range from low (although seldom nonexistent) to extremely high in some neighborhoods.
- Many communities offer out-of-school activities that are unavailable to those young adolescents who cannot travel to, pay for, or be admitted to them (because of skill requirements or membership restrictions).
- Nonschool discretionary time represents an enormous potential for either desirable or undesirable outcomes in the young person's life—a potential that many parents, educators, and policy makers fail to appreciate. (Carnegie Corporation, 1992, pp. 29-30)

As one can see from viewing this analysis, the nonschool hours present great opportunities, as well as challenges for youth. The fact that youth are spending a great deal of time without adult mentorship or supervision is important. Further, there is a great need for youth to use their leisure in ways that result in positive outcomes. It is evident that one of the factors that lead to negative behaviors is a misuse of nonschool hours. There is a myriad of organizations that address youth needs in nonschool hours within which participation by youth is often voluntary and noncompulsory. Such environments create great opportunities for learning, discovery, reflection, positive peer interaction, and a host of other significant outcomes.

SUMMARY

As has been the case with many areas of social reform in the United States, the youth service field remains in transition. As a professional area, youth services is very fragmented, lacking coherence in terms of accepted definitions, concepts, and strategies of intervention. Perhaps this fragmentation reflects the public's view of the overall effort made on behalf of youth by nonprofit organizations, government agencies, and other institutions concerned with the well-being of this age grouping.

Several fundamental questions emerge in our review of the youth services field in the United States. One of the most interesting is that of the public's perception of the movement. Pittman, Irby, and Ferber (2000) have suggested that there is a tremendous need for the public to better understand the concept of youth development. In fact, they call for a major focus of the field to assist in securing "youth development as a powerful, public idea." They suggest that it is very important that we work to help the public better understand the issues and have youth work become a fixture of public debate and action.

A second factor that emerges is whether or not there is, in fact, a youth development field. Does the youth development field exist as a professional area? A well-developed analysis by Hahn and Raley (1998) suggests that progress is being made using normative and other criteria used in defining professions. Youth work is becoming better understood as a professional occupation. Although the professionalization of youth work in the United States has not kept pace with our colleagues in Europe, there is evidence that we are beginning to distill a unique, common body of knowledge and are evolving programs and institutions to disseminate and prepare individuals for careers in this area. However, there is work to be completed in this area.

Last, we are beginning to realize that time spent without adult supervision, time that is usually defined as discretionary or leisure time, has great potential for the development of youth. Informal education is being viewed as a powerful tool for creating opportunities for youth as exist in formal educational venues. In fact, the view is emerging that while academic competence is important, it is not enough. Informal learning environments with programs and services that are planned intentionally to achieve selected ends have as much potential in the development of youth as other opportunities.

REFERENCES

American Humanics, Inc. (1996). *Certification competency requirements for youth and human service nonprofit entry-level professionals.* Kansas City, MO: Clevenger & Company and American Humanics, Inc.

Bronfenbrenner, U. (1979). *The ecology of human development.* Cambridge, MA: Harvard University Press.

Carnegie Corporation of New York. (1992). *A matter of time: Risk and opportunity in the nonschool hours.* Woodlawn, MD: Wolk Press, Inc.

Carnegie Council on Adolescent Development (1989). *Turning points: Preparing American youth for the 21st century.* New York, NY: Carnegie Corporation.

Connell, J .P & Kubisch, A. C. (2001). Community approaches to improving outcomes for urban children, youth and families: Current trends and future directions. In A. Booth & A. C. Crouter (Eds.), *Does it take a village? Community effects on children, adolescents, and families* (pp. 177-201). Mahwah, NJ: Lawrence Erlbaum Associates.

Delgado, M. (2002). *New frontiers for youth development in the twenty-first century: Revitalizing and broadening youth development.* New York, NY: Columbia University Press.

Dewey, J. (1916). *Democracy and education.* New York, NY: The Free Press.

Dryfoos, J. (1990). *Adolescents at risk.* New York, NY: Oxford University Press.

Edginton, C. R., & Edginton, S. R. (1994). *Youth programs: Promoting quality services.* Champaign, IL: Sagamore Publishing.

Hahn, A. B., & Raley, G. A., (1998, Summer). Youth development: On the path toward professionalization. *Non-Profit Management & Leadership, 8*(4), 387-401.

Jeffs, T., & Smith, M. K. (1999). *Informal Education.* Ticknall, Derbyshire: Education Now.

Lave, J. (1996). Teaching, as learning, in practice. *Mind, Culture and Activity, 3*(3), 149-164.

Leffert, N. (1997). Building assets: A positive approach to adolescent health. http://www.mnmed.org/np/mn-med.html" *Minnesota Medicine, 80,* 27-30.

Magnuson, D. (1999). *Social interdependence: The goal structure of moral experience.* Unpublished doctoral dissertation, University of Minnesota, Minneapolis, MN.

Moore, M. (1998). What sort of ideas become public ideas? In R. Reich (Ed.), *The power of public ideas.* Cambridge, MA: Harvard University Press.

Murphy, N. (1995). Design effective state policies for youth services. Symposium conducted at the National Service Learning Conference. As cited in B. Miller's (1995, July) *The Role of Rural Schools in Community Development: Policy Issues and Implications.* Rural Education Program.

Pittman, K. J., Irby, M., & Ferber, T. (2000). *Unfinished business: Further reflections on a decade of promoting youth development.* Takoma Park, MD: The Forum for Youth Investment.

Putnam, R. (1993). The prosperous community: Social capital and community life. *The American Prospect,* 35-42.

Randall, S., Coleman, M., Magnuson, D., & Stringer, A. (2003). Situated friendship: Goal and identity in an after-school girls program. Relational *Child & Youth Care Practice. Vol. 16*(1), 21-34.

Sampson, R. (Ed.) (2002, November 9). *Edwin H. Sutherland address.* Atlanta, GA: American Society of Criminology.

Task Force on Education of Young Adolescents. (1989). *Turning points: Preparing American youth for the 21st century.* New York, NY: Carnegie Council on Adolescent Development.

Wenger, E. (1998). *Communities of practice: Learning, meaning and identity.* New York, NY: Cambridge University Press.

William T. Grant Commission on Work, Family and Citizenship. (1988). *The forgotten half: Pathways to success for America's youth and young families.* Washington, DC: William T. Grant Commission on Work, Family and Citizenship.

Witt, P. A. (2002, October). *Youth development: The importance of intentionality.* Paper presented at the meeting of the National Recreation and Park Association, Tampa Bay, FL.

Young, K. (1999). *The art of youth work.* Dorset, UK: Russell House Publishing.

Appendix A
Pioneers in Youth Service

Jane Addams	1860-1935	Social Reformer Co-founder, Hull House (1889), author of *The Spirit of Youth and the City Streets* (1909)
Agnes Baden-Powell	1858-1945	Founder, Girl Guides (1910) United Kingdom
Lord Robert Baden-Powell	1857-1941	Founder, Boy Scouts (1909) United Kingdom
Daniel Beard	1850-1941	Founder, Son's of Daniel Boone (1909)
William Booth	1829-1912	Founder, Salvation Army (1865)
William D. Boyce	1858-1929	Founder, Boy Scouts of America (1910)
Murray A. Crane	1853-1920	Co-founder, Junior Achievement (1919)
Francis E. Clark	1851-1927	Founder, Christian Endeavor (1881)
Ernest K. Coulter	1871-1952	Founder, Big Brothers/Big Sisters of America (1904)
Henry S. Curtis	1870-1954	Promoted scouting and playground movement, author *Education Through Play and The Play Movement and It's Significance* (1917)
Charles M. DeForest	1878-1947	Founder, Knighthood of Youth Program
Henry Drummond	1786-1860	Author, *The Natural Law in the Spirited World,* (1904) honorary vice-president of Boys Brigade (1883)
William R. George	1866-1936	Founder, Fresh Air Camps (1877)
Wilson Gill	1851-1941	Author of award-winning School Republic Plan

Appendix A

Lottie (Charlotte) Gulick	1865-1929	Co-founder, Camp Fire Girls (1910)
Luther H. Gulick	1865-1918	Co-founder, Camp Fire Girls (1910) First president of the Playground Association of American. YMCA leader.
G. Stanley Hall	1844-1924	One of the most influential scholars in the modern history of the United States. Author, *Adolescence: Its Psychology and its Relations to Physiology, Anthropology, Sociology, Sex, Crime, Religion and Education* (1905)
William James	1842-1910	One of the most influential philosophers and educators in modern American history. Pro-moted the idea of national service, peace army.
Torrey Johnson	1909-2002	Founder, Youth for Christ (1944)
Joesph E. Lee	1862-1937	Father, playground movement of America Author, *Play in Education* (1915)
Juliette Gordon LowE	1860-1927	Founder, Girl Scouts of America/ USA (1912)
Dwight L. Moody	1837-1899	Founder, Student Volunteer Movement (1888)
Horace Moses	1862-1947	Co-founder, Junior Achievement (1919)
J. B. Nash	1886-1965	Educator, philosopher, promoted child engineering and effective use of leisure time. Author, *Philosophy of Recreation and Leisure* (1960) and *Organi-zation and Administration of Playgrounds* (1938)

Appendix A

James Rayburn	1909-1970	Founder, Young Life (1941)
Jacob Riis	1849-1914	First president, National Boy's Club Association. Author, *How the Other Half Lives* (1890), *Battle with the Slums* (1902)
W. Mark Sexon	1877-1953	Founder, International Order of Rainbow Girls (1922)
C. D. Smith	1870-1948	Advocate, 4-H program (1902)
William A. Smith	1854-1914	Founder, Boys' Brigade (1883)
Ellen Gates Starr	1860-1940	Co-founder, Hull House (1889)
Ernest Thompson Seton	1860-1946	Founder, Woodcraft Indians (1902)
Theodore N. Vail	1845-1920	Co-founder, Junior Achievement (1919)
James E. West	1876-1948	First Chief Scout Executive (1911)
George Williams	1821-1905	Founder, YMCA movement (1844)
Maria E. Zakazewska	1929-1902	Early playground advocate Co-founder, first women's infirmary in American (1853)
Julia Lathrop	1858-1932	Chief, Federal Children Bureau (1912)

Appendix B
Chronological History of Youth Services

1820 - Sunday School Movement for Children started

1823 - Young Men's New York Bible Society established

1826 - Young Men's Missionary Society of New York started

1831 - Juvenile Missionary Society of the First Reformed Presbyterian Church establishes first youth program in Philadelphia

1833 - The Young Men's Guide published

1840 - London clerks meet in room of George Williams for prayer

1842 - Young Peoples Total Abstinence Society formed

1844 - Young Men Christian Association (YMCA) established in London by George Williams

1851 - First YMCA established in the United States, Boston, Massachusetts

1855 - Young Women Christian Association (YWCA) started in England

1860 - First Boys' Club established in Hartford, Connecticut

1860 - Young Riflemen started

1861 - First Organized camp - Gunnery Camp

1862 - Brookline, Massachusetts purchases land for playgrounds

1864 - First Girls' Club established in Waterbury, Connecticut

1865 - Salvation Army established in London

1866 - First YWCA in the United States, Boston, Massachusetts

1868 - Boston school yard devoted to play sponsored by First Church of Boston

1869 - Young Women, Church of Jesus Christ of Latter Day Saints started

1874 - Young Men Hebrew Association (YMHA) established in New York

1874 - Vacation camps established by YWCA

1876 - Playground established in Washington Park in Chicago

1877 - Fresh Air Movement born

1877 - First settlement house, New York

1878 - Primary Association, Church of Jesus Christ of Latter Day Saints started

1880 - 1890-Muscular Christianity Movement

1881 - Christian Endeavor established

1881 - American Association of Red Cross started

1881 - Youth work begins in the YWCA, Oakland, California

1883 - Boys' Brigade founded in Scotland

1885 - First YMCA camp established, Camp Dudley, New York

1885 - Dr. Marie Zakrezewska starts sand gardens in Boston

1886 - Student Volunteer Movement begins

1886 - University Settlement House started in New York

1886 - The International Order of the King's Daughters and Sons founded

Appendix B

1887 - Boys' Brigade established in United States
1887 - Women's College Settlement House started in New York
1887 - Settlement House movement introduced with establishment of Neighborhood Guild in New York
1887 - YMCA started in New York
1887 - National Christ Child Society, Inc. created
1888 - Young Women Hebrew association (YWHA) established in New York
1888 - Boston opens school halls
1889 - Jane Addams starts Hull House in Chicago
1889 - YMCA established in Chicago
1890 - Epworth League started
1890 - First playground established in Boston
1890 - Free public lectures in New York schools
1891 - South End Settlement House started in Boston
1892 - Model playground started at Hull House
1896 - Junior Daughters of the King founded
1897 - School Republic Plan promotes citizenship
1901 - Young Judaea created
1901 - Thomasites provide service in the Philippines
1902 - Woodcraft Indians established by Ernest Thompson Seton
1903 - Public School Athletic League started in New York
1904 - Big Brother movement started
1905 - G. Stanley Hall authors *Adolescents*
1906 - Boys Clubs combined into national organizations
1906 - National YWCA organization established
1906 - National Boys Club Association established
1906 - Playground Association of America established
1907 - Rural Youth organized by C. D. Smith
1908 - Big Sister movement started
1908 - Boy Scouts started in England by Robert Baden-Powell
1909 - Normal Course in Play published
1909 - Girl Guides established in England by Agnes Baden-Powell
1909 - Jane Addams authors *The Spirit of the Youth and the City Streets*
1909 - Marine Brigade created
1909 - Royal Ambassadors, Southern Baptist Convention started
1909 - Report of Country Life Commission promotes youth needs
1910 - American Camping Association established
1910 - Boy Scouts of American started by William D. Boyce
1910 - Camp Fire Girls started by Luther H. and Charlotte Gulick (first national nonsectarian, interracial organization for girls)
1911 - National Education Association promotes opening school for nonschool use

Appendix B

1911 - National Community Center Association established
1912 - William James proposes the idea of national service, a peace army
1912 - National Council of Young Israel Youth established
1912 - Girl Scouts established by Juliette Gordon Lowe
1913 - The New Convention Normal Manual for Sunday School Workers published, mixes administration, psychology, ecclesiastic activities
1916 - Smith-Lever Act established 4-H Program
1916 - Histadruth Ivrith of America founded
1917 - Junior Red Cross established
1918 - National Education Association publishes *Cardinal Principles of Secondary Education*
1919 - Iowa Plan promotes character education
1919 - Junior Achievement established
1919 - United Calvinist Youth founded
1921 - Job's Daughters started
1922 - International Order of Rainbow Girls created
1924 - American Youth Foundation created
1924 - Cincinnati Community Service establishes youth baseball tournaments
1924 - B'nai Brith Youth Organization founded
1924 - Collier's Magazine promotes codes of morals for youth
1924 - Junior Optimist Clubs established
1924 - Knighthood of Youth program established by National Child Welfare Association
1925 - Colombian Squires founded
1925 - American Legion Baseball established
1925 - Key Clubs established by Kiwanis Clubs
1926 - Junior Achievement started
1927 - Tackle football for youth established in Denver
1928 - Junior Pentathlon founded in Los Angeles
1928 - Southern California Tennis Association established Junior Program
1928 - Youth and Children's Ministries established
1928 - National Future Farmers of America started
1928 - Pentecostal Young People's Association founded
1928 - U.S.A. Youth Volleyball Program founded
1928 - World Association of Girl Guides/Girl Scouts established
1929 - National Junior Honor Society established
1929 - Pop Warner Football started
1930's - Lanham Act provides for day care centers
1930 - American Junior Academy of Science founded
1930 - First Police Athletic League established
1930 - National Association of Youth Clubs founded

Appendix B

1931 - The Religious Zionist Youth Movement, - Bnei Akiva started
1933 - Civilian Conservation Corps established
1933 - Masada of the Zionist Organization of America founded
1935 - Boys State founded
1935 - Works Progress Administration started
1935 - National Junior Horticultural Association started
1936 - Milwaukee starts Stars of Yesterday and Kid's Baseball School
1936 - Academy of Model Aeronautics started
1936 - George Khoury Association of Baseball League founded
1936 - National Junior Classic League established
1937 - Christian Service Brigade started in Illinois
1938 - Girls State founded
1939 - High School Evangelism Fellowship established
1939 - North American Federation of Temple Youth founded
1939 - Little League Baseball, Inc. founded in Williamsport, Pennsylvania
1939 - Pioneer Clubs established
1939 - Pioneer Girls established
1941 - Co-Ette founded
1941 - American Youth Commission prepares report Time on Their Hands
1941 - Young Life started
1942 - Future Business Leaders of America created
1944 - National Association of Police Athletic Leagues established
1945 - Future Homemakers of America established
1945 - Girls Club National Organization established
1945 - Youth for Christ founded
1946 - Big Brothers of America founded as an international program
1946 - Habonim-Dror Labor Zionist Youth Movement founded
1948 - Amateur American Union (AAU/USA) Youth Sports Program
       established
1948 - Western Youth Buddhist League started
1948 - Ezrah Youth Movement created
1949 - Girls' Brigades of American founded
1950 - Awana Clubs International started
1950 - Junior Engineering Technical Society established
1950 - Junior Missionary Volunteers Pathfinders Club started
1951 - Babe Ruth League, Inc. established
1951 - Pony Baseball, Inc. founded
1952 - National Little Britches Rodeo Association created
1953 - National Conference of Synagogue Youth established
1956 - Dixie Baseball, Inc. created
1956 - The President's Council on Physical Fitness and Sports started
1958 - Cinderella Softball Leagues founded

Appendix B

1959 - Future Scientist of America established
1961 - Royal Rangers created
1961 - Peace Corps established
1961 - ASPIRA Association, Inc. started in New York
1964 - American Youth Soccer Organization started
1964 - VISTA volunteers started
1964 - Young Marines of the Marine Corps League, Inc. founded
1965 - Job Corps created
1965 - Young Entomologists Society, Inc. created
1966 - Soccer Association for Youth established
1967 - North American Simulation & Gaming Association started
1968 - National Youth Sports Program created
1968 - Society of Physics Students started
1968 - Special Olympics International established
1969 - National Junior Tennis League founded
1969 - WAVE, Inc. founded
1971 - Youth Conservation Corps inaugurated
1972 - Equal Rights Amendment, Title IX
1974 - U.S. President's Science Advisory Committee Panel on Youth
endorses vocational/career development
1974 - National Network of Runaway and Youth Services created
1974 - United States Youth Soccer Association founded
1975 - Camp Fire Girls becomes Camp Fire Boys and Girls
1977 - Big Brothers/Big Sisters of America merged
1980 - Students for the Exploration and Development of Space founded
1984 - Young Astronaut Program started
1985 - Moslem Youth of North America founded
1987 - Invent America! founded
1988 - *The Forgotten Half: Pathways to Success for America's Youth and
Young Families* published
1989 - Youth Basketball of America, Inc. established
1989 - *Turning Points: Preparing American Youth for the 21st Century*
published
1990 - National Community Service Act addresses community service
programs
1990 - Points of Light Foundation established
1990 - YouthBuild, USA started
1992 - Carnegie Corporation of New York published report *A Matter of
Time: Risk and Opportunity in the Nonschool Hours*
1993 - National Service and Trust Act creates Corporation for National and
Community Service
1993 - AmeriCorps established

Appendix B

1997 - Elementary and Secondary Education Act reauthorized, includes the 21st Century Community Learning Center Program

2000 - *Unfinished Business: Further Reflections on a Decade of Promoting Youth Development* published

2001 - Consistent with the Elementary and Secondary Education Act as reauthorized by the No Child Left Behind Act of 2001, the 21st Century Community Learning Center Program is transitioned to a state-administered effort.

Appendix C
Professional Organizations

Administration for Children and Families
370 L'Enfant Promenade, S.W.
Washington, DC 20201
http://www.acf.dhhs.gov

American Educational Research Association
1230 17th Street, N.W.
Washington, DC 20036
Phone: (202) 223-9485
Fax: (202) 775-1824
email:webmaster@aera.net

American Evaluation Association
16 Sconticut Neck Road, #290
Fairhaven, MA 02719
Phone/Fax (888)232-2275
email: AEA@kistcon.com

American Humanics, Inc.
4601 Madison Avenue
Kansas City, MO 64112
Phone: (816) 561-6415
http://65.108.172.202/ahindex.php

America's Promise
909 N. Washington Street,
Suite 400
Alexandria, VA 22314-1556
Phone: (703) 684-4500
Fax: (703) 535-3900
http://www.americaspromise.org/
contactus.cfm

Association of Experiential Learning
2305 Canyon Boulevard, Suite 100
Boulder, CO 80302-5651
Phone: (303) 440-8844
Fax: (303) 440-9581
http://www.aee.org

Big Brothers Big Sisters of America
Boys and Girls Clubs of America
National Headquarters
1230 W. Peachtree Street, N.W.
Atlanta, GA 30309
Phone: (404) 487-5700
e-mail: Info@bgca.org

Boy Scouts of America
Camp Fire Boys and Girls
4601 Madison Avenue
Kansas City, MO 64112-1278
Phone: (816) 756-1950
Fax: (816) 756-0258
http://www.campfire.org/start.asp

Child Welfare League of America
440 First Street, N.W., Third Floor
Washington, DC 20001-2085
Phone: (202) 638-2952
Fax: (202) 638-4004
http://www.cwla.org

Communities in Schools
277 South Washington Street,
Suite 210
Alexandria, VA††22314
Phone: (703) 519-8999
http://www.cisnet.org

Appendix C
Professional Organizations (con't)

Girls, Inc.
120 Wall Street
New York, NY 10005-3902
Phone: (800) 374-4475

Girl Scouts of the USA
420 Fifth Avenue
New York, New York 10018-2798
Phone: (800) 478-7248
http://www.girlscouts.org/

Institute for Youth Development
P.O. Box 16560
Washington, DC 20041
Phone: (703) 471-8750
http://www.youthdevelopment.org

Junior Achievement
One Education Way
Colorado Springs, CO 80906
Phone: (719) 540-8000
Fax: (719) 540-6299
http://www.ja.org

The National Assembly of Health
and Human Service Organizations
1319 F Street, N.W., Suite 601
Washington, DC 20004
Phone: (202) 347-2080
Fax: (202) 393-4517
http://www.nassembly.org

Association for the Education of
Young Children (NAEYC)
1509 16th Street, NW
Washington, DC 20036
Phone: (800) 424-2460
http://www.naeyc.org

National Association of
Extension 4-H Agents
c/o Affinity Plus
1235-E East Boulevard #213
Charlotte, NC 28203
Phone: (704) 333-3234
http://www.nae4ha.org

National Education Association
1201 16th Street, N.W.
Washington, DC 20036-3290
Phone: (202) 833-4000
Fax: (202) 822-7974
http://www.nea.org

Search Institute
The Banks Building
615 First Avenue, N.E,. Suite 125
Minneapolis, MN 55413
Phone: (612) 376-8955
Fax: (612) 376-8956
http://www.search-institute.org

U.S. Department of Health and
Human Services
200 Independence Avenue, S.W.
Washington, DC 20201
Phone: (202) 619-0257
http://www.hhs.gov

U.S. Department of Education
400 Maryland Avenue, S.W.
Washington, DC 20202
Phone: (800) USA-LEARN
Fax: (202) 401-0689
http://www.ed.gov/index.jsp

Appendix C
Professional Organizations

YMCA of the USA
YWCA
1015 18th Street, N.W., Suite 1100
Washington, DC 20036
Phone: (202) 467-0801
Fax: (202) 467-0802
http://www.ywca.org

Index

work, youth. *See* youth work
writing skills among contemporary youth, 10,
12

Y

YMCA (Young Men's Christian Association)
founding of, 35
and youth work, 3
Young Life, 40
youth
See also adolescence
challenges facing, 13–15
culture. *See* youth culture
crime. *See* crime
development. *See* youth development
mentoring, 175–186
policy formulation role, 246–247
programs, programming. *See* programming,
youth
relationships, importance of, 161–163
resilience in, 61–62
services. *See* youth services
'special needs' of, 35
work. *See* youth work, youth workers
Youth and Shelter Services of Ames, Iowa, 42
youth centers (exhibit), 144
youth culture
contemporary, 1–13
definitions, 198–199
robust, described, 38–39
youth development
and assumptions about adolescence, 24–27
communities and, 5–7
competencies, 55–60
and concept of adolescence, 24
field of, 256
framework for, 273–280
implications of multiculturalism, 200–201
language of, generally, 49–51
orientations toward (table), 101–103
practices, principles of, 3–5, 59, 128
remedial approach to, 240–241
settings that promote (exhibit), 66
stakeholder initiatives, potential (table),
242–243
term described, 2
theoretical perspectives, applications, 100,
104–105
Youth Men's Missionary Society of New York,
35
youth policy
affect on youth work, 239–248
described, importance in youth work, 233–
239

and role of youth worker, 249–250
youth service organizations, increasing prominence of, 1–2
youth services
chronological history of (table), 296–301
pioneers in (table), 293–295
professional organizations (table), 302–304
youth work
in 1980s, 41–42
in 21st century, 42–45
approaches to, 85–93
and assumptions about adolescence, 24–25,
29–30
challenges, issues, 271–289
character education as, 117–119
definitions of, 62–71
and democratic learning, 93–95
diversity and, 190–198
ethics in, 211–230
evolution of volunteerism in, 45–46
federal involvement in, 39–40
historical perspective on, 33–47
interdisciplinary approach to, 284–285
language of, generally, 49–51
leadership and, 155–157
in mid 1900s, 40–41
multiculturalism, diversity, 190–198
nature of, 280–284
organizations, 71–80
orientations toward (table), 101–103
policy, affect on, 239–248
policy, importance of, 235–239
practice of care, extending to, 285–286
professionalization of, 256–257
reform movement, 36–37
as social instrument, 119–120
theoretical perspectives, applications, 100,
104–105
Youth Work Central, 266
youth workers
culture shock and, 199–200
education levels among (table), 262
ethics of, 15, 217–221
increasing prominence of, 1–2
professional development, 255–268
purposeful attitude toward programs, 171
role in formulating, implementing policy,
249–250
roles of, 67–71, 114, 223–230
self-fulfilling prophesies and, 196
strategies for successful career, 265–267
typical titles of (table), 68
values of, 64–67